MW01627342

Greenville-Spartanburg International Airport

Upstate South Carolina's
Gateway to the World

Greenville-Spartanburg International Airport

Upstate South Carolina's Gateway to the World

A HISTORY

BY DAVE PARTRIDGE

Published for the
Greenville-Spartanburg Airport Commission

THE REPRINT COMPANY, PUBLISHERS
Spartanburg, South Carolina
2007

ISBN 978-0-87152-557-4
Library of Congress Control Number 2007933112
Manufactured in the United States of America

Index by History4All, Inc.
Post Office Box 1126
Fairfax, Virginia 22038

The paper used in this publication meets the minimum requirements of American National Standard for Information Science—Permanence of Paper for Printed Library Materials, ANSI Z39.48-1984.

To all who use this airport
as their gateway to the world

Contents

Acknowledgments

Like the building of an airport, the documenting of an historical account is a team effort. Though the author may research and write the story, a team of people must help supply the information and produce the book. I am grateful to the Greenville-Spartanburg Airport Commission for giving me this opportunity. Each commissioner and airport senior staff member has been helpful in providing information and insights. I appreciate the several hours that Chairman Roger Milliken spent discussing his valuable perspectives and memories, and the insights provided by Vice Chair Minor Shaw. Thanks also to Executive Director J. Garrett Jackson and Airport Manager Larry Holcombe for giving so much time to share from their many years with GSP, to CFO Jack Murrin for supplying maps, graphs and statistics, and to Director of Public Relations Rosylin Weston for coordinating many details of the project.

Writing this book was made easier and more interesting by the encouragement of retired executive director Dick Graham, who managed GSP for twenty-three years. I shall always be grateful for the many hours he spent sharing memories and reviewing the manuscript. I appreciate Commissioner Wallace Storey providing details and context on several important developments and Richard C. Webel giving me insights on landscape architecture and the work of his renowned father, Richard K. Webel.

The team effort to which I referred also includes more than one hundred other people whom I interviewed. They are listed in the bibliography along with research sources whose assistance I appreciate, including Elaine Rohr at the South Carolina Department of Archives and History in Columbia and Kate Moore at USC's South Carolina Political Collections room in Columbia. I am grateful also to Executive Director Sidney Thompson of the Greenville County Historical Society; to Greenville City Clerk Cheryle Ratliff; to Mannie Jefferies, museum administrator at the Spartanburg County Historical Association; to Debra Hutchins, local history librarian at the Spartanburg County Public Libraries; to Carol Crowe, senior administrative assistant at the Spartanburg County Legislative Delegation office; and to Charlotte Lynch at the Greenville County Legislative Delegation office; to Peter Cevallos and the late Vardry Ramseur at Donaldson Center; and to Joseph Frasher, director of the Greenville Downtown Airport and Josh Houston at the Spartanburg Memorial Airport. Phil Davis and Francis Earle Hendrix also spent many hours sharing information to help me understand the character of the proud Flatwood community on whose land the airport and BMW were built.

Thanks also to the photographers and sources who have supplied the book's pictures, and to our publisher, Tom Smith, owner of The Reprint Company, Publishers, in Spartanburg, for his patient direction in transforming this story from simple manuscript to attractive book. His long years of publishing experience, and the work of his professional team, especially copy editor Susan Snowden, and graphic artists Katie Severa, who designed the book, and Rob Cook, who designed the dust jacket, have been invaluable and much appreciated. Two others deserve special mention: my cousin, Dr. Carol Hennessy, longtime director of teacher education at the University of Toronto, and my sister, Ruth Stratton, a world traveler who worked thirty-six years with Air Canada in Vancouver. I value their critique of the manuscript.

Personal thanks to my daughter and coworker, Laura Brenneman, for her computer entry and editing, and to my wife, Betty, for her encouragement and patience during the past two years.

It is my hope, and that of the Airport Commission and staff, that this story will give the reader greater understanding of and appreciation for the fascinating history of aviation and for the important role of the Greenville-Spartanburg International Airport in the development of the South Carolina Upstate during the past forty-five years.

Greenville-Spartanburg International Airport ...in 2007, its 45th year

Official name	Greenville-Spartanburg International Airport (GSP)
Location	South Carolina Upstate—15 miles east of Greenville, 16 miles west of Spartanburg, 160 miles northeast of Atlanta, 80 miles southwest of Charlotte
Covers	3,800 acres, five square miles
Runway	11,001 feet, SW to NE, 960 feet above sea level Accommodates world's heaviest aircraft
Second runway	Site available for 8,000-foot runway
Flights per day	64 as of April 2007
Nonstop service to 16 cities	Atlanta, Charlotte, Chicago, Cincinnati, Cleveland, Dallas-Ft. Worth, Detroit, Houston, Las Vegas, Memphis, New York (LaGuardia), Newark, Orlando, Philadelphia, Tampa/St. Petersburg, Washington (Dulles and Reagan National)
Airlines	Delta, US Airways, Continental, United Express, American Eagle, Northwest AirLink, Allegiant Air
Fixed-base operator (FBO)	Stevens Aviation
Turboprop Service Center	Stevens Aviation
Cargo facilities & services	Cargo buildings, customs port, Inland Port of Entry, federal agricultural inspection station, daily services by UPS, DHL, FedEx
Automobile parking	4,700 spaces in garages and lots

Rental cars	Hertz, Avis, Budget, Thrifty, Alamo/National (counters opposite baggage claim; cars in parking garage across from terminal)
Limousine service	Eastside Transportation Services
Transportation network	• Adjacent to I-85; ten miles to I-26; interchanges within 150 miles with I-77, I-40, I-95, I-75, I-20. • Within twenty-four hours' driving time of 70 percent of nation's population; three hours from South Carolina's major East Coast seaports • Nearby rail traffic service
Food concessions	Windows restaurant and counter in terminal and concourse concessions
Gift shop	Hudson News
Weather Forecasting Office	Regional National Weather Service office and radar center
Oversight	Six-member board of commissioners serving in 2007: Roger Milliken, chairman; Minor Shaw, vice chair; Leland Burch, Valerie Miller, Henry Ramella, Wallace Storey
Administration	• J. Garrett Jackson, Executive Director • Larry Holcombe, Airport Manager • Jack Murrin, Chief Financial Officer and Chief Information Officer • Rosylin Weston, Director of Public Relations
Environs protection	Airport Zone Planning Commission Chairs: • Robert E. Coleman, 1995–2005 • Jackie Moore, 2005–2007 • Les McCraw, 2007–
GSP opened	October 1962
Expanded	1989–90

Greenville-Spartanburg International Airport

Upstate South Carolina's
Gateway to the World

Upstate

The term "Upstate" in this book refers to ten counties in northwestern South Carolina that are crossed by or located close to Interstate Highways 85, 26 and 385 and U.S. Highways 25, 29, 76, 123, 176, 178, 221 and 276. They are Greenville, Spartanburg, Anderson, Pickens, Oconee, Cherokee, Union, Laurens, Abbeville and Greenwood counties.

The airport's official name is Greenville-Spartanburg International Airport. It was first proposed in 1958 by the name Piedmont Area Airport. Since it opened in 1962, it has generally been referred to as Greenville-Spartanburg Airport or simply by its FAA code designation, GSP.

www.gspairport.com

The Story

This is the story of a unique airport, and much more. It is a story about the people and progress of Upstate South Carolina, about the triumph of a regional vision, about an emphasis on quality and the success of creative teamwork. It is a story that has its roots in the early days of the twentieth century when aviation pioneers and heroes returning from World War I forged an interest in flying; a story that developed in the middle of the twentieth century when the South Carolina Upstate, our nation and the world were struggling with troubling crises and momentous changes. This is the story of families and communities for whom the path of progress was sometimes painful. Yet amid that pain came opportunity.

In this story you will find accounts of people and places, events and issues, and revealing facts of history and curiosity. You will discover the courage and commitment, the relationships and resources, the planning and skill required to build and operate a business as complex as an airport. Hopefully, you will find stories to enjoy and much to appreciate about the context of how this airport developed and its impact on our region's economy and environment.

This is the story of a *gateway*. A gateway for regional residents and businesses to explore the opportunities of travel and trade. A gateway for the world to discover the beauty and culture of Upstate South Carolina, the spirit and cooperation of its communities, the efficiency and products of its business firms, the work ethic and hospitality of its people and the vision of its business and governmental leaders. This is a gateway—a regional symbol—made possible because enough people cared about the *region*, not just *individual* communities. This is the story of Greenville-Spartanburg International Airport, Upstate South Carolina's Gateway to the World.

The story begins with Flatwood.

CHAPTER I

Before the Airport

Flatwood 1952

The crowd roared as the ball cracked off the bat and shot toward the shortstop. Thinking he had hit a line drive to the outfield, the batter raced toward first. But Witty Davis leaped high, snagged the ball and fired it to first baseman F. E. Hendrix, who scooped up the low throw and doubled the runner off first base. Game over. The big crowd cheered wildly. The Flatwood Peaches had won another game.

It was the season of 1952. Winning was a way of life for the Peaches. In fact, in more than a season of baseball, from July 5, 1951, to September 20, 1952, the Peaches won thirty-eight of their forty games. For decades, watching the Peaches play had been a Saturday afternoon tradition in this quiet farming community of the South Carolina Upstate between Spartanburg and Greenville. Quiet, that is, except on game days. Many fans would follow the team when they went on the road to play in the nearby communities and mill villages; but back home in Flatwood the games were extra special and when the team from nearby Reidville came to play, the crowds were the biggest. From April to October every Saturday afternoon at four the Peaches played. They couldn't start earlier. The players had to finish their mill shifts or complete their farm chores first. That's why the teams and their fans called this the Spartanburg County Twilight League. The games often lasted until dusk. In 1952, the Flatwood Peaches were league champions.[1]

Flatwood lived up to its name. It covered a high, mostly flat plateau with a few gently rolling hills and scattered forests. Stretching across several hundred acres of western Spartanburg County from Highway 14 east to Highway 101, and from where Interstate 85 would later be built north to near the town of Greer, Flatwood had been a farming community since the 1850s. First there was cotton, then peaches, grains, corn and cattle. Just like many of his neighbors, before his Saturday afternoon games, Peaches manager Paul Wood was usually on his farm, caring for his peach trees, working to ensure a good crop this year and another next year. He would never want to leave Flatwood; but that flat land which had made it a great place to grow crops would also make a prime location to build an airport. Within a decade the Flatwood community would be different.

The legacy of World War I

The change that would transform Flatwood—and the world—had its roots in World War I. In the long history of military conflict, that was the war in which the airplane was first used.

In the early years of the twentieth century, much of the world was controlled by empires, the Ottoman, Russian, Hungarian, German, British and others. Many of them were linked by alliances and secret diplomacy. World War I grew out of years filled with disturbing developments: the growth of nationalism and the unrest of ethnic minorities across Europe and the Middle East, increasing global competition for territory and resources. The war's trigger was the July 28, 1914, killing of Archduke Ferdinand, heir to the Austrian-Hungarian throne, and his wife, Sophie. They were shot while riding through crowds in Sarajevo, capital of the Austrian province of Bosnia. A young Bosnian who had lived in neighboring Serbia was the killer. Austria-Hungary claimed he was carrying out a Serbian plot and declared war on July 28. Within three months, the conflict had widened and the allies of the Central Powers—Austria-Hungary, Germany and the Ottoman Empire—were at war with Serbia and its allies—Great Britain, France, Russia and Belgium. Eventually, the conflict engulfed much of Europe and the Middle East and several other nations around the world in the battle that ultimately became the first world war. The "Great War" it was called. It was to be "the war to end all wars." It failed to live up to that slogan.

When the war began, not even eleven years had elapsed since Orville and Wilbur Wright's first successful flights of their flimsy heavier-than-air machine on December 17, 1903, at Kitty Hawk, North Carolina. The war had been raging with devastating loss of life for almost thirty-two months before America finally joined the conflict on April 6, 1917. In September of that year, speaking at the British Munitions Ministry in London, Munitions Minister Winston Churchill declared, "There are only two ways left now of winning the war and they both begin with A. One is aeroplanes and the other is America."[2] Indeed, America and aeroplanes, as Churchill had called them, did make the difference. Just nineteen months after the United States entered the conflict, the Great War was over. The Central Powers had been defeated, but at great cost. Four and a half million Americans had served, two million of them on the battlefield. More than 116,000 were killed or died of disease or other causes; 204,000 were wounded.[3] Of those who survived World War I, some were America's pioneering pilots who returned from the war and created a legacy that had a profound influence on the United States and the world, an interest in flying.

With skills honed by their wartime experience and already addicted to the excitement and freedom of flight, many of those warriors could not wait to get back into the air. Aircraft were plentiful. Most pilots bought them for pleasure and performance. The more adventurous found large farm fields over which they could perform some of the sophisticated maneuvers they had perfected in the war. Some had no trouble attracting crowds to watch their stunt-flying shows. Americans were introduced to a new and exciting type of entertainment. Because many of those aerial showmen loved to thrill the crowds by flying low over barns and other buildings, they became known as barnstormers. In South Carolina and across the country people were paying these pilots to watch their shows. Flying was still in its infancy, daring and dangerous. For most of the pilots and their audiences, flying was fun and it was adding to the decade's still lingering moniker "the Roaring Twenties." World War I had changed America. It had a new confidence. The nation was fast becoming an economic and military superpower.

For several years, designers and builders had been busy creating aircraft that would expand the experience of flying from exciting adventure to practical application. Men whose names would still be familiar a century later, William Boeing, Donald Douglas, Glenn Curtiss and Henry Ford, were introducing aircraft that could carry cargo and people. Just as World War I's pilots had sparked interest in flying for fun and adventure, it was these aircraft designers and builders, along with the federal government, that produced interest in flying for business.

Airfields to airports

Since America's birth, its major cities had developed first along coasts, lakes and rivers, then beside railroad lines. Now cities would grow along air routes. Primitive airfields would have to become more spacious and sophisticated. By the mid 1920s, communities and private interests across America were considering or already establishing airfields. Many of those airfields soon took on a new name: "airport."

Aviation pioneer Orville Wright, however, was not satisfied with the pace of airport development. Testifying before the House Committee on Interstate and Foreign Commerce in Washington on October 12, 1925, Wright told the congressmen, "The greatest present drawback to the use of aircraft for civil purposes such as commerce, mail, travel and sport is lack of suitable airports."[4] Wright's comments came almost twenty-two years after he and brother Wilbur had, in effect, established America's first airport. It was just one hangar for a small, one-person plane, a shovel and a tiny runway from which they made their first flights on windy Kill Devil Hills at Kitty Hawk, North Carolina. By 1925 Wilbur was long dead, the victim of typhoid fever, which had taken his life at the age of forty-five in 1912. Still busy working at his aeronautical laboratory, Orville Wright spoke alone before the congressional committee. His testimony was a major impetus in the development of the nation's airport system.

As early as 1919, that term "airport" was used by an Atlantic City, New Jersey, newspaper reporter to describe Bader Field. Since the 143-acre field just southwest of downtown was bordered on three sides by water, Robert Woodhouse called it an "air-port."[5] The name stuck and eventually "airport"—without the hyphen—was a universal term. Meantime, Bader Field grew into a busy airport that welcomed commercial flights until 1990 and private aircraft until it was closed. City engineer Bill Rafferty was ready to turn off the runway lights at midnight on September 30, 2006. But he and his wife had to wait a few minutes. About half a dozen small planes had landed, each wanting to become the last to land and take off from the old field. When all of the planes had lifted off into the darkness that night, Rafferty turned off the runway lights for the last time.[6] But the name Bader Field will linger in aviation history. The Civil Air Patrol was founded there on December 1, 1941, just six days before the bombing of Pearl Harbor, which prompted U.S. entry into World War II. Thousands of volunteer CAP pilots played a key role flying coastal patrols, helping to protect American shipping interests from marauding enemy submarines. Sixty-four of those volunteer aviators lost their lives. In the decades since, as the civilian auxiliary of the United States Air Force, the Civil Air Patrol has continued to fly search and rescue missions and to deliver critical supplies, operate command posts and provide radio communications during natural disasters and emergencies.

Airmail's influence

The first regular airmail route was started in May of 1915 from New York to Philadelphia and Washington using U.S. Army pilots. The postal service took over airmail service in 1918 because those army pilots had gone to war. In 1925, it began adding routes and awarding contracts to private carriers. The government had no difficulty attracting bidders. One of the first was automaker Henry Ford, who was already beginning production on the first metal airplane, which he called the Ford Trimotor. Ford was using planes to fly automobile parts and supplies among his plants in Chicago, Detroit and Cleveland. He was successful in gaining a contract to serve those cities with airmail delivery.[7]

To make some routes work more efficiently and be financially successful, more communities would need airports and the federal government was willing to help if communities would contribute land. So it needed to find cities that already had an airport or were interested in having one. In 1926, Greenville was extended an opportunity. That's when Charles Stanton, an official of the Federal Airways, precursor of the Civil Aeronautics Board (CAB), later the Federal Aviation Administration (FAA), visited Greenville while looking for a designated airmail stop in the South Carolina Upstate. Stanton met with a small Chamber of Commerce committee, chaired by George Wrigley of J.E. Sirrine Company and whose members included Mayor Richard Watson and George Barr, a local businessman and pilot who had served in the Army Air Corps during World War I. Stanton explained that a route was to be established between New York and Atlanta. There would be a stop in Greensboro, North Carolina, and since the route would cross the South Carolina Upstate, an airmail stop on the east side of Greenville would be his first choice. If Greenville could provide land, the federal government would prepare the site for an airport. Mayor Watson's reply to Stanton's inquiry: the city has no available land and cannot afford to buy any. Years later, George Barr remembered that meeting.[8] The mayor's response had cut short the discussion and the airport opportunity went next to Spartanburg. Undeterred by the mayor's refusal and still convinced that Greenville needed an airport, Barr led efforts to find a location in or near the city. It took time.

Charles Stanton's next stop was Spartanburg. It was a step ahead of Greenville. Chamber of Commerce President W.G. Jackson had already appointed James Grier to chair a study committee to explore the possibility of developing an airport. When Stanton arrived in Spartanburg with his offer of government help and his question if the city could provide a field for an airport, the answer was positive. After necessary negotiations,

Spartanburg was designated as the coveted Upstate site on the airmail route. The city had to work fast. On June 22, 1927, City Council authorized purchase from the Wingo estate of 105 acres southwest of downtown Spartanburg. The federal government funded the preparation of two runways, one 2,700 feet, the other 2,500 feet, and the building of two small hangars. Less than three months later, on September 10, 1927, Wofford College president Dr. Henry Snyder spoke at opening ceremonies and dedicated the new Spartanburg Memorial Airport to the memory of those Spartanburg County World War I fighters in France.[9] Spartanburg had the state's first commercial airport.

Back in Greenville, George Barr did not let the mayor's dismissal of the airmail opportunity discourage him. He and his friend Errett Williams, a barnstormer who had been flying out of a field on Cedar Lane Road west of Greenville, had been searching for a suitable airport site. They finally located about two hundred acres of farmland east of Greenville and asked representatives of the Federal Airways to come and check it out. Two engineers examined the site and sent their recommendation to Charlie Stanton, the man who had sought Greenville's interest in an airmail stop two years earlier. Barr next had to find twenty-five thousand dollars to pay for the land. Ward 4 Councilman J. H. Huff proposed that Barr ask the city, the county, the Park and Tree Commission and the American Legion Post each to pay a fourth of the price. Huff also suggested that Barr first meet with City Council to share his airport idea.

On October 26, 1927, George Barr went before the council with his persuasive argument on why Greenville should have an airport. He was encouraged when Alderman L. B. Clardy moved that Mayor Alvin H. Dean appoint an airport committee to work with committees from other organizations to help Barr develop his idea. The vote was unanimous. Having received pledges from the American Legion, the county and the Park and Tree Commission, on February 7, 1928, George Barr was back at Greenville City Hall where, according to minutes of that evening's council meeting, he asked the city for its contribution. Two weeks later, on February 21, 1928, Alderman L. A. Mills moved "that the city put up

$5,500.00 for their part of the airport, provided the other parties put up theirs and it is approved by the city attorney." Mayor A.H. Dean asked for a vote. The city's contribution to the airport property was unanimously approved.[10] The airport, George Barr knew, was assured. On November 11, 1928, thousands attended the dedication of the Greenville Municipal Airport—later known as Greenville Downtown Airport since the city had long ago grown closer to the airport.

Charles Lindbergh in Spartanburg

By the spring of 1927, sixty-six people had already flown across the Atlantic Ocean. Charles Lindbergh, however, wanted to fly a longer route and he wanted to fly it *alone*. At twenty-five, Lindbergh already had plenty of flying experience. He had been a barnstorming pilot and, in 1925, had flown the first airmail between Chicago and St. Louis.[11] On May 20, 1927, Lindbergh left muddy Roosevelt Field on Long Island, New York, at 7:42 a.m. His single-engine *Spirit of St. Louis* barely clearing the phone wires at the end of the runway, he headed out over the Atlantic. Beside him were five sandwiches and some water. Seventeen hours into the flight, Lindbergh was exhausted. He had to slap his face several times and open the cockpit window for fresh air to stay awake. Twenty-six hours into the flight he spotted Ireland. Then while heading toward the coast of France, he ate his first sandwich. Finally, he was over Paris, flying around the Eiffel Tower before heading to his planned destination.[12] Thirty-three and a half hours after leaving Long Island, he landed at Le Bourget on the outskirts of Paris. More than one hundred thousand wildly excited fans were there to greet him. Twenty-five-year-old Charles Lindbergh became an instant hero, a worldwide celebrity.

Just nineteen weeks after his triumphant greeting in Paris, Lindbergh landed his *Spirit of St. Louis* at the new Spartanburg airport. Lindbergh was visiting airports across the country to promote the government's new airmail service. The young aviator was greeted by Mayor Ben Hill Brown and a host of local and state dignitaries. He had never expected his daring flight would attract such attention and excitement. Thousands cheered and waved as he rode into downtown Spartanburg on the afternoon of October 12, 1927, atop the back seat of an open car.[13] That evening during a dinner at Converse College, Governor Richards, Mayor Brown and other leaders paid him tribute for his bravery and for what his daring accomplishment would mean to the still new era of aviation.

There was no doubt. Interest in aviation was skyrocketing because of Charles Lindbergh. Elinor Smith Sullivan saw it firsthand. In the years after Lindbergh's visit to Spartanburg, during the Great Depression of the early 1930s, the young woman aviator and stunt pilot flew in air shows with Lindbergh to raise money for the unemployed. Decades later Sullivan wrote:

> It's hard to describe the impact Lindbergh had on people. Even the first walk on the moon doesn't come close. The Twenties was such an innocent time, and people were still so religious—I think they felt like this man was sent by God to do this. That kind of public adulation is something that I doubt could ever happen again. And it changed aviation forever because all of a sudden the Wall Streeters were banging on doors looking for airplanes to invest in. We'd been standing on our heads trying to get them to notice us but after Lindbergh, suddenly everyone wanted to fly, and there weren't enough planes to carry them.[14]

Aviator Amelia Earhart also attracted the public's attention to aviation. She had been introduced to flying while serving during the last year of World War I as a Red Cross volunteer at a medical facility in Canada. She acquired a thirst for flying while listening to Royal Flying Corps (RFC) members recount their wartime exploits. With those stories fixed in her mind, Earhart moved to California and in 1920 took her first lessons from a pioneer woman pilot. She was soon flying solo and in 1922 bought her first plane. In it she set a record as the first woman to fly at fourteen thousand feet. Then for two years she performed stunt exhibitions across southern California before moving to Massachusetts. In 1930, Earhart landed at the Spartanburg airport for a brief visit to the city to promote aviation. In 1932, she was the first woman to fly the Atlantic alone. Three years later, she was the first pilot to fly solo from Honolulu to the United States mainland. On June 1, 1937, she and navigator Fred Noonan, former chief navigator for Pan American World Airways, left on their ill-fated round-the-world flight. They flew to Brazil, across the Atlantic to Africa, on to Saudi Arabia, Pakistan and India, then to Southeast Asia and on to Darwin, Australia. On June 28, they began their long flight from Darwin to Howland Island in the South Pacific and disappeared.

Another famous American who promoted aviation in those early days was auto maker Henry Ford. His Ford Trimotor planes had become popular and were being used to deliver mail on several routes. Ford even sent planes around the country to give rides and promote flying. When one of his planes came to Spartanburg, young Bruce Littlejohn and a friend went to the airport and paid fifty cents for their first flight—a short ride over the city. They made a big impression when they reported the experience to their friends. Littlejohn had remembered seeing his first plane when he was just ten years old. It was 1923 and the small biplane was flying over Littlejohn's home in the Spartanburg County town of Pacolet, following the railroad track to its destination.[15] Bruce Littlejohn grew up to be a lawyer, a circuit and appeals court judge before serving as Chief Justice of the South Carolina Supreme Court. He died in April of 2007 at the age of ninety-three.

Airmail comes to South Carolina

Less than eight months after the Spartanburg Memorial Airport had opened in September of 1927, it made history. At 9:35 p.m. on May 1, 1928, a Pitcairn Aviation Mailwing arrived with the first shipment of airmail into South Carolina. Spartanburg postal messenger Robert Fowler was there to pick up the mail. The specially designed biplane could carry up to six hundred pounds of mail on a New York City to Atlanta route that included Spartanburg.

The fascinating new service of airmail and the development of airports became intertwined. Early airplanes and airports spawned the idea of airmail. In turn, the reality of airmail encouraged communities to develop airports. Airmail was the twentieth century equivalent of the nineteenth century's Pony Express. It quickly became popular and spawned the establishment of several major airlines.

Captain Rickenbacker's Visit

By 1943, most commercial aircraft flying in the United States carried twenty-seven or fewer passengers, but larger aircraft were being designed and within a few years some planes would be carrying a hundred passengers or more. The small airports in Greenville and Spartanburg were already more than fifteen years old. They had not been built to accommodate the need that the fast growing aviation industry would soon have.

J. P. Williamson and his friend Tom Hartness were pilots who had often discussed the need for increased air service to the small Spartanburg and Greenville airports. Hartness had moved from Sanford, North Carolina, to work in his uncle's Pepsi bottling operation in Spartanburg. He had an idea. He would write a letter to Eastern Airlines' president Eddie Rickenbacker inviting him to Greenville to talk about Eastern's service to the area and the need for new airport facilities.[16] The idea was supported by area leaders. The letter of invitation was sent in early 1945, Rickenbacker accepted, and leaders across Spartanburg, Greenville and Anderson counties, along with several state officials, were invited. Organizers thought they would have no problem attracting people to hear someone of Rickenbacker's stature.

Captain Eddie Rickenbacker was America's top flying ace of World War I. Pilots credited with shooting down five or more enemy planes were honored with the title "Flying Ace." In the months between April 29 and October 30, 1918, Rickenbacker shot down twenty-six planes. Edward Vernon Rickenbacker was born in Columbus, Ohio, in 1890. He left school at thirteen following the death of his father. The rest of his education was by correspondence and included some engineering courses. He also trained as an auto mechanic. His fascination with cars sparked his interest in auto racing, and in 1914 he placed tenth in the Indianapolis 500. In 1917, Rickenbacker arrived in France as an Army Sergeant First Class and by the spring of 1918 was flying combat battles. His experiences in the Army Air Corps earned him both the Medal of Honor and the French Croix de Guerre.[17]

Several years after returning from World War I, Rickenbacker bought the world famous Indianapolis Speedway and ran it until World War II began. In 1938, he became president of Eastern Airlines and for more than two decades led Eastern through some of its most prosperous years. While at Eastern, in February of 1941, Rickenbacker was critically injured when a DC-3 on which he was a passenger crashed near Atlanta. The next year, Secretary of State Henry Stimson asked Rickenbacker to conduct an inspection trip of some South Pacific battle areas and deliver a message to General Douglas MacArthur. On the way from Hawaii to Canton Island, the B-17 in which he was flying went off course and the pilot ditched in the Pacific near Japanese-held territory. Rickenbacker along with other passengers and the crew drifted on rubber rafts for twenty-four days before being rescued. One had died before rescuers reached them.[18] Those experiences increased the mystique surrounding the dangerous and adventurous life of Eddie Rickenbacker.

On Thursday evening, April 5, 1945, more than three hundred filled the main dining room of Greenville's Poinsett Hotel. Governor Ransome Williams, U.S. Senator Burnet Maybank, Congressman Joseph Bryson, the mayors of Greenville, Spartanburg, Greer, Anderson and other cities and one of Rickenbacker's old flying buddies were in the audience. Chairman D. S. Burnside of Spartanburg's Aviation Committee introduced Bob Cates, the Spartanburg resident who had flown with Rickenbacker in World War I. Also in the crowd were representatives of several airlines seeking permission to serve the region.

"I say to you with all my sincerity, get together," Rickenbacker told the crowd. He was speaking as the president of Eastern Airlines, but to a war-ravaged world he was still Captain Eddie Rickenbacker, hero of World

War I. He could inspire a crowd as he often did in speeches throughout the country. "It just doesn't make sense," Rickenbacker claimed, "to cheat yourself with each city getting only half of the air service that would be available with one strategic airport." He noted the advantages already being enjoyed by the North Carolina cities of Raleigh and Durham and by the Texas cities of Port Arthur and Beaumont where joint airports had already been built. "The people in those cities don't know why they waited so long to reap the benefits of that sort of arrangement," said Rickenbacker. "That same benefit can and must happen between Spartanburg and Greenville."

Rickenbacker was promoting the concept of a regional airport as much for his company's benefit as for the cities of the Upstate. Eastern Airlines had for years been providing passenger service to the local airports of Spartanburg, Greenville and Anderson, airports that were only thirty miles from each other. As planes grew bigger and heavier, as the age of jet engines, which he predicted, approached, bigger airports with larger runways would be needed. His and other airlines would not be able economically to continue service to small airports in nearby cities. A joint airport "built halfway between the two cities," said Rickenbacker, "would serve to connect the 600,000 people living within fifty miles with the rest of the country."[19]

Reaction to Rickenbacker's passionate and eloquent speech was positive. Vice President Tom McGee of the Spartanburg Chamber of Commerce, reflecting on past inability to foster regional cooperation, declared, "the hatchet is gone now." Congressman Joseph Bryson, who represented the 4th District, which included both Greenville and Spartanburg counties, told the audience, "I'm the happiest man in the room over seeing Spartanburg and Greenville get together." The enthusiasm of the evening and the statements of inter-city cooperation notwithstanding, it would be twelve more years before serious movement began toward establishing a regional airport and another five years before that airport opened. However, Eddie Rickenbacker had given area and state leaders plenty to think about. Attitudes in the South Carolina Upstate were gradually changing. More time was needed.

As the leaders left Greenville's Poinsett Hotel that April evening, they did not know how drastically our nation and the world would change in the next week. As Rickenbacker addressed the crowd in Greenville that night of April 5, 1945, in Washington the Joint Chiefs of Staff made a critical wartime decision. They assigned General Douglas MacArthur and Admiral Chester Nimitz to lead American army and naval forces in an attack on Japan.[20] A new phase in World War II's Pacific Theater was about to begin. That was not the only change our nation would experience in the week following Rickenbacker's Greenville speech. The next Thursday, April 12, President Franklin Delano Roosevelt died in mid-afternoon at his retreat in Warm Springs, Georgia. A cerebral hemorrhage had taken his life at sixty-three. Exactly a week after the Rickenbacker dinner in Greenville, the United States had a new president. Harry Truman was sworn in that evening at 7:08. The next day fifteen thousand people gathered at the railroad depot in Greenville as the train carrying President Roosevelt's body stopped briefly on its sad journey from Georgia to Washington.[21]

Realizing that there would soon be bigger planes that would need longer runways and demand more support and services, there were short-lived and unsuccessful efforts during the 1940s to develop interest in a regional airport in the South Carolina Upstate. In early 1945, members at Woods Chapel Methodist Church, just east of Highway 101 near Greer, learned that land north of their church was being considered as a possible site for an airport. They sought help in opposing the airport from at least one nearby church. At a called "business conference" on February 18, 1945, the deacons of Abner Creek Baptist Church "agreed to appoint a committee to work with a liaison committee from Woods Chapel Methodist Church to oppose the building of an air base [sic] in that nearby community." Minutes of the meeting note that the members elected to the committee were Pastor D. R. Hill, J. O. Hendrix, R. B. McHugh, John P. Snow, Clyde Hughes and T. J. Hendrix.[22] The airport idea died.

Separate or together

Despite the passion and plea of Eddie Rickenbacker's "work together" message and the immediate impression it made on his audience of leaders, it would be another twelve years before serious efforts finally led to establishment of a regional airport in the South Carolina Upstate. There was progress in upgrading the local airports in Spartanburg and Greenville; however, there were some legitimate reasons for the inability to develop a larger regional airport in the Upstate.

In the 1940s, the distance between the downtowns of Greenville and Spartanburg—just thirty miles—was still a barrier to communication. In that pre-television era, the communities hardly knew each other. There were no regional organizations like the I-85 Alliance or the Appalachian Council of Governments, the International Center for Automotive Research or the regional programs of universities as there would be decades later. There was federal Highway 29 but no interstate highway. There were miles of fields and orchards and only occasional residences between the two cities rather than the almost continuous strip of industry and business that is there today. There were no regional shopping centers or regional entertainment and sports venues. There was no University of South Carolina Upstate, no University Center in Greenville, and, until 1947, no Bob Jones University. Furman University was deep in the center of Greenville, still years away from moving to its expansive campus north of the city. Thirty miles to the west of Greenville, Clemson College was a relatively small institution. South Carolina's statewide technical education system was years in the future. There were few activities or interests to attract people from one city to the other. As a result, the idea of working together as a region did not even occur to most leaders. Besides, each city had enough of its own challenges. The entire region was still struggling from the effects of the Great Depression a decade earlier.

If the Depression had been damaging to Greenville, it was devastating for Spartanburg. Before World War I, Spartanburg was the bigger of the two cities. It had actively pursued the railroads. By 1910 it already had rail lines going in all directions, leading to its well-deserved moniker "The Hub City." There were many textile mills, thanks in large measure to the Montgomery family and to northern textile baron and philanthropist Dexter Converse. A native of Swanton, Vermont, Converse had moved to Spartanburg in the 1850s. He bought and built a number of textile mills. He was to Spartanburg in the last half of the nineteenth century what Roger Milliken was to Spartanburg in the last half of the twentieth century. Spartanburg benefited greatly from Converse's largesse, especially his founding of Converse College in 1889.

When the Great Depression descended in October of 1929 banks closed everywhere. In an effort to save the banks, President Roosevelt imposed a "bank holiday." When the banks were allowed to reopen, Spartanburg's six banks remained closed. They were all locally owned. None survived. Since most of Spartanburg's mills were locally owned and the local banks had collapsed, the mill owners were hard hit. To add to the disaster, Spartanburg's biggest insurance company, Southeastern Life, moved to Greenville where some of the banks had survived because they were not all locally owned.[23] Greenville was home to more textile plants that were owned by large companies, which had been better able to withstand the financial strains of the Depression. Greenville also had Daniel Construction Company and J.E. Sirrine Engineering Company. Sirrine had designed Milliken's DeFore plant at Clemson in 1945, the first one-story, windowless, fluorescent-lighted, and air-conditioned plant in the country. Sirrine and Lockwood Greene in Spartanburg were two of the largest engineering companies in the United States. Daniel had moved its headquarters from Anderson to Greenville in 1942 and was quickly expanding from residential housing to constructing mills, educational and military facilities.

In Spartanburg, after the U.S. military closed Camp Croft following World War II, the Spartanburg County Foundation, which had been founded by Walter Montgomery Sr., acquired the base. With sewer, water and a railroad spur already serving the property, it was ready for civilian use. The foundation managed to recruit a major non-textile industry to move to the city.[24] Kohler built a large plant on the old Camp Croft property, the first move south for the Wisconsin-based manufacturer of plumbing fixtures and bathtubs, commodes and sinks. It was the beginning of industrial diversification for the city.

Economic challenges were not confined to the cities. Upstate farmers faced great difficulty prompted by declines in the cotton market and the results of poor farming techniques. By the 1940s, conservation measures had succeeded in restoring much of the Upstate's farmland, but the days of cotton as king were over. Peach trees were planted on much of Spartanburg County's agricultural land where cotton had bloomed a decade or two earlier.

In the early 1940s, electricity had only recently arrived at many rural homes. In the textile towns and cities across the Upstate, most of the mill workers lived in mill villages supplied by the companies for whom the people worked. Those villages with their own stores and churches, sometimes ball fields and meeting halls, were the centers of interest and activity for those who lived and worked there, many of whom did not have cars. Then, in 1953, came television. WFBC in Greenville, later to be renamed WYFF, was the first to go on the air, as an NBC affiliate, on New Year's Eve 1953. Little more than a year later, WSPA-TV in Spartanburg introduced CBS to the area. Television became popular as quickly in the mid-1950s as radio had in the 1920s and '30s. And not only popular, but influential as well. Any family who could find a way to afford a television—and many did—could now watch the world from their living room. They were not only entertained, they were informed. Informed in a way they had not been before. Television was bringing a powerful visual awareness of what was happening across our nation and around the world, every day. The residents of Spartanburg and Greenville could now see what was happening in each other's communities and across the Upstate. They saw advertisements for products and services in each other's cities. Soon markets that had been strictly local would become regional. Soon an interstate highway would be completed across the Upstate. Soon travel would be easier and faster, not only across the Upstate but also beyond. Television ads showed places that many people had only heard of before. Now many wanted to travel to see them. The influence of television, the prospect of easier and faster transportation and the hope of better economic days ahead were fueling excitement and anticipation across the South Carolina Upstate. The climate was right for regional cooperation. But it would still require some leaders with enough influence to transform vision to action.

The Flatwood Peaches were champions of the Spartanburg County Twilight League in 1952. Front: J. Wohonick, Dude Waddell, P. Wood, Poss Dillard, H. Davis, R. Duncan, J. Davis; back: W. Davis, B.C. Hawkins, G. Carlton, R. Cox, F.E. Hendrix, C. Davis, Hoss Owens, Bob Cox, Les Tillotson. COURTESY OF FRANCIS EARLE HENDRIX.

Flatwood Peaches manager Paul Wood plows a field in 1952 next to his 2,800-tree peach orchard in Flatwood. COURTESY OF KATHY WOOD EDGE.

Paul Wood (standing second from right) and his family in front of their Flatwood community home in 1919. The large home stood in the middle of what is now the GSP runway.
COURTESY OF KATHY WOOD EDGE.

A home is prepared for moving from the Flatwood community on July 20, 1961, as site preparations begin for the new airport. COURTESY GSP ARCHIVES.

This August 6, 1962, picture shows rapid progress on the airport terminal, concourse building, runway garden, control tower and runway since clearing of the land had begun just thirteen months earlier. The airport opened only nine weeks later. PHOTOGRAPH BY JOE F. JORDAN.

Crowds greet famed aviator Charles Lindbergh as he rides through downtown Spartanburg on October 12, 1927, less than five months after he had been the first to fly across the Atlantic alone.

COURTESY OF *HERALD-JOURNAL* WILLIS COLLECTION, SPARTANBURG COUNTY (SC) PUBLIC LIBRARIES.

At a testimonial dinner at Converse College on October 12, 1927, Charles Lindbergh stands with Spartanburg mayor Ben Hill Brown on his right and Henry Ligon Jr. and Governor and Mrs. John Richards on his left.

COURTESY OF *HERALD-JOURNAL* WILLIS COLLECTION, SPARTANBURG COUNTY (SC) PUBLIC LIBRARIES.

Lindbergh's Spirit of St. Louis*—the same monoplane he had flown to Paris on May 21, 1927—sits where Lindbergh parked it at Spartanburg Memorial Airport on his October 12, 1927, visit. The Spartanburg airport had been open just one month. Lindbergh's visit sparked great interest in flying.* COURTESY OF *HERALD-JOURNAL* WILLIS COLLECTION, SPARTANBURG COUNTY (SC) PUBLIC LIBRARIES.

Eastern Airlines began operations as Pitcairn Aviation with this Mailwing biplane. It first arrived in South Carolina at the Spartanburg Memorial Airport on May 1, 1928. COURTESY OF *HERALD-JOURNAL* WILLIS COLLECTION, SPARTANBURG COUNTY (SC) PUBLIC LIBRARIES.

Spartanburg's airport opened in September of 1927, the first commercial airport in South Carolina. On May 1, 1928, it received its first shipment of airmail. COURTESY OF *HERALD-JOURNAL* WILLIS COLLECTION, SPARTANBURG COUNTY (SC) PUBLIC LIBRARIES.

Greenville's "first aviator," Errett Williams, was one of the area's first "barnstormers." He flew out of a large field off Cedar Lane Road on Greenville's west side where he and other pilots would present air shows. He also helped his friend George Barr find property on which the Greenville Downtown Airport was built in 1928. Inset: Errett Williams in his plane. COURTESY OF THE GREENVILLE COUNTY (SC) HISTORICAL SOCIETY.

CHAPTER 2

From Dream to Design

Master salesman

More than twelve years had passed since Eddie Rickenbacker issued his call for Greenville and Spartanburg to "work together" to build a regional airport. Nothing had happened yet. Eastern Airlines loyally continued its service to the local airports in Greenwood, Anderson, Greenville and Spartanburg. That made it more convenient for Rickenbacker to hitch a ride into Spartanburg on one of his planes for an occasional visit with his old World War I flying buddy Bob Cates. On one of those visits in the mid-1950s, Cates invited a few friends to his home to meet Rickenbacker and hear about some of his adventures. Spartanburg textile executive Fred Dent never forgot that evening. "He was a fabulous human being," said Dent. Rickenbacker recounted that night the same story he had told the Greenville dinner crowd in 1945, the one about him and several others drifting on life rafts for twenty-four days after their military inspection plane had ditched in the South Pacific. But he added another detail. "A seagull landed on my head," Rickenbacker told Dent and the other guests. "I carefully reached up and grabbed its leg. That was my food for the next couple of days." Dent remembers thinking, "This man must have nine lives."[1]

By the summer of 1957, the jet age was looming. Airplanes were bigger and Rickenbacker's and other airlines no longer wanted to serve small local airports that were inadequate for those bigger planes. The cities that had the foresight to build larger regional airports were trumping economically those cities that lacked the vision.

Charlie Daniel believed Eddie Rickenbacker in 1945. He still believed him in 1957. He could see it happening on either side of the South Carolina Upstate's two biggest cities. Seventy miles east of Spartanburg, Charlotte's airport had opened its new passenger terminal in 1954. Growing numbers of Upstate residents were already driving to Charlotte to board flights. A hundred and sixty miles southwest of Greenville, Atlanta's fast-growing airport was starting construction on its new terminal. By 1961 it would be open. Then residents from far northeast Georgia and far western South Carolina could be driving to Atlanta to board flights, if they weren't already. There was an even bigger concern. Upstate business and industry could soon be using the greater capacity of those airports for cargo shipments. If Greenville and Spartanburg did not soon heed Rickenbacker's long-ago plea for a regional airport, South Carolina's Upstate would be left behind in the inevitable rush toward the jet age. That could be an economic disaster.

Charlie Daniel loved Upstate South Carolina. It had been kind to him. He had been good for the Upstate, indeed for all of South Carolina. For years, he had regularly been riding the rails between Greenville and New York and other cities selling the benefits of his construction company and the state to anyone who would listen. As soon as he learned that a company might be considering a new plant or a move south, Daniel would be on the next train north to New York or wherever that company's headquarters was located. He would tell the top officer about South Carolina, why it would be a good place to build a plant and why he would be a good one to build it. Daniel had also been an enthusiastic supporter of the State Development Board that formed in 1945 to promote recruitment of industry to South Carolina.[2]

Textile executive Robert Small had traveled with Daniel and remembered how he could captivate people. "The South was looked down upon (in that era) as an underdeveloped part of this country," Small explains. "He had a vision to lift up South Carolinians and the whole South both economically and educationally." Referring to a dynamic early twentieth century evangelist and preacher, Small said of Daniel, "He was a Billy Sunday of industry."[3]

Daniel Construction Company had developed into one of the largest general contracting firms in the country. The company had built numerous industrial plants and World War II defense installations, including the Army Air Base (later Donaldson Air Force Base) near Greenville. It had constructed the Greenville campus of Bob Jones University in 1947 and had built several facilities at Clemson College.[4] Charlie Daniel had become South Carolina's most effective salesman for business and industry. By 1957, his lofty leadership position was worlds apart from the humble family into which he had been born on November 11, 1895, in Elberton, Georgia.

Daniel was just five when his father moved the family thirty miles northeast across the Savannah River to Anderson, South Carolina, to look for better job opportunities. Mr. Daniel was a millwright and he knew there were mills in the Upstate that could use his skills of setting up and repairing machinery. He taught those carpentry skills to young Charlie, who worked several high school summers making pallets at the Townsend Company in Anderson. After two years at the Citadel in Charleston and service in World War I, Daniel returned to the Townsend Company in 1919 and was allowed to build houses. Soon he began building several at a time and by 1924 he gained Townsend a contract to construct a 175-house mill village in Anderson for a textile company. A 350-house contract in Rome, Georgia, soon followed. By 1934, Daniel had decided to take advantage of the new post-Depression business climate. In December, he chartered Daniel Construction Company, occupied office space in the Townsend Building, and began broadening his services. In February 1942, Daniel moved his growing company to a new building it had constructed on North Main Street in downtown Greenville.[5]

In 1956, Governor George Bell Timmerman Jr. appointed Daniel chairman of a three-member planning committee that the state legislature had created to study and recommend financing for maintenance and construction at South Carolina's ports in Charleston, Georgetown and Beaufort. It was a short-lived assignment since Daniel and the other two committee members resigned a few months later, disagreeing with the Ports Authority over how to proceed with policy making and administrative functions.

His brief volunteer effort with the ports system behind him, Charlie Daniel by 1957 had time to focus on another of his concerns: a regional airport for the Upstate. He had been talking about that need for some time with two of his friends. Alester Furman Jr. had deep roots in the Greenville community. He had been the chairman of Furman University's board of trustees when the decision was made to buy property for a new campus north of Greenville. Furman had also for many years been vice president of the Woodside National Bank.[6] Walter Brown was a Georgia native who had served in Washington as an aide to Charlie Daniel's old friend, former Spartanburg attorney James F. Byrnes. President Roosevelt had appointed Byrnes as the nation's director of war mobilization during the early years of World War II. When Roosevelt elevated Byrnes to the U.S. Supreme Court, Walter Brown moved to Spartanburg and bought WSPA radio from the owner, who had put it on the air in 1930 as the state's first radio station. After Roosevelt's death in 1945, President Truman appointed Byrnes Secretary of State and Brown returned to Washington to work with his former boss. He was with Byrnes, Truman, Stalin and Churchill at the famous Potsdam Conference on the outskirts of Berlin in the summer of 1945. That was the conference at which defeated Germany was divided among the four major Western allies. After Brown left the Truman administration he returned to Spartanburg and in 1956 put WSPA-TV on the air.[7]

Daniel, Furman and Brown discussed the names of others in both Greenville and Spartanburg counties whom they thought could be helpful in building support for the regional airport idea, including Spartanburg textile industry leader Walter Montgomery Sr. They knew the man they needed to lead the project. He was a successful business leader and an excellent planner, thorough and detailed. He was a good motivator, had great connections, was younger than the three of them and had boundless energy. All three knew him, but would he be available? They scheduled a luncheon to ask him.

Roger Milliken had not lived long in Spartanburg. After years of commuting between New York City and Spartanburg, in 1954 he moved his family into their new home in the city. In 1958, he would move his textile company's headquarters from New York to land along where Interstate 85 would soon be built on the city's north side. Milliken already knew Spartanburg well. He had begun visiting the city in the 1930s when he would accompany his father on train trips south to promote the company's business.

Deering Milliken had been founded by his grandfather and a friend in 1865. Twenty-one-year-old Seth Milliken was the proprietor of a small country store in the town of Minot, near Portland, Maine. Young Seth loved trading and he often made trips to Boston to buy goods, not only for his own store but for other country stores as well. The more he bought, the better prices he obtained from wholesalers. So he joined with William Deering to represent textile mills in the area. They would sell the mills' greige goods—unfinished fabrics that had not yet been dyed or printed—to wholesalers. Deering soon left the company because of illness, but Milliken kept the Deering name and continued to grow his company. Around 1900, Seth Milliken moved his operations to New York City and began investing in textile mills that needed cash. He bought several failing mills and soon became a major mill owner.

When Seth Milliken died in 1921 at the age of fifty-eight, his son Gerrish took over. By then, Deering Milliken had evolved into a manufacturing company with several mills, some of them in the South. It wasn't long before Gerrish Milliken bought another one. Judson Mill in Greenville, South Carolina, was one of the first rayon manufacturing plants. During the years that followed, Gerrish Milliken, often accompanied by son Roger, made many an overnight train trip south to check on his plants in the Carolinas and to acquire additional ones.[8]

By the time Roger Milliken had graduated from Yale in 1937 and had worked for a brief time at Mercantile Department Stores, another family business, he was ready to begin helping his father locate and build or renovate plants. Throughout the next decade and a half, Milliken spent half of every month in the South, often staying at Greenville's Poinsett Hotel and, after 1941, working out of an office at the new Daniel Construction Company headquarters on North Main Street in Greenville.[9] The rest of the month he worked at company headquarters in New York City. One day in 1947, he and his father were hosting a group of textile suppliers for a day of golf at a course on Long Island. Roger and his foursome had just started their round when his father, who was playing two holes ahead, suffered a fatal heart attack. He was sixty-nine. A short time later, the Deering Milliken board named thirty-two-year-old Roger Milliken president of the company.[10]

Ten years later, by the time he sat down with his friends for lunch that day in the fall of 1957, Roger Milliken was a seasoned industry leader. He shared the concept that Spartanburg and Greenville needed to take a bold step to ensure their economic viability. Milliken agreed that a new airport in the area was needed. However, it had never occurred to him that he might be involved in, let alone lead, such a project. So did he accept the job immediately? "Instantly," he remembers, "because I respected Charlie Daniel and he said this would be a monumental decision for the future.[11] I had driven all over the country, often with Charlie Daniel, looking for plant sites. I loved designing a plant. Charlie knew that and he knew how much detail would have to go into planning an airport. So he knew it would interest me." During that time in his life, though, Roger Milliken hadn't thought much about airports. His emphasis was on building and renovating textile plants. His preferred method of long distance travel had usually been trains. That's how he had made many of those trips between New York City and South Carolina. "I hated flying. I was scared of it," Milliken admits. "When I did book a plane trip," he chuckles, "some of my colleagues teasingly called me 'Cinders.'" His other nickname was "Big Red" because of his six-foot-two-inch frame and red hair.

Charlie Daniel shared Roger Milliken's preference for trains. His company didn't even buy its first airplane until 1956. It was then that Daniel quickly became a fan of flying.

A UNIQUE RELATIONSHIP

Life is often a strange matchmaker. Here was Charlie Daniel, a Georgia boy from a modest family who had attended the Citadel, served in the

Army during World War I, and had labored hard as a builder. Then, while building what grew to be one of the country's largest construction companies, he meets a man from New York City, a graduate of Yale who had majored in French history, named Milliken.

It was 1939. Roger Milliken had taken possession of the Excelsior plant in the Upstate textile town of Union, a few miles south of Spartanburg. The building needed major renovation and construction. He asked some friends for the name of a good builder. They suggested Charlie Daniel. The two men met for the first time at the Union plant, where Daniel found Milliken sweeping the floor. Daniel helped finish the cleaning job. Then they sat down on the front steps of the plant's office to get acquainted and talk business.[12] Daniel was forty-four. Milliken was twenty-four. It was the beginning of a friendship that grew quickly as the two men began designing, renovating and building plants together. Milliken was the conceptual designer of their first joint projects. He would share ideas with Daniel, who would comment and add suggestions. Then the two would refine the concept. When engineers had completed the plans, Milliken would give his approval, then Daniel and his company would do the job, quickly and well. There was never a contract between the two, just respect, confidence, trust and a handshake.

Charlie Daniel and Roger Milliken came from such different backgrounds. Yet they were so much alike in some ways. Each had a seven-day-a-week capacity for work. While many South Carolinians went to church on Sunday mornings, Daniel went to work. In the one-story headquarters that he built in 1942 on Greenville's North Main Street—next to a church—his Sunday morning meetings with executives were legendary. When he finished his meetings, he would drive to job sites and conduct a walk-around inspection. If he found a problem or had a question or wanted to meet with the project manager, he would drive back to North Main Street and leave a note on that project manager's desk. Robert Yeargin was one of Daniel's early project managers who later started his own construction firm. Early Monday morning, Yeargin would always stop by the office to check his desk. If there was no note from Charlie Daniel, he could breathe easier.[13]

Roger Milliken shared Daniel's attention to detail. Anyone who has worked with or for Milliken remembers his questions. They were questions generated not only by his thoroughness but also by a genuine curiosity and a passion for quality. Hard, smart work and exacting detail and thoroughness were attributes the two men shared. Attributes that revealed their absolute commitment to any task they assumed or to any organization with which they worked. Robert C. Edwards had the unique opportunity to work with both men. For ten years, Edwards was in Abbeville overseeing Milliken plants there and in nearby towns. During that decade, he became well acquainted with Milliken's questions. He also met Charlie Daniel, whose firm was working on some of the plants. In 1956, as a life trustee of Clemson College, Daniel was looking for a vice president of development for the school. On Daniel's recommendation, Clemson's board offered Edwards the job. Soon, Bob Edwards was riding the overnight train north. Daniel would take the young vice president along to introduce him to contacts in New York who might be candidates for making contributions to Clemson. Edwards was amazed at Daniel's commitment to the school, especially knowing how busy he was running his company. Edwards was vice president only a short time. Just two years after he took the job, he was elevated to acting president of Clemson following the sudden death of President Robert F. Poole. Ten months later, on April 19, 1959, Robert C. Edwards was named Clemson's president. Decades after he retired in 1979, Dr. Edwards remained convinced that "Clemson College could not have developed into Clemson University on July 1, 1964, had it not been for the vision and leadership of Charlie Daniel."[14]

Both Daniel and Milliken were also politically active. Daniel even served briefly as a United States senator. He replaced former Charleston mayor and governor Burnet Maybank, who had defeated former governor Olin D. Johnston of Anderson in 1941. Near the end of his second full term, Maybank suffered a fatal heart attack on September 1, 1954, at his vacation home in Flat Rock, North Carolina. Two months later, Governor Byrnes appointed Daniel to fill the remaining weeks of Maybank's senate term. After just six weeks, Daniel resigned in order to give his friend, write-in candidate Strom Thurmond, the advantage of gaining extra seniority by allowing him to begin his senate term early.

Roger Milliken neither served in nor sought political office. However, he used his resources of money and influence to support conservative political candidates and causes. He was a major supporter of Republican Barry Goldwater's 1964 presidential campaign. The candidates who benefited from his support were usually, but not always, Republicans. He supported Democratic Senator Ernest Hollings for reelection in the 1990s because of his support of the beleaguered American textile industry. The causes that attracted his attention were almost always conservative organizations and issues. He strongly opposed the long-running GATT, the General Agreement on Tariffs and Trade. Milliken thought its agreements, which were updated regularly, undermined America's textile industry by allowing unfair imports and taking American jobs. For some of the same reasons, he was an ardent opponent of NAFTA, the North American Free Trade Agreement. To combat the nation's troublesome trade imbalance, and what he regarded as unfair and damaging trade policies, Milliken created and funded his Crafted with Pride in America campaign. For years it has promoted the quality and integrity of American-made products.

The Crafted with Pride campaign reflected Milliken's longstanding commitment to quality within his own company. By the time he dropped the name "Deering" and renamed it Milliken & Company in 1976, the firm had become one of the largest privately held companies in the world. It was also widely regarded as the most successful of America's textile companies, partly because of its heavy emphasis on research and development. Since Milliken had assumed leadership of the firm in 1947 and had built its Spartanburg research center in the late 1950s, Milliken & Company by 1990 had been granted more than fifteen hundred patents on a wide range of products.

One of Milliken's proudest achievements was his company earning the Malcolm Baldrige National Quality Award from the National Institute of Standards and Technology (NIST), an agency of the U.S. Department of Commerce. Created by Congress in 1987, the award recognizes American companies that improve quality and productivity. It is named for Malcolm Baldrige, a U.S. Secretary of Commerce in the 1980s known for his managerial excellence, which helped improve government efficiency. Secretary Baldrige was killed in a 1987 rodeo accident.

In 1989, the Baldrige Award recognized Milliken & Company for its Pursuit of Excellence program. One of the program's results was that by 1988, Milliken & Company had improved its on-time delivery to an industry best of 99 percent. The award also specifically recognized the company's chief executive officer, Roger Milliken, for playing what the award citation called "a key role in pioneering quick response as an important strategy for American industry."[15] By the early years of the twenty-first century, Milliken & Company had 11,000 employees worldwide, 9,300 in the United States. It had for years been the largest privately-held company in South Carolina and the largest privately-held textile company in the world. In 2006, Roger Milliken stepped aside after fifty-nine years as chief executive officer. He retained his role as chairman of the board.

By the time Charlie Daniel turned his attention to the need for a regional airport, Daniel Construction Company had long since grown beyond a regional firm. Known for its ability to build high quality projects and deliver them on time, Daniel not only built facilities of all types throughout the United States, but it also had projects in the Caribbean, Europe and the Middle East. In the years ahead, Charlie Daniel's brother, Hugh Daniel, and his wife's nephew, Buck Mickel, would assume leadership of the company. Mickel eventually merged it with one of the nation's largest engineering and construction firms, California-based Fluor Corporation.[16] Fluor would maintain a major presence in Greenville where the name of Charlie Daniel would never be forgotten.

Now, in the fall of 1957, the unique relationship enjoyed by Charlie Daniel and Roger Milliken since their meeting eighteen years before continued. They would bring all of their business experience to the proposed building of a regional airport for the Upstate. It would be a challenge, but they thrived on challenges. First, they had to assemble a team, develop a design, and then sell the idea.

Assembling the Team

Charlie Daniel and Roger Milliken knew they needed to have a good, comprehensive plan designed before they took their airport idea to the people who would have to approve—first, the state legislators from Spartanburg and Greenville counties, and then the entire South Carolina General Assembly. Until they had that plan prepared, they would work quietly and proceed quickly. They would need money to retain the necessary experts on airport design and planning. That would be no problem. They would pay those initial bills themselves. They also wanted a good team, the best experts they could find. Roger Milliken liked to say, "If you want the *best* job, find the *best* people." In fact, he wanted *world-class* people, as he was fond of calling them.[17]

Assembling the team progressed rapidly. Both Daniel and Milliken had been in business a long time. Their circles of influence and connections were wide and impressive. No committee needed to conduct interviews and decide on selections. They knew whom they needed and wanted. They started with their choice for engineer. That was simple. A graduate of Clemson College, Alex Crouch, along with his brother, owned Piedmont Engineering in Greenville. For years, their firm had provided engineering services for many of Daniel's building projects. Crouch was eager to participate in the project. His first assignment was to begin looking for some appropriate properties to consider for an airport site. Daniel and Milliken also retained Leigh Fisher & Associates of San Francisco to conduct a survey, prepare a long-range forecast of aviation activity in the South Carolina Upstate, and then recommend airport facilities to accommodate that forecast. There was another obvious local choice whom Charlie Daniel offered as a team member. Like Daniel, a native of Elberton, Georgia, by 1958 Buck Mickel was assistant to the chairman at Daniel Construction. In November of 1960, Daniel would name Mickel his executive vice president. During the years of airport planning and preparation, Mickel would coordinate many of the project's details.

Milliken and Daniel needed an architectural firm, one with plenty of experience in airport design. Their choice was Skidmore, Owings & Merrill in New York City. But Skidmore was a huge firm. Founded in 1936, it had already established a reputation as one of the world's leading architectural, urban design and engineering firms. During the decades before and since the 1940s, its projects have included the 109-story Sears Tower and the 100-floor John Hancock Tower in Chicago, the Bank of America pyramid-shaped tower in San Francisco and the U.S. Air Force Academy in Colorado Springs. It also has designed major airports and some of the world's tallest skyscrapers in other countries. Roger Milliken had used the firm on some of his projects, but would Skidmore be interested in working on a small regional airport in Upstate South Carolina? There would be no harm in asking. Milliken had recently dined with Skidmore's Chicago office director during a meeting at banker David Rockefeller's home in New York City. He called Chicago and asked if this "world-class" architectural firm would consider designing a regional airport in South Carolina. The answer was yes.[18] The designer assigned was a young, fast-advancing New Jersey native. Mike Keselica would be sent down to Spartanburg for a meeting with Milliken, Daniel and Alex Crouch. The team was starting to take shape. Now a good land planner and landscape architect were needed. Roger Milliken found them both in one man.

~

When Milliken was growing up in New York City, his family had what he described as "a very nice family place up in Maine in an area where there were lots of beautiful gardens." His mother had a friend, Beatrix Farrand, who was at the time "the most famous woman landscape architect in the United States," as Milliken remembers. Mrs. Farrand would help his mother with her gardens. Although he had never taken a course in landscaping, Roger Milliken had developed an appreciation for landscape architecture and design. He knew he wanted the best landscape architect he could find for the new airport.

Some of the best advice Milliken ever received came from his friend and neighbor Virginia Russell. She was the wife of Spartanburg attorney

Donald Russell, who served as governor, federal judge, University of South Carolina president and briefly as United States senator during a long career of public service in South Carolina. Mrs. Russell suggested the name of a landscape architect she thought was the man Milliken needed to meet: Richard K. Webel, a partner in the Long Island, New York, firm of Innocenti & Webel. The Russells were Spartanburg neighbors and longtime friends, so Milliken took Mrs. Russell's advice seriously. Virginia Russell was right. Milliken and Webel were a good match. By the time their first meeting had concluded, the two men had struck a friendship that lasted until Webel's death in 2000 and which Milliken continues today with Webel's son and protégé Richard C. Webel.[19] It is a relationship that has resulted in the site design and beautifully landscaped setting that has won the Greenville-Spartanburg Airport many awards and thousands of compliments.

Innocenti & Webel has left its creative and beautiful imprint on several areas of South Carolina. In Greenville, the Furman University campus, the Fluor Corporation engineering center, and parts of the city's downtown owe much of their beauty and design to the philosophy and creativity of Innocenti & Webel. In Spartanburg, Milliken & Company's headquarters and research and development complex along I-85, the campus of Wofford College and much of the redesign and restoration of the city's downtown bear the marks of Innocenti & Webel's design expertise. It is expertise that most of those clients still retain. Richard K. Webel's experience in South Carolina began in the early 1930s when two of his wealthy New York clients bought Hilton Head Island with the intention of developing a hunting estate. Over the next twenty years, Webel and his partner, Umberto Innocenti, provided land planning and landscape architectural and design services for wealthy coastal landowners who were developing plantations in South Carolina's Low Country.

Webel had been working on the master plan for the new Furman University campus being developed along Poinsett Highway, six miles north of Greenville. The school had no room to grow and its gracious old buildings were declining on its small campus near the Reedy River in downtown Greenville. Furman University's trustees bought 972 acres of gently rolling agricultural land in the shadow of Paris Mountain. They retained noted Boston architect Robert Dean, who asked his longtime friend Richard K. Webel to assist in designing a master plan for the future campus of the university. Dean had designed the reconstruction of Colonial Williamsburg in Virginia. Furman's leaders liked Dean's proposal to include some of the ideas he had used at Williamsburg in his design for the campus buildings. They also liked the complementary land planning and landscape ideas that Webel brought to the proposed design.[20] Campus design and construction continued for more than five years before the first of Furman's students began moving to the new campus in 1958.

Roger Milliken retained Richard K. Webel to work on the airport project. The more Milliken learned about Webel's education, experience and philosophy, the more he became convinced that Webel was exactly the right man for the job. After earning a bachelor of science degree from then Harvard College, Richard K. Webel had enrolled in Harvard's Graduate School of Landscape Architecture in 1923. The most influential mentor during his three graduate school years was the man for whom he worked during his last summer. Ferruccio Vitale was a young army engineer. He had spent some time in the diplomatic service and had an aristocratic and dignified bearing that helped him make friends with prominent architects. That gave Webel his first opportunity to work with architects on an interesting project, the national competition to design the Jefferson Memorial, which would be built in Washington, D.C.

In the mid-1920s, New York architects could not keep up with the demand for work created by the large number of emerging industrialists moving to New York City and wanting to build estates in places like Long Island, where Ferruccio Vitale's office was located. Vitale had convinced many of the architects to conceptualize site work as they developed their architectural designs instead of treating land planning and site development as an afterthought. It was a different approach that emphasized the *architecture* in the profession of landscape architecture instead of concentrating simply on the *landscaping*. Many architects liked the approach. For

Vitale, it was successful. While Vitale met with architects onsite to design concepts, summer intern Webel and the other staff in Vitale's studio worked on the details.

Vitale's partner, Alfred Geiffert, had been observing the twenty-three-year-old Webel's work. Geiffert thought Webel started drawing plans and pictures before he did enough thinking. "He taught me," Richard K. Webel told his son and protégé decades later, "to put down my pencil and stop drawing pictures—to 'wiggle my *mind* before I wiggle my *pencil*.'[21] He would encourage me," Webel explained, "to visualize the topography as it was and as I wanted to make it. Then, he would require that I throw out the first image and develop an alternative one. When this had been repeated three or four times to his satisfaction, Geiffert allowed that I would be reasonably prepared to speak with the client and be able to think on my feet. This was helpful advice." Indeed. It was advice that permeated Webel's work for the rest of his career. It was advice that helped him win a coveted prize that sent him to Italy for training, and it was advice that Roger Milliken watched Webel use when the Greenville-Spartanburg Airport was being designed. It was advice that ultimately would save the airport project considerable time and money.

When Richard Webel returned to Harvard that fall of 1925 for his final year of graduate school, his confidence was high and his grades were excellent. He applied to be considered for the coveted Rome Prize, so called because it provided a year of study as a fellow at the American Academy in Rome, study which included observing and learning in the famed gardens of Tuscany and Florence. Harvard's Graduate School of Landscape Architecture was the oldest in the United States, but no Harvard student had ever won the Rome Prize, which was awarded only once every three years.

Richard K. Webel was selected as one of that year's finalists. Each finalist was assigned a hotel room and given a demanding assignment: produce a design complete with working drawings and details. They had two weeks to complete the assignment. All of the finalists stayed in their hotel rooms and started working, except Richard Webel. "While everyone else was madly drawing," Webel recalled years later, "I took a whole week off and just wandered around the city, drank coffee and thought. Then I went back and spent almost a week making paintings and sketches of what I wanted the place to look like. Only when that was finished did I go to my working drawings, grading and planting plans to support those sketches." Webel's solution was radically different in approach from that of the other finalists. He won the Rome Prize. "I still think the reason I won," Webel told his son years later, "went back to the training I had received from Geiffert."[22] Webel had remembered Alfred Geiffert's advice. He had wiggled his mind before he wiggled his pencil.

During the next year in Italy, those gardens of Tuscany and Florence taught Webel a valuable lesson that would shape his approach to landscape architecture and delight his clients: the enormous potential for beauty and elegance in tightly constrained places. "I was just amazed," he told his son, "that on those great huge pieces of land, the intensively developed areas were kept to an absolute minimum, just around the dwelling and its dependencies. They didn't want to give up one inch that could be cultivated for vineyards or agriculture."[23] The gardens of Tuscany and Florence were forever fixed in Webel's mind. The lesson became a key to his designs. One has only to observe the beauty and efficiency of the landscaping at GSP or Furman University, at Wofford College or on the University of South Carolina campus in Columbia, or at any of the other Webel client properties to understand why Richard K. Webel and his partner, Umberto Innocenti, designed and planted the way they did.

Years later, when Roger Milliken would reflect on the team he and Charlie Daniel assembled to design and build the airport, he enjoyed sharing his philosophy and reflecting on his good fortune. "I was lucky to have been introduced to the best," he would say. "If you are going to do something, you find the best firm to do it. The difference between good and best is all the difference in the world. All this has been a team effort," he was quick to emphasize. "What I believe in so desperately is that making projects successful is a *team* sport and not an *individual* sport."[24]

One of the team of people who helped garner support for the airport in the late 1950s was textile baron Walter Montgomery Sr. He was already an influential and generous leader by the time Roger Milliken moved to Spartanburg in 1954. The two men became good friends and, as an example of the respect that Montgomery had earned in his industry and the Spartanburg community, Milliken often told a favorite story about him. Walter Montgomery and a friend from Georgia took their wives on a European vacation. When the wives decided to fly home early, the men stayed a little longer and returned to the United States by ship. True to his sociable nature, once on board, Montgomery obtained a passenger list, checked off everyone who had a South Carolina address and sent each one an invitation to an on-board cocktail party. Talking to one of the guests at the party, Montgomery's friend asked where she lived. "Spartanburg," the lady replied. "Well," said the gentleman, "you must know my friend Walter Montgomery." "No," she replied, "I don't know him personally, but I can tell you that Mr. Montgomery is to Spartanburg what the Statue of Liberty is to New York City." Roger Milliken thought that was an accurate way of indicating Walter Montgomery's valuable leadership in his community.[25] It was the kind of influence that had been needed in generating enthusiasm and support for the airport. For almost a year, beginning in the autumn of 1957, Milliken, Daniel, Montgomery, Furman, Brown and their friends assembled a team of like-minded and concerned leaders and worked on their plan of designing an airport. One of the first jobs was finding a site.

Looking for the land

It was just before lunchtime when the phone rang in Alex Crouch's office in Greenville. The head of Piedmont Engineering immediately recognized the voice. "Alex," said Charlie Daniel, "be out front with some of your maps and information on Greenville and Spartanburg counties. Roger and I will pick you up. We're going to look at something." Crouch had just enough time to gather his topographical maps, quadrangle sheets and other items he might need before the Daniel limousine arrived.

As soon as Crouch was settled in the back seat with all those maps and sheets, Roger Milliken said, "Alex, where can we put a new airport to serve Greenville and Spartanburg counties?" Crouch had been looking at some possible airport sites but until that moment he had not realized the exact purpose of this trip. Surprised and scrambling to find the sheets he needed in the information he had brought, Crouch directed Daniel to a site near where Interstate 85 was being planned between the towns of Greer and Pelham. Crouch said he had found some land that looked "very promising." He told the men it was the only site in the area that looked appropriate for an airport. It sat astride the county line, near utilities, next to where the interstate would be built, with a spine facing the right direction and on high terrain almost midway between Spartanburg and Greenville. Arriving at the site a short time later, the three men looked around, studied Crouch's quadrangle sheets and discussed many details. It appeared to be an ideal site.[26] It was a rural area known locally as Flatwood.

On a plateau at about nine hundred feet above sea level, the site offered ample long, flat stretches next to gentle ridges. It also lay in a southwest to northeast direction that would reduce runway crosswind problems because prevailing winds in this area were usually out of the northeast. Engineer Crouch was a pilot. Since this land was higher than much of the surrounding property, he thought pilots would find approaches easy, clear and safe. And if more property were needed, there appeared to be adjacent land that could be available. Interstate 85 was not yet finished. Greenville and Spartanburg were still miles away. Nearby Greer was just a small town; Pelham was a village. The whole area was mostly farmland with scattered houses, wide expanses of undeveloped acreage and almost no business activity. The site appeared to be ideal for development of the airport that Daniel, Milliken and Crouch thought would be vital to the economic future of South Carolina's Upstate. Within forty-five minutes, impressed and satisfied, they had found the site they wanted. They really liked this land. Problem was, many other people liked it too. The residents of Flatwood called it home.

Designing the airport

If they were to be successful in selling the idea of a regional airport to local public officials, Charlie Daniel and Roger Milliken knew they would need to have a solid proposal with a realistic, functional and exciting design. Developments in aviation were moving at a startling speed in 1958. Airport and airline competition was growing. Bigger and faster planes were being built. Passenger numbers were rising and the demand for air cargo was increasing. The design for this airport would need to be innovative and flexible to accommodate inevitable changes over many years. Adequate land was needed to allow for long-term growth to provide necessary buffers between the airport and its future neighbors. They had assembled an experienced team to design the plan, as thoroughly and quickly as possible. "Quickly" in airport planning can mean years. There was no time to waste. Every year that passed, the South Carolina Upstate might be losing economic opportunities to other airports and markets. Right now, though, the idea of regional airports was novel. Time was crucial. "When we decided we wanted to build the airport, we wanted to build it expeditiously, with all due haste," Roger Milliken recalled decades later.[27]

One of Milliken's first meetings was with the design team sent from Skidmore, Owings & Merrill (SOM) in New York. Senior designer Art Widhoff, design partner Roy Allen, project manager Frederick Ganns and junior designer Mike Keselica visited the site where engineer Alex Crouch showed them the proposed location of the runway. They also listened to Roger Milliken explain his vision for the airport. Since three of the designers were already involved with other projects, Keselica was soon assigned as SOM's project manager on the GSP job.

A graduate of the Rhode Island School of Design, Keselica had spent two years in the army before earning a master's degree in architecture from the Massachusetts Institute of Technology. SOM had a job waiting for him in its New York office just across the river from Keselica's New Jersey home. In the fall of 1957, he had been at SOM for little more than a year but already had been exposed to airport design. Later in his career,

Keselica would work on several airports overseas, including as project manager for the new Ben Gurion Airport in Israel.

Roger Milliken wanted Keselica and others from SOM's conceptual group to see other U.S. airports. They went to Miami to meet with Eastern Airlines officials. Among others, they visited what was regarded as an innovative regional airport in Wichita, Kansas. There, some of the service functions had been submerged in a "tunnel arrangement." The designers also visited some airports that were joint-use civilian-military facilities. They quickly determined "that was not a viable way to go," Keselica recalls. Some of the survey trips to other airports were aboard Milliken & Company's DC-3. Engineer Alex Crouch piloted his own plane on other journeys. Keselica says, "Alex Crouch was an affable Southern gentleman. He was competent and always wanted to do things properly. It was a pleasure working with him." It was also frightening, at times, to fly with him. "We would frequently fly with Alex," Keselica remembers, "and I had some white knuckle rides." Crouch and his passengers always returned safely and with some worthwhile observations and ideas for their airport design.

During the design process, Keselica was also consulting with other experts. He interfaced frequently with Wayne Wells at Arthur Andersen. Wells supplied the financial analysis as design work progressed. In those days, Arthur Andersen was highly respected in the accounting world. Roger Milliken regarded the firm as "the best in the world." That was before they had a "bad apple in the barrel," he noted, referring to the firm's demise in the wake of the Enron scandal in the early 2000s.

Mike Keselica and his team set to work on ideas for a terminal design. "At first, we pressed the idea of a terminal with a tunnel to remote holding areas." Roger Milliken was not impressed. "Damned if they didn't want us to build mushrooms," Milliken chuckled years later. "It was a unique architecture. I told them we live in South Carolina. If we have to spend a lot of money, people will want to see how we spend it and I didn't want it to be underground." Keselica and his team looked at other design possibilities for the terminal. "At the time," Keselica recalled, "we were doing a lot of buildings that were complete glass structures." However, Keselica and his colleagues soon discovered that "Roger Milliken was averse to a glass building." It was the normal back-and-forth exchange of tastes and opinions in which designers and clients often engage. The designers wanted to propose concepts for a jet age airport. Milliken and his fellow airport commissioners wanted a building that was jet age as well, attractive and appealing, but affordable. They had to be thinking cost.

"Eventually," said Keselica, "we acceded to Mr. Milliken's wishes and created a solid building with a strip of windows. It was a good concept with the great hall (terminal) and the open finger concourse. It had good scale and proportion. It was very simple with concrete and stucco." Keselica remembers that the concept was "very well received."[28]

Richard K. Webel liked the fact that his advice was being sought early in the airport design process. He enjoyed projects where the overall use of the land and the landscape architecture would be planned and designed at the same time as buildings, runways, parking areas and roads were being considered and designed. That's the way he and his partner, Umberto Innocenti, preferred to work with clients. Innocenti and Webel had established a reputation not only as good landscape architects but also as astute land planners. They were, they believed, most useful when they could have influence on the overall design and use of the client's property.[29] So Webel appreciated Roger Milliken's invitation to come frequently to the early planning sessions.

"In the beginning when we were planning this," Milliken recalls, "every second weekend Mr. Webel would come down from New York City and we would spend two days together." Webel stayed at Milliken's guest house on Milliken & Company property in Spartanburg where the planning meetings were held. Milliken remembers one of those first meetings, after engineers and architects had been working on where and how to locate the terminal and runway on the land. Several people were at the weekend meeting, including engineer Alex Crouch, the man who had selected the property.

"Mr. Webel comes in, rolls up his sleeves, and puts our plan on the table," Milliken recalls. "He has a big rubber eraser and a soft pencil and he starts looking at the plan. After several minutes of looking and silence, somebody whispers, 'What's he doing?' I said, "Don't disturb him. It's important. But I don't know what it is." Webel worked intently and silently for a long time, frequently using his big eraser and his soft pencil. Finally, Webel broke his silence and said to engineer Alex Crouch, "I think if we move the runway a hundred feet in that direction we can save three hundred thousand cubic feet of earth moving." Crouch and Milliken were excited. To Milliken, that was the advantage of using what he liked to call *the best people in the world*. "So we made the change and it made all the difference," recalled Milliken. "We much better utilized the property and we were talking about a lot of money saved."[30]

Richard K. Webel's long and careful study of the airport site plan that day was an example of what he had learned during that summer internship while at Harvard University thirty-five years earlier. He had remembered the advice from mentor Alfred Geiffert: wiggle your mind before you wiggle your pencil. What Webel did that day, and at other weekend planning sessions with Milliken and the design team in Spartanburg, was more than move a proposed runway. Webel was struggling to balance design criteria with the reality of the site's valleys and ridges. He didn't want to see the native character of the beautiful rolling site destroyed by leveling *all* of the land. As Webel's son and future GSP consultant Richard C. Webel noted about his father's work in his 1998 book *Making a Landscape of Continuity*, "the results were unconventional for an airport: a terminal building cross-section that steps up with the site to accommodate the arrival/departure level split." What resulted from Richard K. Webel's land planning ideas was a terminal ultimately with three levels, designed to fit the contours of the land. Webel would have much more influence on the airport's design before its opening. His early advice had been crucial and cost-saving.

An unusual idea

Years before he became involved with planning an airport, Roger Milliken was sitting alone one day at the airport in Frankfurt, Germany, waiting for a flight that was late. He was watching the planes land and take off while having a drink in a pleasant little biergarten.[31] Memories of that experience came back to him one day shortly after design began for the Greenville-Spartanburg Airport. "Let's be brave," Milliken told Richard Webel, Mike Keselica and other members of the design team. "Let's take the best airplane position at the terminal and make it a garden instead." The best airplane position, of course, would be right in the middle of the gate positions, on the runway side of the terminal. That's exactly what Milliken wanted. It was an idea that was virtually unheard of. What airport would reserve prime space like that for a garden? What airline would like that idea? Didn't matter. Roger Milliken was serious. He thought passengers and visitors would enjoy it. He was sure it would be good for the airport's image. He was positive people would talk about it. He was right. "We've never had a complaint," he would often say years later. "Never. Nothing but excitement."[32] Architect Mike Keselica had been surprised by the idea when it was suggested but he agreed with the results. "The airlines told Mr. Milliken it would be wasted money. People said the plants and flowers would die. But they didn't. It was," said Keselica, "a real innovation. One of the nicest features of the airport."[33] Somehow, Roger Milliken was sure that would be the result. So, he instructed the airport's designers to make a runway-facing garden part of the plan for the proposed airport.

While the initial design work on the airport continued, the aviation survey and traffic forecast were completed. Financials were compiled. Alester Furman and Walter Brown, along with Walter Montgomery Sr., were quietly gathering support from other leaders and communities. They gained endorsements from Mayor Neville Holcombe in Spartanburg and Mayor Kenneth Cass of Greenville. Before the end of the year, Roger Milliken, Charlie Daniel and Alex Crouch would be ready to take their proposal to the Spartanburg and Greenville county legislators and go public with their plan for a regional airport.

CHAPTER 3

Building the Airport

Selling the plan

"This part of the country has been losing industry to other areas. A major reason has been lack of adequate new air facilities." Forty-three-year-old Roger Milliken was addressing members of the Spartanburg and Greenville county legislative delegations. If this airport was going to fly, these were the elected officials who first must be sold on the idea. Then they would have to persuade their colleagues in the South Carolina General Assembly. A regional airport would require public funding, at least for the design and construction.

Milliken's assessment of the area's airport facilities was in no way intended to be critical of either the Spartanburg Memorial or Greenville Downtown airport. They had been operating for three decades, both serving general aviation and both served by Eastern Airlines. However, neither had the capacity to handle the new breed of commercial aircraft on aviation's horizon. "This airport project could super-charge development of the entire Piedmont area," Milliken told the local legislators.

The public selling of the Piedmont Area Airport proposal began at the Greenville County courthouse on the evening of Tuesday, November 11, 1958. Roger Milliken and engineer Alex Crouch presented the plan, complete with preliminary design drawings. The plan's major points:

- The airport is designed to accommodate "ultra modern turbo jets" and future jet aircraft.

- At least 2,000 acres must be acquired in Spartanburg and Greenville counties.
- Proposed site is almost halfway between Greenville and Spartanburg, north of I-85, with all but five hundred acres in Spartanburg County.
- A terminal and runway will be built. An additional parallel runway can be added later.
- An airport tax district must be created with six commissioners, three from each of the two counties.
- The commission's duties will include purchasing land and overseeing design, construction, operations and maintenance of the airport.
- The proposed name will be Piedmont Area Airport. (By the time the airport opened, it was usually called Greenville-Spartanburg Airport or "the jetport." In later years, it was generally referred to by its FAA code designation: GSP.)
- The estimated cost: $5,509,000.
- Each county will contribute $2 million to be raised through an increase in the tax millage.
- $1.5 million in federal funds will be sought.
- The airport could be in operation by 1961.[1]

As Milliken and Crouch explained their airport plan, "there was an atmosphere of excitement in the room," Rex Carter remembers. A Greenville attorney, Carter had been elected to the South Carolina House of Representatives in 1952. Later, he would serve as Speaker of the House for seven years before retiring from the legislature in 1980. As a still-young member of the legislature on that night in November of 1958, Carter was impressed with the scope of the airport plan and the thoroughness of the presentation.[2]

Roger Milliken told the legislators about steps that had already been taken: the studies, the retaining of top experts in the field of engineering, design, landscaping and financial analysis. He said experts had been asked for a plan by which the best possible airport could be built, for today and the future. "The potential," Milliken assured the lawmakers, "is even greater than we had anticipated." He projected that the joint airport could build the South Carolina Piedmont into what he called the distribution center of the Southeast. "If we do this thing right," Milliken declared, "we will have an advantage that few such communities have ever realized." He noted that the growth of cities throughout America had been tied to available transportation facilities. "This decision," he said, "is the same type faced by towns one hundred years ago that wanted to build beside a railroad. Here, we have a facility in keeping with the growth of our time."[3] Roger Milliken and Charlie Daniel deeply believed in the need for an airport. They were committed to it. They had paid all the bills so far.

After the presentation and questions, the two delegations met, each to appoint four members to a joint study committee to consider the proposal. The study committees were asked to make a report with their recommendations in two weeks. The Greenville County study committee was headed by Senator Bradley Morrah; the Spartanburg County committee by Senator Charles Moore. (Prior to 1966, counties had only one senator who was usually the chairman of the county legislative delegation. House members were elected at-large rather than from separate districts in their counties.)

Reaction to the airport proposal came quickly, most of it positive. The next morning's *Spartanburg Herald* called the airport proposal "a magnificent concept...enough to send the imagination soaring." *The Greenville News* on November 14 called the proposal "a boldly conceived and sound plan. Without this proposed airport," said the editorial, "industrial development could stagnate." Even Buck Moss, manager of the then thirty-one-year-old Spartanburg Memorial Airport, was positive. "Traffic might increase here if the joint airport is built," Moss predicted. "The private pilot on business isn't going to fly into a big airport if there is one close by in Spartanburg."

Chambers of Commerce in Greenville, Spartanburg and other cities endorsed the plan, which also drew support from communities to the north like Landrum and Campobello in northern Spartanburg County, and Tryon across the border in North Carolina. It was especially well received by many of the business executives in those towns who had long been hoping for improved air service to other parts of the country and overseas.

Even before word of the November 11 meeting with the legislative delegations hit the newspapers, television and radio, the residents of Flatwood had heard of the airport plan. Some of them had stood at their front doors or gazed from their front lawns or farm fields and watched the surveyors sizing up the land. Some of them asked questions. And when the surveyors told them about the airport possibility, some Flatwood residents began marshalling their opposition. Within ten days after the November 11 meeting, Paul Davis, his neighbor James Byars, and other Flatwood volunteers had collected 325 names on a petition asking the Spartanburg delegation members to vote against the proposed site. The petition said the airport "would disrupt the whole community and have an adverse effect on our churches and excellent farmland. We would be forced out of our homes where we have prepared for our families and with no satisfactory place to go. There must be," said the petition, "some less populated, less valuable land that would be suitable."[4] Byars and Davis asked the Spartanburg delegation for a public hearing on the issue. They and their fellow residents did not know how much of their Flatwood community would be needed for the airport. They were sure, however, that it would be enough to change their quiet way of life forever. They were right.

The committees appointed by the legislative delegations went to work quickly, meeting with their local airport managers and commissions and studying the traffic and financial estimates supplied by the proposal's supporters. Leigh Fisher Associates of San Francisco had developed the survey statistics. Passenger traffic was estimated to increase 800 percent over seventeen years, from almost 61,000 currently at the two local airports to 490,000 at the new airport by 1975. A review of 1947 to 1957 traffic at the two local airports had already showed growth higher than the national average. Growth estimates for cargo were also healthy, from 457 tons in 1956 to an estimate of almost 4,200 tons by 1975. And the Piedmont Engineering study noted that with even greater community and industrial expansion expected, a higher growth rate in air travel could be anticipated.

The proposal's operating budget predictions for the first fifteen years of operation were also positive. From 1960 to 1975, operating expenses of $2,360,000 were estimated against revenues of $4,835,000 from landing fees, terminal space rentals, concessions, parking, rental cars and newsstands. If close, that prediction would mean a "profit" of as much as almost $2.5 million, which would provide reserves and allow for some expansion. It would also bolster the promise, important to legislators and county officials, that after the initial general obligations bonds to fund construction were paid off, the airport would seek no more local property tax money. It was a promise that was kept. Operationally, the airport has been self-sustaining from the day it opened. Even its multimillion dollar major expansion in the late 1980s was underwritten by the airport selling bonds that it paid off with its own revenues.[5]

On Monday, November 18, 1958, the Spartanburg delegation's airport committee met with Alex Crouch of Piedmont Engineering to review details of the plan and then expressed "strong approval" of it. The next day, the full Spartanburg delegation accepted the committee's recommendation and unanimously approved the plan. Said delegation chairman Senator Charles Moore, "I am hopeful we can work it out (in the legislature) for the benefit of both counties and the entire Piedmont."

The same evening, the Greenville members of the joint study committee met with commissioners of the Greenville Municipal Airport: Chairman William T. Adams, Hugh Aiken, Olin Spann, Ed McCardy, William Coxe, and their airport manager O. L. "Andy" Andrews. "We want to ask questions because these are our airport experts," said committee member and Greenville County delegation chairman Bradley Morrah. The local airport commissioners told the delegation committee that the best interests of the community demand that a new airport facility be established and that the local airport commission "vigorously sponsors the development of the proposed Piedmont Area Airport."[6] The reasons for the local commissioners' recommendation were clear. They said it would be "grossly impractical economically, if not impossible physically, to develop the present site to meet the minimum foreseeable and predicted need in the coming decade. The economic well-being of our community, to a great extent," the local commissioners said, "is pivoted around a long-range, progressive air transportation program; such a program could not be launched from the present site." The recommendation concluded that the development of a joint-usage airport between Greenville and Spartanburg would allow the Greenville Municipal Airport to continue rendering "invaluable service to our city and county, devoid of financial liabilities." When the joint study committee took the recommendation of the Greenville airport commissioners to the full Greenville County legislative delegation, former representative Rex Carter recalls, "There was no debate. The consensus was to go forward." The delegation approved the airport plan.[7]

The two delegations met together the next Monday, November 24, to ratify the joint airport proposal. It had been less than two weeks since the plan had been presented to them. That rapid local approval was greeted by more positive response. Editors of *The Greenville News* applauded the legislators for moving on the proposal "with admirable speed" and for pledging to seek enabling legislation in the next General Assembly session beginning in January 1959. "All this is encouraging," wrote the editors, "because the airport is a must." Representative Rex Carter agreed. "Had we not taken this step, our economy would have been in bad shape," Carter observed years later. "It was the first time I could ever recall Greenville and Spartanburg doing something together and I give Charlie Daniel and Roger Milliken all the credit."

With local legislative support assured, the airport plan and the federal money required to help fund it needed to be discussed with members of the state's congressional delegation and with officials of the Federal Aviation Administration. Senators Moore and Morrah and four House members from the two counties headed to Ft. Worth, Texas, to brief regional FAA officials. They took with them engineering consultant Alex Crouch, who explained details of the plan and answered questions. The officials were "interested and impressed with the cooperation evidenced by both counties and by the detailed engineering data presented," the two senators reported. The FAA officials also told them the next step would be to coordinate air space requirements with other aviation agencies. That would be accomplished at a meeting the next month in Atlanta. The FAA officials thought the proposed site would be acceptable. They indicated that a commitment for funding would take longer. There were no federal funds in the current fiscal year, but perhaps next fiscal year, beginning July 1, 1959, money might be available. The local legislators were also told that the proposed state legislation creating a new airport commission and approving construction would need to meet certain FAA requirements to ensure maximum federal participation.

Meantime, Greenville representative Rex Carter and a small group of legislators traveled to Washington to pursue the needed federal funding. They met with the state's two senators, Strom Thurmond and Olin D. Johnston, and members of the Senate and House appropriations committees. They also received a favorable response from 4th District Congressman Robert Ashmore, who pledged support in seeking federal dollars for the project.[8]

Back in Columbia, since the Greenville and Spartanburg legislative delegations were in accord on the airport plan, the General Assembly approved by unanimous consent the bill creating the airport tax district. Within twenty-four hours of the bill's approval, the Greenville and Spartanburg delegations proposed an amendment to satisfy an objection that had been raised in the financing part of the bill. It called for each county to contribute a total of $2 million toward the estimated initial cost of the airport. The proposal was for each county to be taxed two mils. However, since Greenville County had a greater assessed evaluation, a district-wide tax levy would raise more money in Greenville County than in the smaller Spartanburg County. Moreover, most of the proposed site—about two thousand acres—was in Spartanburg County; just a small portion—less than five hundred acres—in Greenville County. Spartanburg County stood to lose ten thousand dollars a year in property taxes. So the two delegations agreed that Spartanburg County would be credited for ten thousand dollars each year in determining the share of each county's obligation. Imbalances beyond that, the delegations agreed, would be adjusted by payments from one county to the other so that each county's annual contribution would be on parity with the other. The General Assembly approved the amendment, and the act creating the district with six commissioners, three from each county, was passed on March 25, 1959, and signed into law by Governor Ernest F. Hollings.[9] The work on the proposed airport was now ready to move from the informal stage, led and funded personally by Roger Milliken and Charlie Daniel, to the formal stage led by the new six-member Greenville-Spartanburg Airport Commission.

The men who made it work
The original commissioners

On April 6, 1959, Governor Hollings appointed the six initial commissioners nominated by the Greenville and Spartanburg county delegations. By law, each commissioner would serve a six-year term without remuneration and each would be eligible for reelection at the will of his or her county's legislative delegation.

At forty-three Roger Milliken was the youngest of the appointees and the only one not a South Carolina native, although he knew the state well as a result of conducting business there for more than two decades. A native of New York City, he graduated from Yale University and by 1958 had for more than a decade been the president and CEO of Deering Milliken, the world's largest privately-held textile company. He, his wife, Justine, and their five children had moved to Spartanburg in 1954.

The other Spartanburg County representatives on the commission were L. A. Odom and S. J. Workman. Odom was a sixty-two-year-old attorney who had been Spartanburg's city attorney under Mayor Ben Hill Brown. The owner of an oil company and founder of a savings and loan association, he had served in the South Carolina House and Senate in the 1920s. A native of Bennettsville and a graduate of Wofford College, Odom came to the commission with long years of airport experience as a twenty-five-year member of the Spartanburg Memorial Airport board. In fact he had spoken at the dedication ceremonies for that airport in September of 1927. In his law practice, he had also represented aviation companies and had appeared several times before the Interstate Commerce Commission and the Civil Aeronautics Board. S. J. Workman of Woodruff had served as mayor of that southern Spartanburg County community and as a state highway commissioner. A native of Woodruff, he had been president of the local Chamber of Commerce and had business and agricultural interests both in Spartanburg and Greenville counties.

The three commissioners representing Greenville County were Hugh Aiken, John Ratterree and W. T. Adams. Sixty-one-year-old Hugh Aiken was a native of Laurens County and a graduate of Davidson College in North Carolina who had long ago moved to Greenville, where he founded Piedmont Print Manufacturing Company and was still its president. Sixty-eight-year-old William Taylor Adams had worked his entire career for Fiske-Carter Construction Company. A native Greenvillian, he had served on the Greenville Municipal Airport Commission for thirty years and had been its chairman since 1946. Licensed in 1916, Adams was one of the nation's early pilots. When he entered the military in 1916, the Army Air Corps had only eleven planes. He served in Italy and in Tours, France, where he was chief of the U.S. Army Air Corps Flying Field. John Ratterree owned five firms in his native Greer. He was also vice president of Columbus, Ohio-based State Auto Insurance Company. Ratterree was active in many civic and industry organizations and had served on the Greer City Council.

At its first meeting, the Airport Commission elected Roger Milliken as chairman, L. A. Odom as vice chairman and W. T. Adams as secretary. Milliken appointed Adams as the commission's representative to oversee construction of the airport. Individually and as a group, these six original commissioners brought to their role considerable business and aviation experience. It would be needed because they would soon be facing major challenges.

The Donaldson Question

Just four days after the December 7, 1941, Japanese attack on Honolulu's Pearl Harbor, the U.S. Army notified Greenville officials that an airbase would be built just south of Greenville.[10] Built quickly by Daniel Construction Company and opened in mid-1942, the Army Air Base was used primarily to train B-24 and B-25 bomber pilots fighting in World War II. In the late 1940s, the base played a support role in the post-war Berlin airlift and conducted other humanitarian airlifts. In the early 1950s, it was renamed Donaldson Air Force Base, in memory of Lt. John Owen Donaldson. Born in South Dakota, raised in South Carolina, Donaldson attended Greenville High School and later joined Britain's Royal Air Force. He became a flying ace credited with shooting down eight enemy planes during World War I. In the 1920s, he operated a charter flying service in Brooklyn for several years. He died in 1930 while performing at an air show in Philadelphia.[11]

In 1953, Donaldson's mission changed when the 63rd Troop Carrier Wing was assigned there. Two years later a young officer from New Jersey was promoted to public information officer of the Wing. Ron Copsey's father had been commander of the same Wing when it was a reserve unit twenty years before in New Jersey.[12] During 1955, huge C-124 Globemasters flew supplies to the ice of the Alaskan and Canadian arctic for the building of the Distance Early Warning Radar (DEW) line. It was a series of remote radar installations across the Arctic to provide the United States and Canada with an extra thirty minutes of warning should Russia fire missiles at the two countries. Those same large planes from Donaldson also for several years in the late 1950s and early 1960s supplied America's research efforts in Antarctica. As part of Operation Deep Freeze, the planes flew to Christchurch, New Zealand, where they refueled and flew on to McMurdo Sound on the coast of Antarctica, then to the South Pole. A sign over Donaldson's front entrance proudly proclaimed it the Airlift Capital of the World. Built by Douglas, the C-124 at that time was the largest cargo plane in the air force. The 63rd Troop Carrier Wing had the motto "anything, anywhere, anytime." Its reputation was well deserved. C-124 crews were in the air on all sorts of missions: national defense projects, scientific research and exploration, humanitarian airlift and for supporting the U.S. military.[13]

By the time federal funding for the new joint airport was being requested and promised in 1960 and early 1961, Donaldson's days were numbered. The base had outlived its usefulness and the government was preparing to announce its eventual closing. Some local legislators saw the soon-to-be-deactivated Donaldson as a logical, lower-cost location for the proposed regional airport. Among them was Rep. Fred Fuller, who had been a member of the Greenville County legislative delegation's original four-member committee appointed in November 1958 to study the proposal for the new airport. He had second thoughts about the proposed location and still wanted Donaldson considered. If it became available, said Fuller, Greenville city and county, which had donated the site for the base to the federal government in the 1940s, would have to develop an industrial park. "One of the finest things would be to have the leading airport of the Piedmont sitting right in the middle of it," Fuller told the *Greenville Piedmont*. "I'm afraid we may be giving up something awfully good for Greenville," he warned. As late as April 1961, months after federal funding had been promised, Fuller and Representative Charles Garrett were still urging a "go slow" policy on the project.[14]

The fight for funding

The Federal Aviation Administration was the agency that approved federal funds to help build airports. The first notification of the initial plans for the airport had been sent to the FAA in November 1958, shortly after the Greenville and Spartanburg county legislative delegations had approved, in principle, the preliminary airport plans and cost estimates. The request for Washington's help was formalized a few months later after the Greenville-Spartanburg Airport Commission had been created by state law and its initial members appointed by Governor Hollings.

It wasn't until August 1959 that the FAA responded, saying the Airport Commission's request would be considered for inclusion in the FAA's 1961 plan only if a complete regional economic study were conducted. In addition, both the FAA's regional office in Dallas and the Airport Division of the Washington office would have to concur with all proposals in the economic study. Only then would the FAA consider making it part of the 1961 plan.

Each year, the FAA budgeted a certain amount for airport construction and improvements. Only those requests that made it into each annual plan were considered for funding. The original local request had contained some economic information on the Upstate, but the FAA said the Greenville-Spartanburg Airport plan was unique. The proposed new regional airport would replace two existing local airports that already had regularly scheduled airline service. So the FAA said it needed a more detailed economic study "in order that we may be in a fair position to support a proposal of this type." (The local airports did not close.)

On August 31, the FAA broadened its requirements. It said the new study of the area's air transportation needs should include an engineering study on both the Spartanburg and Greenville local airports, along with studies on the costs of developing Donaldson Air Force Base and on costs for building and developing the new airport through 1970. The agency also wanted projections on how Donaldson Air Force Base could be included in the plan either as part of a joint military-civilian airport or as a strictly civilian airport.[15] All those requests represented a tall order. Realizing it needed help with such a study, the newly-appointed Airport Commission retained Leigh Fisher & Associates of San Francisco to conduct the air transportation needs study and the engineering costs study on the proposed new airport site as well as at Donaldson and the two local airports. Working with Leigh Fisher would be the two firms that had already been retained: Skidmore Owings & Merrill and Piedmont Engineering.

The future of Donaldson Air Force Base had been the object of conjecture and rumor for several years. In the late 1950s the air force was starting to abandon some of its bases and questions about Donaldson's future began to circulate. Finally, on November 28, 1960, Brigadier General Andrew Cannon told a news conference that the air force was changing Donaldson's status to a "reserve installation." As commander of the 63rd Troop Carrier Wing, Cannon was Donaldson's senior military officer. The air force decision was a blow to the area's economy. At the time, five thousand military and civilian personnel were employed at the base. The *Greenville Piedmont* reported that, based on reports circulated before Cannon's announcement, five hundred homes were already for sale and that soon more than thirteen hundred rental properties would flood the local real estate market.[16]

Since moving a base to reserve status is often the prelude to closing, speculation increased concerning the possibility that the base could be transformed into the new regional airport. However, when Leigh Fisher & Associates reported results of its economic study to the Airport Commission in January 1961, it called any development of Donaldson Air Force Base "the most costly solution" for a regional airport location. The firm's survey revealed that the opinion expressed by all agencies contacted indicated that Donaldson could not adequately serve the civilian aviation needs of the Upstate.[17] A major problem was its location. It was southeast of Greenville, many miles from Spartanburg. Based on the Leigh Fisher conclusions, the Airport Commission decided that Donaldson was unsuited to serve as a regional civilian airport and it removed the base from further consideration. The economic and engineering reports were forwarded to the FAA with the commission's concurrence.

Moving swiftly the FAA in mid-January 1961 authorized the commission to proceed with detailed development plans for making the Greenville-Spartanburg Airport operational as soon as possible and it promised to help fund about one-third of the project, which by latest estimate stood at seven million dollars. But the idea of Donaldson as a site for the new airport still had its supporters.

The airport is approved

Wednesday, January 18, 1961. The headline in the afternoon *Greenville Piedmont* blared the long-awaited news: "Work to Begin Soon on Modern Facility. Money Allocated for Joint Jet Airport."

It was the privilege of Senator Strom Thurmond and 4th District Congressman Bob Ashmore to make the official announcement: the first federal money—$550,000—had been granted so that airport site preparations could begin. Senator Thurmond had kept the pressure on his close friend General Elwood Quesada, who released the funding just two days before he retired as head of the Federal Aviation Administration. John F. Kennedy was about to become president and General Quesada would soon be switching his attention from airports to baseball as leader of a new major league baseball franchise in Washington, D.C.

"This will be a great boon to the future development of the great Piedmont area of South Carolina," Thurmond safely predicted in his official announcement. No one was happier or more relieved by the news than the Airport Commission chairman. "I am thrilled with the news," said Roger Milliken, who was in New York City. "I think I speak for all the people who have looked forward so long to the time when we could start on a new, modern joint airport." He promised, "It will be the objective of the Airport Commission to proceed with a view toward having the airport available for use at the earliest possible date."

"We will proceed immediately," Andy Andrews told reporters. Andrews was the longtime manager of the Greenville Downtown Airport. Just a week after the initial federal funding was announced the new Airport Commission, with permission of the Greenville Downtown Airport Commission, hired Andrews as executive director for the new airport. Until it opened, Andrews would have two jobs—running the local airport and working with the Greenville-Spartanburg Airport commissioners preparing for the new one. "We'll begin with land acquisition," Andrews announced.

Construction

The six airport commissioners knew they had plenty of work ahead of them. Since most of the land needed was in Spartanburg County, vice chairman L. A. Odom asked John Rigby and T. B. Thackston of Spartanburg to begin calling on Flatwood residents and appraising property. Each owner was to be offered the appraised value. Odom asked Spartanburg attorney Milton F. Smith to do the legal title work. The land acquisition proceeded quickly. Smith recorded the first deed on April 7, 1961. By early summer, most of the land needed had been acquired with only about half a dozen parcels going to condemnation proceedings. Smith had prepared titles on more than two hundred fifty parcels of land.[18]

At the February 28, 1961, commission meeting, Roger Milliken reviewed his tentative construction and development schedule. He wanted construction to begin by August 15, 1961, and the airport opened by October 15, 1962. That would be a fifteen-month construction schedule. It was an ambitious one because this was already the last day of February. If the chairman had his way, construction would begin in just five and a half months.

No one took the chairman's proposed project timetable lightly. Milliken had a habit of setting seemingly impossible goals for project completions. He also had a reputation for accomplishing those goals. So commissioners, airport staff, architects, engineers—everyone—had to take his seemingly impossible tentative schedule seriously. They knew that in Milliken's mind, it was more than a *tentative* schedule. The details that had to be addressed were mind-boggling.

Richard K. Webel and the engineers began negotiating and planning with the South Carolina Department of Highways on relocating a stretch of Highway 14 on the west side of the airport property. They also had to negotiate with state and federal officials on an interchange that would be needed off Interstate 85 for an entry road to the airport. Then there were roads on airport property that would have to be relocated. Skidmore, Owings & Merrill architects began working on design of a terminal. Some current utilities had to be removed, the location of future ones planned and all of the proposed land had to be acquired. Even as land acquisition was underway at that site halfway between the major cities of Greenville and Spartanburg, the question of Donaldson had to be put to rest.

Notwithstanding the Airport Commission's January action in rejecting further consideration of the Donaldson site and the FAA's agreement and positive attitude toward funding help, some critics of the proposed I-85 site near Greer continued to lobby for the Donaldson site. Three months after the commission's decision not to consider Donaldson, an open letter carried in *The Greenville News* on April 21, 1961, raised the level of debate, as much for who wrote it as for what it said. The author was Alester Furman Jr. Surprising, since Furman was a good friend of Charlie Daniel and one of the men who had joined in asking Roger Milliken to head the airport effort. But Furman was an astute business leader who felt strongly that if local and federal money could be saved by locating the airport at Donaldson, and if enough regional support for the site could be generated, the air base location should be considered. Furman suggested that ten Upstate counties — Greenville, Spartanburg, Oconee, Pickens, Anderson, Abbeville, Greenwood, Laurens, Cherokee and Union — "do the patriotic thing" and ask the federal government to make Donaldson available for civilian use. Emphasizing that he intended no criticism of the Airport Commission for planning a new airport, he did not think selling bonds at this time was necessary. He thought that the air base site would be "ideal for a regional airport" with its hangars, runways, airfreight warehouses, railroads, and water and sewer service. "We could save the federal government and Greenville and Spartanburg counties a large sum in taxes," he declared. Furman asked the Greenville and Spartanburg county legislative delegations to request that the bond sale be deferred until Donaldson's future was made clear. "We do not believe they (Charlie Daniel and Roger Milliken) would advocate the spending of unnecessary federal and municipal funds for something we already have," said Furman.[19]

Furman's letter appeared as part of an article by William D. Workman Jr. on April 21, 1961. Airport Commission Chairman Roger Milliken wasted no time in responding. In a statement released the next day to reporters he explained why Donaldson would not be appropriate and why the site already selected near Greer was ideal and met FAA specifications. Answering Furman's assertion that the Donaldson site could save federal and local tax dollars, Milliken said the conclusions of the study that Leigh Fisher had conducted indicated that developing Donaldson as a civilian airport would cost taxpayers virtually as much as building on a new site. "Based on the most expert counsel obtainable," wrote Milliken, "the commission believes that the site at Greer is the solution that provides the way to obtain the maximum amount of air service to and from this community, that it offers the cheapest answer to this problem for each of the two counties, and that it would be an airport that will generate the most income at the lowest possible cost of operation." He closed his statement by giving his assurance that "when completed, this airport will be one of the most modern facilities of its kind in the country, adequate to serve the needs of the area for many years to come."[20] As far as Milliken and the Airport Commission were concerned, the Donaldson question had been laid to rest. Now that local funding had been assured, federal funding had been approved and the first federal monies received, it was time to proceed with building the airport.

The Airport Commission on April 27 authorized issuance of $3 million in bonds to help cover the local share of land acquisition and initial airport construction costs. On May 10, the commission approved the basic layout plan for the terminal and ordered architects to proceed with working drawings.

At its June 28, 1961, meeting the commission agreed to negotiate with the Greer Public Works Commission to supply water and it began discussions with Southern Bell regarding future phone service. However, commissioners did face one obstacle. The Federal Bureau of Roads would not approve the proposed construction of the interchange that would be needed to link the airport terminal with Interstate 85. Commissioner

S. J. Workman, a former member of the State Highway Commission, said he would pursue the matter. There was encouraging news. An FAA grant offer of $659,352 was accepted, the second installment of the promised federal funding. That money now assured and most of the initial needed acreage having been acquired, the Airport Commission awarded a site preparation contract to Asheville Construction Company.

Dozens of area leaders joined members of the Airport Commission along with staff and members of the design and construction team for groundbreaking ceremonies on July 7, 1961. One of the attendees that day was Leigh Fisher, owner of a San Francisco firm that was a consultant to the airport. Fisher shared with several people at the ceremonies, and made the mistake of telling Chairman Roger Milliken, that he did not see how the airport could possibly open on the date Milliken had set, October 15, 1962. When, in fact, the airport did open on that date, Milliken would have some fun at Fisher's expense.

Less than three weeks after the groundbreaking, commissioners reviewed the architects' proposal for design of the terminal. According to minutes from that meeting on July 24, the estimated cost of $1,550,000 "far exceeded the budget." Commissioners ordered a redesign within the $1 million budget that had been established. At the same meeting, they also ordered removal of about ten of the Flatwood-era homes that had been bought as part of land acquisition.

The Buttonhole and Rotary Speeches

For years in the middle of the twentieth century, the Greenville Buttonhole Club was a popular platform for speakers wanting to advance a cause or for local leaders wanting to be informed or entertained. On July 25, 1961, the largest crowd in club history came to hear an update on construction of the new regional airport. The occasion was the Greenville Chamber of Commerce Aviation Day observance. Club president Belton O. Thomason, an always enthusiastic leader and a member of the state legislature, welcomed more than 230 political and business leaders from across Spartanburg and Greenville counties who filled every seat in the Hotel Greenville dining room on Washington Street.[21]

Roger Milliken reviewed the hurdles that had been crossed and those that remained in the design and building of the airport. He made clear that the site chosen along I-85 between Spartanburg and Greenville was the right choice. Answering again the critics who had proposed the soon-to-be-closed Donaldson Air Force Base as the best site for the new airport, he said, "Fine runways and buildings are not the answer. Service and location are." Besides, said the chairman, the federal government could decide to take back the Donaldson property.[22] As far as Milliken and his Airport Commission were concerned, the Donaldson question was a closed case.

Milliken assured his audience that the new airport, even while still under construction, was attracting the attention of industry to the Upstate, but he had a warning. "An area like this will grow not just because you have provided such facilities as this airport. It will grow only because of the kind of business climate you have maintained here." Noting that the project was a month ahead of schedule, he said the target date for opening of the airport was October 15, 1962.

Milliken applauded leaders of the two counties for their willingness to work together in supporting the airport project. He related the words of FAA officials who had told him they had never seen two communities work so well together for one purpose. Reflecting on some critics who were still provincial in their attitude, Milliken drew laughter when he told the crowd about the small town politician who, when he learned of the airport plan, was reported to have said, "I don't go to Duncan to get on a train and I ain't goin' to Greer to get on a plane."

Three months after his Buttonhole Club speech in Greenville, Milliken delivered a similar address to the Spartanburg Rotary Club on October 17, 1961, with an update on construction progress. He confirmed the date for the airport's opening. With most of the airport still remaining to be built, Milliken said the target for having it open was still October 15, 1962.

The new airport could not be finished too quickly. Area leaders could see what airport development was occurring on either side of the South Carolina Upstate. To the east, Charlotte's airport had opened its new passenger terminal in 1954. United and Eastern both had a major presence and Eastern was planning to begin jet service there by 1962. Even more troubling, 160 miles to the southwest, Atlanta's airport had already overtaken Chicago's O'Hare as the busiest airport in the country. As a result, Atlanta's economy was booming. The Atlanta airport had already started construction on a new terminal when Roger Milliken, Charlie Daniel and Alex Crouch were still looking for land. That terminal had opened in May. The enlarged Atlanta airport in its first year had drawn 9.5 million passengers. Now, in October of 1961, the new joint airport for Greenville and Spartanburg was still a year from opening.

Triangle Construction Company of Greenville was awarded the job of building the terminal and control tower. Howard Suitt, then a project manager for Daniel Construction Company, remembered what a dark day that was at Daniel's headquarters on Main Street in Greenville. "Our people had worked very hard on our bid and they were greatly disappointed," Suitt recalled.[23] The disappointment, of course, was made sharper by Charlie Daniel's long support of the airport project. He and his firm wanted the job. They also understood the rigors of competition. Years later, twenty-five years after Charlie Daniel's death, the firm would win a big airport project. But this day—November 29, 1961—deep disappointment was felt at the Daniel headquarters.

At the February 28, 1962, Airport Commission meeting, the next FAA grant was accepted. That $1,397,000 would cover runway and taxiway paving, runway lighting and construction and equipping of the fire and rescue building. The commission also awarded the runway paving contract to a joint venture of Sloan Construction and Ballenger Paving and approved design of the parking lot. It had been a busy and productive year. A year before on this day, February 28, 1961, Roger Milliken had shared with his fellow commissioners his schedule calling for the airport to open on October 15, 1962. Now, just seven and a half months remained.

The big airport project was on the schedule that the chairman had established. Opening day was still planned for October 15.

Herb Howell and his family lived a short distance from the airport. They would often go to watch the land being cleared, the terminal and runway being built. Clearing land for and paving the runway was a huge job. The runway was built of concrete and steel twelve inches thick resting on an eleven-inch stabilized base, giving the runway a load-bearing thickness of almost two feet. Howell remembers "how exciting it was to have an airport almost in our backyard." The airport would become a big part of his life. As a teenager, Howell cut grass and did other jobs at the airport. He began his career with Southern Airways as a ground handler at GSP. Then after serving at other airports for several years, he returned to GSP as station manager for Northwest Airlines.[24]

By mid-April, terminal and control tower construction was progressing well. Final plans and specifications for the fire and rescue building were ready and at the April 19 meeting the Commission approved revised plans for a six hundred-car parking garage. Just a month later, however, the FAA issued a warning: it must be given the control tower by July 15 in order to have all of its control systems installed, tested and ready by October 15. Meanwhile, the State Highway Department had awarded a contract for the I-85 interchange bridge to connect with the airport entry road. Commissioner S. J. Workman said he would see "that this work starts at the earliest date possible." The project was moving smoothly. At the May 18 meeting, the commission approved the runway lighting contract, awarded a contract for the observation court garden to Terry Construction Company of Greenville, and the Weather Bureau said its facilities would be ready on schedule. And the commissioners made one of their biggest decisions. They approved a final agreement with the firm that would serve as GSP's fixed-base operator.

FBO: STEVENS AVIATION

During the design phase of the airport, textile executive Robert Stevens told Charlie Daniel and Roger Milliken that he would move his aviation division to the airport when it opened. It was just four months before the opening of the new airport that the commission in June 1962 signed an agreement with J. P. Stevens & Company.[25] Stevens would offer services at GSP to all civil and military aviation including "aircraft and fuel sales, flight training, air taxi service and one of the finest aircraft maintenance facilities to be found in the Southeast." Stevens Aviation would be GSP's fixed-base operator (FBO). It had already established an excellent service reputation during its ten years at the Greenville Downtown Airport. When the new airport opened, the company would transfer its services there. In the four months before GSP's scheduled opening, Stevens would begin building a three hundred thousand dollar hangar and negotiate with Gulf Oil to establish a fuel storage facility at GSP.

Stevens Aviation had grown out of a friendship between the CEO of J. P. Stevens textile company, Robert T. Stevens, and the legendary founder and president of Pan American World Airways, Juan Trippe. As a twenty-eight-year-old pilot, Trippe had started Pan American in 1926 to fly airmail between Miami and Havana. In the decades ahead, it was Trippe who pioneered several long distance air routes, including the first passenger routes across the Pacific.

On a flight that Stevens took with Trippe in 1949, the J.P. Stevens executive realized the value airplanes could be in moving his executives among the many plants and offices that his huge textile company owned across the Southeast. Soon after, Stevens added the aviation division to his company, bought one plane and hired one of Juan Trippe's veteran pilots, Ralph Cuthbertson. A native of Columbia, South Carolina, Cuthbertson had been flying for Trippe since the early days of Pan Am. He was based for several years in Miami flying Latin American routes. Gaynelle Cuthbertson remembers that her husband was flying the Clipper Ships. They were huge seaplanes that landed in and took off from harbors.[26] Cuthbertson was later transferred to New York and flew routes to Europe. Hiring a veteran pilot from a premier airline like Pan Am was a coup for Stevens.

The 1962 contract with Stevens was an important development. Ralph Cuthbertson was now president and the breadth of services Stevens could provide and its wide contacts in the corporate aviation community would be valuable to the success of the new regional airport.

Keeping the promise

"At the present pace of construction on the terminal, it cannot be completed on schedule," engineer Alex Crouch warned the Airport Commission on June 11, 1962. Not to be deterred, Commission Chairman Roger Milliken ordered a review of dates "on which certain phases of the terminal construction must be completed in order to maintain the schedule." That wasn't the only problem. Construction progress was lagging on the Interstate 85 interchange as well. Nevertheless, all other phases of the project—runway paving, lighting, highway signage—appeared to be on schedule. A contract was pending and Daniel Construction would soon start work on the fire and rescue building.

By the July 27 commission meeting, the terminal construction was "a little behind," but closer to schedule than it had been six weeks earlier. All other jobs, including the fire and rescue building construction, observation court garden and development and access roads, were on schedule. The land use plan was being reviewed. Most of the remaining thirty-four houses that had been retained after land acquisition were sold at public bid. The last of the peach orchards were disposed of and were being replaced by loblolly pines.

By mid-September 1962, only a month remained until the promised opening date. The 7600-foot runway and its taxiways had been paved. Workers were still busy installing infrastructure inside the terminal. Technicians were installing the last of the equipment in the seven-story control tower where testing would soon begin. Next to the tower the fire and rescue building that would house all of the fire-fighting and other emergency equipment was nearing completion. Richard K. Webel was still overseeing landscaping details.

Greenville-Spartanburg would be the first jet age civilian airport built from scratch to be completed in the United States. Others being built would either be open later than October or were enlargements of existing fields. This had been a big job and it would be accomplished in just over fifteen months from groundbreaking to opening.

Leigh Fisher, the man who had said he would eat his hat, wasn't the only one who laughed when Roger Milliken said the airport would be built that quickly. Lots of people were laughing, doubting. Now, with only thirty days remaining, an October 15 opening date seemed possible. It even amazed William Johnson. He was the FAA's Southeast regional engineer, the man who supervised the federal government's investment in the payment, making sure the airport was built right and funds were spent properly. As he watched the last phase of construction and the other preparations in the final months of the project, Johnson admitted, "If you had asked me a year ago if they would be this far along, I would have said *no*. It's fantastic how things have worked out." Johnson was asked how the new airport compared to others in his Southeast region. "It has the latest equipment and design," he replied. "It is the best, by far, in the region."[27]

The "latest equipment" to which the FAA engineer referred included the lights that had been installed down the center of the runway. Until then, airport runways had lights only on each side. Greenville-Spartanburg was the first civilian airport in the nation with centerline runway lighting. The runway was built with grooves across it to guard against hydroplaning. It was also the first new airport built in the United States with high-speed, curved taxiways.

By the time construction was finished, the new airport would cost $10 million. That would include $3.6 million for site preparation and paving, $310,000 for airfield lighting, $210,000 for utilities, $2.2 million for terminal and control tower construction, $2,950,000 for land acquisition, $730,000 for road work, landscaping, equipment and miscellaneous costs. Of that, $2.5 million came from FAA funding and the Airport Commission paid

$7.5 million,[28] which was provided through general obligation bonds underwritten by a property tax levy on the residents of Spartanburg and Greenville counties.

Finally, it was October of 1962. Construction on the new airport was rushing to completion. The last employees were being hired. Preparations for the opening ceremonies were underway. After years of dreaming and planning, designing and building, the Upstate's regional airport was ready to open. True, the coming of a major airport would forever change the way of life in Flatwood. But the airport was needed.

CHAPTER 4

The Early Years: 1962–1969

Opening day 10-15-62

Eastern Airlines agent Jim Chandler and Captain E.W. Anlage waved good-bye to one another as the airliner pulled away from the terminal, the last Eastern plane to leave Greenville Downtown Airport. It was 11:30 p.m. Sunday, October 14, 1962. The Eastern flight board in the terminal lobby said simply, *That's all.* After serving Greenville and Spartanburg and Anderson for more than three decades, Eastern's service was moving from the local airports to the new regional airport.

As Flight 263 disappeared into the night sky and headed southwest toward Atlanta, a few miles to the east several small, privately-owned planes were jockeying for position in the air over Greer. Each wanted to be the first to land at the new airport. At midnight, Alex Crouch, the engineering consultant who had found the property five years earlier, turned on the runway lights. A Cessna, a Piper Cherokee and a Navion landed within minutes as about a hundred nocturnal spectators applauded. Inside the big new terminal workers were busy polishing floors and making other last-minute preparations for the first day of flight operations.

The midnight fliers were not actually the first to land on the new runway. That same Sunday airport commissioners had hosted a large group of area political and community leaders for a preview look at the airport. The Spartanburg County legislative delegation and Spartanburg County's three airport commissioners had flown fifteen miles in the Milliken & Company turbo-prop from the Spartanburg Memorial Airport to the new airport. The Greenville County legislative delegation and the county's airport commissioners had flown from the Greenville Downtown Airport in an identical plane owned by J. P. Stevens. Both planes arrived shortly after 12:30 p.m. and were greeted by news media personnel who had arrived earlier. Chairman Roger Milliken thanked present and past legislators from the two counties for their "splendid efforts" in helping to make the airport a reality. It was the two delegations who had approved the original plan and the local tax levy. It was they who had helped to secure the federal funding and who developed and forged the passage of enabling legislation in the South Carolina General Assembly. Noting that the airport had been built in record time, the chairman also recognized the "fantastic cooperation of a great many people," many of whom were at the luncheon. "This airport is truly the gateway to this area," Milliken told the leaders. "Through this gateway will pass the people who will make the future of this area. This airport will be a model of cooperation between Greenville and Spartanburg for others to point to."

On a lighter note as he concluded his remarks, Milliken had a score to settle with Leigh Fisher. He was the airport consultant from San Francisco who at the groundbreaking ceremonies in July of 1961 had expressed doubt that the airport could open in fifteen months. Milliken called the other airport commissioners to the platform and they stood with him as Milliken said, "Leigh Fisher said we could not possibly open by October 15, 1962, or he would eat his hat." Milliken intended to hold Fisher to his word. So he and the commissioners donned aprons and chef's hats, dropped a gray checked hat in a bowl sitting on a table that had been placed on the platform and proceeded to marinate the hat. Milliken said the hat would be appropriately boxed and shipped to Mr. Fisher in San Francisco the next morning on the first flight out of GSP. Then Milliken and his commission colleagues took their guests on a tour of the facility that the public would soon see. Spartanburg mayor Bob Stoddard called it "magnificent." Senator Charles Moore said it was "wonderful."

There were many other superlatives used to describe the new airport, but local leaders were not the only ones impressed. Praise came from officials of the Federal Aviation Administration, the government agency that had to approve—and help fund—the airport's very existence and under whose authority the airport would conduct its flight operations. George Gary, chief of the FAA's southern region, called it, "one of the earliest efforts to solve the regional airport need." Strong words of support and appreciation even came from Najeeb Halaby, who had two years earlier succeeded General Quesada as head of the FAA. Quesada was the man who, just days before his retirement in 1961, had given final approval to the FAA's share of the airport's funding.

Forty-seven-year-old Najeeb Halaby was not just a federal agency chief. He was a pioneer of aviation and an expert on airports. A graduate of Yale law school, he had been a navy test pilot in World War II and he would later be CEO of venerable Pan American World Airways. Born in Dallas, Texas, the son of a Syrian immigrant of Lebanese descent, his oldest child, Lisa, in 1978 would marry King Hussein of Jordan and become known as Queen Noor, the Arabic word for light. Lisa Halaby had met Hussein while in Jordan working on development plans for the Amman International Airport.[1]

In 1962, shortly before GSP opened, Najeeb Halaby spoke to the Airport Operators Council in Washington and cited soon-to-be-completed Greenville-Spartanburg as an example of what he called, "suitable planning for airports of the future." He noted the broad support and cooperation of Spartanburg, Greenville and surrounding communities. Halaby warned that federal aid to airports in the future would be granted "only if the FAA finds that they are designed and will function to serve regions." That was exactly what the Greenville-Spartanburg Airport would be doing, serving the region of Upstate South Carolina.

The first official flight into what was then usually referred to as GSA (later GSP) was at 7:33 a.m. on Monday, October 15, 1962. Eastern 580 was en route north with stops in Charlotte and Raleigh-Durham. It had come from Atlanta with some special passengers including Greer mayor Lloyd Hunt.[2] He was the first official passenger off the plane, preceded only by Greenville photographer Joe Jordan, who was taking pictures.

Captain W. E. Waters stopped for photos with dignitaries while about two hundred spectators lined the ramp leading to the gate and the outside concourse. The captain removed the first piece of airfreight and Jim Lindsey, manager of the airport's Eastern office, gave Captain Waters the first airfreight package to leave GSP. That was the marinated hat for consultant Leigh Fisher in San Francisco. Soon after, the four-engine Super Electra departed for Charlotte shortly before Eastern's next flight arrived from Atlanta at 8:30.

The opening of GSP meant a longer drive for Spartanburg postal messenger Robert Fowler. He was one of those who transported mail from the local post office to the airport several times a day. Fowler had been carrying mail to and from the Spartanburg Memorial Airport for almost thirty-four years. That is when he had met the first ever delivery of airmail into South Carolina on May 1, 1928. In those thirty-four years, sometimes making up to four deliveries a day, Fowler had missed only one delivery. He ran out of gas a mile from the airport. So he grabbed the mailbag and ran it the rest of the way. He was too late; the plane had already left. Now he was working at GSP and he wouldn't be able to run with a mail sack anymore. By the time he had worked a few days at the new airport he found the bags much heavier. "I used to meet flights with maybe two or three pounds of mail," Fowler explained, "but now I load between two hundred and three hundred pounds on every flight."

There were twenty commercial flights and a "steady stream of passengers the first day," as *The Greenville News* reported. Everyone passing through the airport, and the guests at Sunday's preview, had been given a brochure touting its facilities and services and welcoming everyone to "the good life of the Piedmont area of South Carolina." The brochure also highlighted the airport's "huge, beautifully-landscaped observation court," which it said "reflects the serenity of a region that has enlarged its activities without losing its appreciation of nature." Hailing it as the "crossroads of the jet age South," the brochure listed cities to which the new airport and Eastern offered direct service: Atlanta, Baltimore, Birmingham, Boston, Charlotte, Chattanooga, Greensboro-High Point, Hartford, Springfield,

Memphis, Montgomery, New York (Idlewild and Newark), Pensacola, Philadelphia, Raleigh-Durham and Washington, D.C. Southern Airways had direct service to Athens, Atlanta, Charlotte and the South Carolina cities of Charleston, Columbia and Myrtle Beach.

Monday, October 15, 1962, was an historic day for the long-dreamed-of airport, but reasonably routine. Betty Thompson was working in the terminal restaurant that overlooked the runway and formal garden. She remembers clearly the best-selling meal that day, for good reason. "As a Southern girl," said Thompson, "I had never heard of sardine sandwiches with mustard and raw onions on rye bread, but we sure served a lot of them that day." Thompson remembers opening day as rather slow and quiet. Dedication day would be entirely different. On the following two Sundays a total of almost twenty thousand visited the airport, but the big celebration would come twenty days later. During most of those twenty days between GSP's opening on October 15 and its dedication on November 4, the world would be gripped with fear and the possibility of a nuclear war. Dangerous days lay ahead.

The Dangerous Days of October 1962

The Days of Crisis Between GSP's Opening and Dedication

As the new airport's first commercial flights arrived and departed on that Monday, October 15, 1962, a secret military airplane flying high above Cuba made a chilling discovery. Flying his U-2 reconnaissance jet, pilot Richard Heyser spotted and took the first pictures of Russian SS-4 nuclear missiles under construction in Cuba, just ninety miles from the U.S. The so-called Cold War had just reached a new level of intensity and anxiety.[3] The days ahead would be some of the most dangerous the world had ever faced. The Cuban missile crisis had begun.

Tensions in the Cold War between the world's two superpowers had been building for years. Russia had tested an intercontinental ballistic missile in 1957. That same year it preempted the U.S. in the space race by launching its first Sputnik rocket. Confrontations between the two countries had occurred in Germany and the Middle East. Then in May 1960, U-2 pilot Francis Gary Powers was shot down over Russia. Powers was captured and admitted he was a spy. President Eisenhower acknowledged that the U-2 had been taking pictures for four years; however, at a conference in Paris with Russian leader Nikita Khrushchev, a few days after Powers had been shot down, Eisenhower refused to apologize. Khrushchev walked out of the conference and just four months later he was in the United States addressing the U.N. General Assembly, criticizing the U-2 flights and—to show his anger—taking off a shoe to pound on the speaker's podium.

Meanwhile, Fidel Castro had taken power in Cuba and turned the island into a communist state. In January 1961, newly-elected president John F. Kennedy met Khrushchev in Vienna where the Soviet leader called for an end to the military occupation of Berlin. Two months later, to stop the wave of East Germans escaping to the West, communist East Germany began building a twenty-six-mile wall across Berlin. Thereafter, those who attempted to escape were killed.

In April 1961, Russia again led the space race with the first manned space flight around the earth. It was almost a year—February 1962—before American John Glenn circled the globe for four hours and fifty-five minutes. Meanwhile, Russia and the United States had resumed nuclear testing in 1961. Russia had secretly begun building missile bases and installing nuclear missiles in Cuba. But the United States needed proof. So on October 15, 1962, when Richard Heyser photographed the Russian missiles from his U-2 spy plane, President Kennedy's worst fears were confirmed. JFK told Soviet foreign minister Andrei Gromyko that the United States would not tolerate Soviet missiles in Cuba. Gromyko denied there were any. But now Kennedy had pictures to prove it. The missile pictures were also being examined by U.S. military intelligence officers, one of whom was a future mayor of Greenville, William D. Workman III.[4] Another future Greenville community leader had a special job during the missile crisis. Cary Fondren had just arrived in Spain when he was ordered back to Andrews Air Force Base. He was met on arrival there several hours later and escorted to the Pentagon where he met several other young officers who were briefed on their new and unexpected duties. They would be carrying top secret documents between the Pentagon and the Strategic Air Command headquarters at Omaha, Nebraska. Why, they wondered, out of all the young officers in their branch of the service had they been chosen? Yes, they had been selected quickly from a long list. Their one impressive common trait that had earned them such an important job in the midst of the missile crisis? They had all been Eagle Scouts.[5]

~

President Kennedy faced difficult decisions; but remembering the bungled Bay of Pigs invasion on Cuba's coast a year earlier, Khrushchev thought Kennedy was weak. The Soviet leader was wrong. Kennedy quickly ordered a naval blockade of Cuba to prevent Russian ships from reaching the island with additional missiles or construction materials. In return, Khrushchev ordered his commanders in Cuba to launch their nuclear missiles if the United States attacked. On October 22, President Kennedy issued his ultimatum to Khrushchev: any attack by Russian missiles based in Cuba on any country in the Western Hemisphere would be considered an attack by the Soviet Union and retaliatory action would be taken. A few days later, Khrushchev backed off and ordered his supply ships to return to their bases in the Soviet Union.

For twelve tense days, the leaders of the world's two greatest powers had held firm to their positions with nuclear missiles aimed at the United States, poised for launch. Kennedy's effort at deterrence had worked, but not in time to save the life of an Upstate South Carolina native. On October 27 a Russian missile shot down another U-2 reconnaissance plane.[6] Its pilot, Major Rudolph Anderson, was a native of Spartanburg who had grown up in Greenville. He was the only one killed during the Cuban missile crisis. A member of the 15th Tactical Reconnaissance Squadron, Anderson died just six weeks after his thirty-fifth birthday. A 1944 graduate of Greenville High School and a 1948 graduate of Clemson

College, during more than a decade in the U.S. Air Force, he had logged three thousand hours of flight time, one thousand of them in a U-2. His service as a reconnaissance pilot in the Korean War had earned him the Distinguished Flying Cross.[7] President Kennedy awarded him the Distinguished Service Medal and the first Air Force Cross posthumously.

Cooper White Jr., who was mayor of Greenville from 1969 to 1971, had been a classmate of Anderson's at Greenville High. The two boys had roomed together one summer in Myrtle Beach while they worked at that city's famous old pavilion. White always enjoyed Rudy's gregarious nature and admired his confident demeanor and adventurous spirit. Anderson and White had played football against each other in an era when "grammar" schools had football teams in Greenville County.[8] At Greenville High, Anderson was the football team manager. Another high school classmate, future South Carolina Lt. Governor Nick Theodore, remembered him as "a clean cut boy, a competitor with a strong interest in the military." Retired *Greenville News* sports editor Dan Foster recalled Anderson's speed on the baseball diamond. "He could fly," says Foster. The two were on the Buncombe Street Methodist Church team.

On November 6, 1962, just two days after GSP's dedication, Major Rudolph Anderson was buried with full military honors in Greenville's Woodlawn Memorial Park. The family asked Dan Foster to work with the military on funeral arrangements and with the media who covered the story. Foster said President Kennedy had Major Anderson's body flown to Greenville on Air Force One.[9]

Six months later, on May 19, 1963, a memorial in his honor was dedicated in Greenville's downtown Cleveland Park on the banks of the Reedy River. Greenville Mayor David Traxler and realtor Frank Halter had headed the fund-raising drive and made arrangements to establish the memorial. Clearly visible from busy McDaniel Avenue, the memorial's centerpiece is an F-86 Sabre jet, Anderson's favorite plane, the same kind that he flew in Korea. The F-86 was one of the last military jets to be flown by a single pilot. Able to carry two thousand pounds of bombs, it flew at six hundred miles per hour at up to fifty thousand feet.

In the Korean War, from 1950 to 1953, F-86 pilots had a fourteen to one kill ratio over pilots flying the Soviet-made MIG15. A tribute to Major Anderson at the memorial in Cleveland Park says:

> In a period of great international stress, he performed his duty of great responsibility with honor. He was awarded the Distinguished Service Medal and gave his life that America could proceed on a course toward peace without the threat of tyrants.

In the few days since the Greenville-Spartanburg Airport had opened on October 15, the world had approached the brink of nuclear war and then retreated. In the months ahead, Cold War tensions would ease and the world, for a time at least, would be a safer place. Now residents of the South Carolina Upstate could relax and look forward to attending dedication ceremonies for their new airport.

Dedication Day, 11-04-62

"Jet Age Airport Comes to Life." That headline greeted readers of the *Spartanburg Herald-Journal* on Sunday, November 4, 1962. Actually the airport had "come to life" twenty days earlier when flight service began. Since then, many people had already driven to the new airport just to walk around and see the place about which they had heard so much. This crisp autumn day was *the* day for the public to come and see their new airport. Come they did, up to fifty thousand some newspapers estimated, maybe more.[10] Nobody knew for sure. There were too many for an accurate count, but few who were there would have argued with the estimate. Some neighbors from the Flatwood community walked. Other people, appropriately, flew in. Private planes began arriving before 8:00 a.m. Dozens of smaller aircraft—all shapes and sizes—filled every available space near the terminal and at the Stevens Aviation site. The airport's control tower was busy all day. It normally had two traffic controllers on duty in those early days. This morning, five controllers were handling the arrivals.

Most people arrived by car, thousands of cars. By late morning roads were clogged. From his helicopter vantage point, *Spartanburg Herald-Journal* state editor Jim Oliphant saw cars bumper to bumper "for about ten miles" in each direction along I-85. "And you wonder where they are going when they finally get to the airport," Oliphant said.[11] Many of them didn't. With the regular and special airport parking areas fast filling up, by early afternoon many motorists escaped the traffic jams on I-85 and sought a place to park near the airport. If they could not reach the airport itself, at least they would have a good location from which to enjoy the thrill of the U.S. Navy's Blue Angels precision flying demonstration at 4:00 p.m.

"Visitors marvel at the size and beauty of it," the *Spartanburg Herald-Journal* reported. The new airport was big. The 7600-foot runway was the longest many in the dedication day crowd had ever seen. For those accustomed to the small terminals at their local airports across the Upstate, the GSP terminal was big. The "finger" of the terminal that contained the open concourse and arrival/departure gates was almost a quarter of a mile long. The size of the airplane parking area amazed many, large enough to accommodate several airliners at one time. With Eastern's big DC-8 jet sitting there, visitors began to realize that this, indeed, was a jet age airport. Although there was no jet service yet, when jets did arrive, this facility had been built to accommodate their size, speed and larger passenger loads.

Big was not all that impressed the thousands of dedication day visitors. Beauty was their other positive first impression. There was the drive up the entryway from I-85, the shrubs and flowers around the terminal, the displays of local art on the bridge section of the terminal. There was also the garden. The observation court, it was called, because you could go outside the terminal and observe the planes taking off and landing while standing amid a beautiful garden of magnolias, azaleas and other flowers and plants that surrounded a pool and fountain. The garden was 220 x 168-feet with a 60 x 25-foot reflecting pool in the middle of it. Around its perimeter was a mass planting of Chinese red berry holly edged with dwarf Japanese holly. The large garden had a total of five thousand plantings of flowers, plants and trees.

For the tens of thousands who arrived early or waited out the traffic jams to reach the airport, there was plenty to do amid a festive atmosphere. Most people, whose curiosity had been raised by more than a year of media coverage on the construction project, explored the airport. Some enjoyed the runway view from Bailey's Coffee Shop where Betty Thompson was working as she had been on opening day. Today she was much busier. "It was unreal," Thompson remembers. "We set up a buffet and kept busy until perhaps four, when we ran out of food, everything. It was so busy, it was unreal." Since flights continued to arrive and take off all that day, Thompson and her colleagues in the restaurant were also busy because the restaurant provided meals for airplane passengers. The staff prepared and boxed the meals in the restaurant and took them to the planes. The menus weren't bad. Thompson said they often included filet mignon, green beans, canned potatoes, salad, dessert and drinks.[12]

While many people kept the restaurant open, some checked out the various concessions; others viewed the exhibits of local artists. Most inspected the aircraft display and virtually everyone took an up close look at Eastern's sleek new DC-8. The jetliner had flown from Miami in less than an hour and a half. Some of the early arrivals were attracted by the opportunity to take a short flight. For a minimum gift of ten dollars to the United Fund (later the United Way), one hundred twenty people, many of them for the first time, had the thrill of riding in a jet, looking down on Greenville, Spartanburg, Donaldson Air Force Base and the new airport. So that passengers had a clear view, the captain flew under a low cloud cover. The air was a little turbulent and the flight was uncomfortable for some, but landing in the DC-8 at one hundred forty miles an hour was a new and thrilling experience for most on board. Meantime, the 7600-foot runway and the air traffic controllers supervising it stayed busy with a steady flow of planes coming and going. Despite the crowds and special activities, the airport remained open to commercial traffic. Before the program began, there was a flyover by planes from nearby Donaldson and from the South Carolina Air National Guard. Donaldson was also represented by its band, which played as the crowd gathered for the program.

By the time the afternoon dedication ceremonies finally began, a cloud cover that had lowered temperatures passed, the sun reappeared, but a cool breeze picked up. Speaking from the roof of the concourse building where the gates were located, several speakers praised the new airport and proclaimed its future importance to the area. Eastern Airlines president M. A. MacIntyre presented an American flag and called the airport "a miracle of the New South which provides unlimited opportunity for growth." Other speakers included Congressman Bob Ashmore, Spartanburg County Senator Charles Moore and Greenville County Senator Bradley Morrah. Senator Strom Thurmond declared, "No state has a brighter future than South Carolina," crediting the airport as a major reason for that claim. Congressman Bob Ashmore, whose 4th District covered both Greenville and Spartanburg counties, observed, "Nothing like this has ever happened to our state before. Our airport is the first jetport opened in South Carolina. It is ahead of other cities that are just now beginning to think of a regional airport." Praising the leaders who had spearheaded the airport effort, Ashmore said, "They had a dream and the dream has become reality." In response, Roger Milliken declared, "We have the finest airport in the nation," assuring the huge crowd that the airport had been designed to serve the Upstate's needs far into the future.

The dedication day ceremonies concluded with the thrilling precision flying demonstration by the navy's Blue Angels. Four of the sleek jets flew in a diamond formation as the other two pilots flew solo. For a few moments the huge crowd was dazzled by intricate formations and dives at high speeds and with the ear-splitting sound of powerful jet engines. A seventh pilot described all the maneuvers. Everyone understood they were watching our nation's most skilled military fliers. These were U.S. Navy and Marine pilots, all between twenty-six and thirty-six, in the best possible condition with lots of flight time and skilled as goodwill ambassadors for our armed forces.

Another special pilot attended dedication day, but his arrival did not go according to plan. Joe Walker was the chief test pilot for the National Aeronautics and Space Administration (NASA). He had recently flown the X-15 experimental rocket plane forty-seven miles above the earth at four thousand miles an hour. Launched from a B-52 bomber, lessons learned from the X-15 flights helped chart the course for flights to the moon later in the decade. Joe Walker was to have flown into GSP that day in a fast and exciting F-104 fighter jet, but it had developed mechanical problems on his flight from Edwards Air Force Base in California. So he diverted to Shaw Air Force Base one hundred miles south, near Sumter, South Carolina. Walker finally arrived at GSP in a small and slow propeller-driven Cessna that he had borrowed at Shaw.

For two special pilots, dedication day brought back memories. Eastern Airlines senior pilot Captain Gene Brown, thirty-four years before, had flown an open cockpit plane on the first northbound airmail route through Spartanburg. The man who greeted Brown at Spartanburg Memorial Airport that day in 1928 was J. C. Grier, chairman of the Spartanburg Chamber of Commerce Aviation Committee. Grier was at GSP to greet Brown again when he arrived for the new airport's dedication. The pilot of the first airmail stop in Greenville also returned for the November 1962 dedication. In the years since his 1930 arrival in Greenville, Eastern Captain Dick Merrill had achieved the distinction of piloting the first roundtrip commercial flight across the Atlantic.

Airport police, aided by thirty auxiliary officers, directed traffic for the estimated fifteen thousand cars that had parked at GSP for the dedication day activities. When the Blue Angels completed their flight demonstration, thousands of those cars headed for the interstate while many visitors delayed their departure and continued exploring the airport. At dusk, cars and planes were still leaving, their passengers excited about what they had seen and encouraged by the promise of the airport's potential.

Dedication day had been an experience to remember, made more pleasant because early November is always the height of the colorful leaf season in the South Carolina Upstate. As reporter Jim Oliphant noted from his helicopter overhead, "Autumn has painted a landscape of color in the bordering trees." It was an appropriate observation. The airport had been designed with beauty as well as function in mind. Mother

Nature, November style, had added an extra touch to the picturesque design of the airport's landscape.

Most important was the impact the new regional airport had already exerted on the area. "It has brought the two counties closer together," Commissioner S. J. Workman of Woodruff told reporters. Fellow commissioner W. T. Adams, who had overseen the construction project for the commission, agreed. The challenge ahead was to meet the high expectations of Upstate leaders and to maximize the airport's positive economic impact.

Roger Milliken and Charlie Daniel were filled with many emotions that happy November weekend as they accepted the congratulations from leaders across the state and observed the huge crowds. It had been a long time, five years, from the day in 1957 when Daniel, along with Alester Furman Jr. and Walter Brown, had recruited Milliken to lead the regional airport effort. It had been seventeen and a half years since Eddie Rickenbacker issued his plea to three hundred Upstate leaders to come together and build an airport. Operating an airport, both men knew, could be even more difficult than building one. Milliken's job was not finished; he was chairman of the Airport Commission. Charlie Daniel, who had not been granted a commissioner's seat by the Greenville County legislative delegation, would still be available to help when needed, but not for long. Just twenty-two months later, the construction executive who had been one of the Upstate's greatest salesmen for more than twenty-five years, would be dead, the victim of cancer.

The dedication weekend of open house and ceremonies had introduced the new airport to tens of thousands and had invigorated many with the idea of flying. The early years of the airport would sometimes be difficult and contentious. The South Carolina Upstate finally had what it needed: a gateway to new and expanded business opportunities and much more. The people of the Upstate had a gateway to the world.

The new airport's first year

Delta Airlines had been serving some of the area's local airports for years, but it pulled its service from the Upstate on the eve of the new airport's opening. That left the new airport with just two airlines: Eastern and Southern Airways. It would be more than two decades before Delta next landed its planes at GSP.

For the first several years of GSP's operation, Eastern was the airport's dominant carrier. As a result, Eastern understandably attracted many compliments and sometimes most of the complaints for GSP's air service. The first major compliments came when it announced that it would soon begin nonstop service to New York City. On Thursday, December 13, 1962, almost two months to the day after GSP's opening, an Eastern Lockheed Super Electra prop jet took off at 7:35 p.m.[13] Seventeen Greenville and Spartanburg business and community leaders along with Governor-elect and Mrs. Donald Russell, other elected officials and some reporters were on board. An hour and thirty-eight minutes later they arrived at Newark, just west of New York City. En route, the two state senators on board shared their thoughts with reporters. Greenville's Bradley Morrah predicted "addition of this type of service should prove to be one of the prime attractions to new industry." Spartanburg's Charles Moore expressed the hope "that the area will support Eastern in its efforts to give us the best of service."

The next morning, the *Spartanburg Herald-Journal* editorialized that the mix of Greenville and Spartanburg leaders on the inaugural flight "once again symbolizes the unity in which the airport was conceived and without which it never could have been built." Noting that the much larger city of Memphis, Tennessee, did not yet have nonstop service to New York, the editorial boasted, "This kind of service puts our facility in the category with major cities." On a more sobering note, the Spartanburg paper's editorial warned, "Airline service cannot be based on a community's desire to have it. It can be justified only on the basis of use. If we have enough passengers to support additional flights profitably, the airlines will be happy to accommodate us." It was a warning that would haunt the airport and the communities it served more than once in the years ahead.

In the airport's first several months, business exceeded most initial expectations. A March 5, 1963, *Spartanburg Herald-Journal* headline told the story: "Air Traffic Up, New Airport Proves Money Maker." From opening day on October 15, 1962, to February 28, 1963, total airline passenger traffic increased 9 percent over the combined traffic of the year before at the two local airports. Eastern had sixteen daily flights; Southern had seven during that period. "All financial projections are being met," reported airport manager Andy Andrews.

Some people from elsewhere found it difficult to believe you could actually get to Greenville or Spartanburg, South Carolina, by plane so easily. Greenville's 1963 Chamber of Commerce president Bill Orders received a call early that year from a business contact in Chicago who needed to visit the city. "But how do I get there?" the man asked. "Fly," replied Orders. "Into where?" asked the man. "Right into Greenville," Orders assured the surprised gentleman.[14] It delighted Orders to be able to tell the caller that this area now had a new airport. "Anyone wanting to bring business to town wants an airport," the president of Orders Distributing Company said. "The airport was as big for business as anything Greenville had ever had."

In an April 1963, headline claiming "Regional Airport That Really Works," *Airlift Magazine* said GSP "is fast proving itself a highly successful model of the regional airport concept favored by the FAA and CAB." It called location "the outstanding feature of the airport," saying it was the result "of far-sighted planning that tended to disregard specific city interests in favor of furthering the economic growth of the area." Throughout 1963, both air freight and passenger traffic remained strong, but there was growing dissatisfaction with Eastern's service.

The Jetless Jetport

During its design and construction days GSP had been touted as a jet age airport. It was often referred to as "the jetport." By early 1964, it had been in operation for almost a year and a half and there still was no jet service. Many, including some in the media, derisively called it "the jetless jetport."

Then in March of that year, Eastern made a decision that prompted a public outcry and strong criticism from airport management. It was cutting two popular daily flights into GSP: 374, which left Atlanta at 4:00 p.m., and 341, which left Newark at 5:45, would cease on April 7. Airport manager Andy Andrews was incensed. "I am disturbed over this latest development and I plan to take action," Andrews assured reporters. "There is no reason for Eastern to further limit our service except they have no competition here. Since Eastern has a monopoly out of GSP, they feel they can cut service here and put it in places where they do have competition." Andrews threatened to appeal to the Civil Aeronautics Board, charging deficiency of service, if Eastern failed to make satisfactory adjustments in its flights to GSP. "If Eastern can't provide us with (adequate) service," said Andrews, "the CAB ought to put someone in here who can."[15] Andrews was also irritated over Eastern's slowness in bringing jet service as it had promised to do. The airline would soon be starting jet service from Greensboro/Winston Salem to New York City but had no plans to extend jets to GSP. The closest Eastern came to providing jets at the new airport was the prop jet Lockheed Electra.

Business and commercial leaders along with elected officials began pressuring Eastern not to reduce service. Senator Thurmond sent Eastern president Floyd Hall a letter asking for his "personal attention" to the matter. Letters and telegrams also went to Hall from the mayors of Spartanburg and Greenville and from more than a dozen towns in those two counties. Meantime, the Greenville and Spartanburg Chambers of Commerce appointed a joint committee to seek ways to improve air service, including adding flights to Chicago and other Midwest cities as well as another one to New York.

Within a couple of days, Eastern delivered its first response to the critics of its plan to reduce flights. The airline, a spokesman said, was dropping the two daily flights based on business needs. Eastern also explained that, despite reducing flights, it was actually offering more passenger seats since it was now using larger four-engine prop jets instead of smaller two-engine planes. Eastern spokesman Jeff Dishough said the airline was still "extremely happy with its growth in this market," noting it was on par with what its forecaster had predicted. Eastern's answers, however, did not satisfy Greenville Mayor David Traxler. He said it was "incongruous" that Eastern should reduce flights when GSP's passenger load had increased 29 percent over the past year. The mayor voiced disagreement with Eastern's claim that the airline would provide service if the community produced the passengers. "If the airline provides the service, we'll get the passengers," claimed the mayor.

Despite the criticism, Eastern held firm to its flight reduction plan. At a news conference on April 2, its director of community relations told the media and business leaders that, although Eastern had record boardings of more than seven thousand in March, its load factor was an unprofitable 48.7 percent. Jeff Dishough said that with the advent of bigger planes, "one of the axioms of airline scheduling is that frequency of service declines as airline capacity increases."[16] Answering complaints of an Eastern monopoly, he doubted that the CAB would authorize additional route competition at GSP. Dishough said Eastern planned to bring jet service to the airport in the fall of 1964—at least six months hence—if passenger traffic continued to increase. Dishough claimed that GSP was still receiving better service than any similarly-sized Eastern market and he said the airline had no intention of leaving the area.

With that promise, Eastern was trying to diffuse the still-growing dissatisfaction with its service and the suggestion in some newspaper editorials that the airline's flight reductions were linked to the airline's "severe financial losses in recent years." *The Greenville News* editorialized on May 19, 1964, that "if Eastern for any reason is not in a position to offer the best service, then its successor should be sought out." The editorial allowed that parting ways with Eastern after so many years would be regrettable, "but the time is rapidly approaching, if it is not already here, when the cold hard facts of economic life must be considered." The newspaper said any delay in facing those facts would only make matters worse and it called upon the Greenville Chamber of Commerce and the Airport Commission "to investigate the matter, make public where the fault lies and research a solution."

At his April 2 news conference, Eastern's spokesman had read a statement by Charlie Daniel, who had been elected an Eastern board member in 1959, in which Daniel said Eastern had promised to provide B-727 jet service after GSP opened. The statement quoted Daniel as saying he was confident that Eastern president Floyd Hall would keep his promise "if we uphold our end of the bargain." That was obviously a reference to Eastern's claim that enough passengers would have to be produced to make flights profitable to the company. Once Eastern did introduce its Whisperjet B-727 to replace the prop jet Lockheed Electra, the airport would have to attract even more passengers because the 727 was bigger and would have more seats to fill.

Meantime, reduced flights were having a negative effect on freight traffic. After living through a month of the new flight schedule, the Tri-County Transportation Association said the cuts had caused "inconvenience and delay." Freight shipments, it said, usually were not ready until late afternoon. Eastern now had only two flights to Atlanta after 5:00 p.m. Both were usually filled with mail and priority shipments, leaving little, if any, room for freight, the association claimed. This was May of 1964, in an era when airlines had to accommodate most airfreight shipments. In the decades ahead, firms like Federal Express, UPS, Emery Worldwide, DHL and others would fill much of that need.

On August 31, Southern Airways announced it would add a flight to Atlanta on its Martin 404 propeller service. It was a schedule that would offer connections to cities north, west and south. Eastern, meantime, maintained its reduced flight schedule. It would be another eight months before it introduced its promised jet service.

Goldwater at GSP

September 17, 1964, was by far the busiest day in GSP's almost two years of operation. A popular presidential candidate came to visit.

Some in the huge crowds—estimated at twenty thousand to twenty-five thousand—had been waiting for hours.[17] Many had brought food baskets and picnicked on the airport grounds. Now they were cheering and high school bands were playing while cars remained backed up along I-85 and on the roads into the airport as the candidate's jet rolled to a stop on the tarmac. It was just about noon on a sunny, warm Thursday in the South Carolina Upstate, perfect for a campaign stop. As they waited for the Republican presidential candidate to emerge, many on the front rows were mystified by the letters on the Boeing 727: Yia Bi Kan. They were Navajo for "house in the sky." For Barry and Peggy Goldwater this plane was their house in the sky these days. They were a long way from their Arizona home, entering the critical stage of an uphill battle against an incumbent. It had been almost ten months since Lyndon Johnson had succeeded to the presidency on November 22, 1963, the day of John F. Kennedy's assassination. Now, Johnson was seeking election to a full four-year term. His Republican opponent was the nation's best-known conservative leader.

As Senator Goldwater left his plane to be greeted by Republican leaders from across the state, he had to be encouraged. This was Goldwater country. Several South Carolina counties had voted for him in 1960. He was still so popular, people had come by car, bus and plane to see him this day. In fact, by day's end, there would be 431 takeoffs and landings at GSP. At one time during the day more than one hundred private planes covered every available piece of aircraft parking space at the airport. It was the biggest crowd at GSP since dedication day almost two years earlier.

Defying the efforts of dozens of state and local officers, many of the younger fans broke through security lines to get closer to the candidate as he and his wife walked down the plane's steps toward the greeting line and onto the platform. The rushing crowd scattered the receiving line of dignitaries who had been assembled to greet the Goldwaters. Security in those days was nothing like it would be in the years ahead.

The crowd was festive for two reasons. They had come to see their candidate and to hear his tough criticism of LBJ and his Democratic administration. They had also come to see the man who would introduce Goldwater, Senator Strom Thurmond. Just the afternoon before, Thurmond had gone to the Spartanburg home of his longtime good friend Judge Bruce Littlejohn to tell the shocked judge that he was leaving the Democratic Party for the GOP.[18] Hours later, Thurmond told his South Carolina constituents on a statewide television and radio broadcast that he was switching parties. Today he was a Republican. His fellow senator Barry Goldwater told the happy crowd—in a lapse into hyperbole—that Thurmond's switch to the GOP was "one of the bravest actions in the history of our nation." The crowd cheered and the regional and national media corps of more than two hundred reported from the airport to media outlets across America and overseas.

It was, said one party official, likely the biggest campaign event in the state's history. People of all ages were there, including many students. For sign-carrying fourth grader Knox White this was his first venture into politics.[19] Thirty-one years later he would be elected Greenville mayor. Fred Bright from Startex was there with his high school government class. Little did he know that day that he would spend many years at the airport working in the operations department. The Goldwater rally remains one of the biggest—and noisiest—events ever at GSP. It didn't last long. At 1:32 p.m., just an hour and twelve minutes after he had arrived, Goldwater climbed aboard his house in the sky and was on the way to Shreveport, Louisiana, the next stop on the journey toward his ultimate November 3 defeat.

Since the candidate had arrived late there wasn't time for the planned reception with the party's leaders. One of his main supporters hadn't even been able to shake his hand. Roger Milliken and his wife missed that opportunity thanks to the fans who had broken through security and disrupted the greeting line. Nevertheless, Milliken told reporters a handshake wasn't important. The event had met its objectives. How that campaign stop at GSP was reported angered some residents of Spartanburg County.

What's in a name?

When he finished watching CBS coverage of the Goldwater campaign at GSP, J.E. Wofford of Spartanburg was so frustrated he decided to call the network. It wasn't how they reported on what Goldwater had said in his speech. It wasn't even what the network had said about Strom Thurmond's switch from Democrat to Republican. What angered Mr. Wofford was how news anchor Walter Cronkite had kept referring to the campaign event at "the Greenville Airport" in South Carolina. When he finally was able to connect with someone at the CBS news department in New York City, Wofford complained that the event was not at the Greenville Airport. It was at a joint airport between Greenville and Spartanburg, South Carolina. "They thanked me for my call," Mr. Wofford told a Spartanburg newspaper reporter. "But at least I got my gripe off my chest." It was a complaint shared by many others that day and in the future, including Spartanburg newspaper columnist John Black.

On September 20, Black wrote a lengthy column in which he noted that, while Greenville and Spartanburg legislators had agreed that the two counties would share the initial taxation for the airport, Greenville gets most of the publicity. He observed that most of the networks and the wire services had used Greenville as their dateline when reporting on the Goldwater story. Black claimed the misnomer was nothing new and he blamed it on "attitudes of news organizations, airlines and some citizens." He congratulated Spartanburg's city manager for asking airlines to use the airport's correct name in their printed schedules and during their inflight announcements. Sounding frustrated, Black wrote, "Come on...when you're in another city and the airline tells you Spartanburg doesn't have an airport and you can't get a ticket to Spartanburg, tell them we *do* have an airport."

The following Wednesday, September 23, *The Greer Citizen* carried its own column with a tongue-in-cheek response to Mr. Black and suggested a solution: "that the airport be known as the *Greer* Airport." The *Citizen* noted that Greenville newspaper reporters covering Goldwater datelined their stories *Greer*, while Spartanburg papers said *Greenville-Spartanburg Airport*. Greer, being closest to the airport, the newspaper reasoned, is the logical dateline choice. Use of a Greer dateline, the editorial claimed, "would eliminate jealousy between our two neighboring cities. Or, if the two are jealous of Greer, we'll give in and let them dateline their stories *Pelham*. We suggest that Greenville and Spartanburg not fall out over what it is called. Just call it the *Greer International Jetport*, gentlemen, and let it go at that."

From Kites to Computers
Early Weather Forecasting

In this age of satellites and computers, it is difficult to believe that many weather forecasters once relied on kites. The weather bureau's kite program began in the 1920s. Kites brought back from aloft valuable information on humidity, temperatures, barometric pressure and, of course, wind speed and direction. The kites were flown with piano wire and brought down with a winch. When a kite got away, its handlers would chase it in a car.

"On a good day, we could get kites up to five thousand feet," recalled Ernest Kliemann. "But many days there was no wind so kites couldn't go up." Kliemann was the chief of the area weather bureau at GSP when the airport opened in 1962. By the time he retired in 1964, he had seen a lot of changes in his thirty-five years as a weather forecaster. "Until 1935, the weather bureau relied almost entirely on ground observations," Kliemann explained. Meantime, the airplane observation program had begun. Kliemann said a pilot could take his plane to twenty thousand feet and transmit the same information to twenty weather bureaus across the country. Airplane observations could provide better information on storm development. "Then in 1937," Kliemann recalled, "the weather bureau mounted radio transmitters beneath huge helium-filled balloons that reached heights up to sixty thousand feet." All the time the balloon was ascending, its radio was sending back vital weather information. Kites needed wind; planes in those days couldn't fly in bad weather. Balloons could fly in all but the heaviest rain.[20]

The jets arrive

Thirty months after its opening, jet service finally came to the Greenville-Spartanburg Airport on Sunday, April 25, 1965. Greenville Chamber of Commerce president, later 4th District Congressman, James R. Mann of Greenville was the first passenger to board flight 152, Eastern's Whisperjet B-727 service to New York City. The 727 was quickly becoming the work horse of Eastern's fleet. The airline already had twenty-seven in service with more on order. It carried ninety-four passengers and cruised at six hundred miles per hour. For a while, the daily flight from and to New York overcame some of the public criticism that had been aimed at Eastern. "This," said airline spokesman Donald Grefe, "is one of the fastest growing areas in Eastern's operations." Indeed, arriving and departing passengers totaled more than 183,000 in 1964, an increase of 25,000 over 1963. Airmail and cargo also had increased substantially.

Dick Tukey, Paul Foerster and Hoechst

From the 1940s to the early 1960s, Greenville's Charlie Daniel concentrated his efforts on attracting industry to South Carolina's Upstate from elsewhere in this country. In the 1960s and 1970s, a Spartanburg leader decided to focus much of his recruiting effort overseas. A New York native, Richard Tukey[21] moved to Spartanburg in 1951 to head the Chamber of Commerce. He became convinced that much of the region's future economic success would depend on its ability to take advantage of global markets, both by increasing trade and attracting overseas firms to invest here by building plants and locating North American headquarters in the Upstate, especially Spartanburg. That is when he met Paul Foerster.

Paul Foerster had escaped the post-World War II Russian occupation of East Germany and earned the German equivalent of a PhD in chemistry. Then he began a long career with Hoechst, one of Germany's major industrial firms. Hoechst had decided it wanted to build a plant in the United States and Foerster was given the job of heading a small team to find an appropriate site and make a recommendation to the company's board. Dr. Foerster's research indicated that he could draw a circle around a twenty-five-mile radius of Spartanburg, South Carolina, and cover 85 percent of the textile spindles in the United States. For a chemical company wanting to manufacture polyester fiber for the American textile industry, Spartanburg sounded like the place for Foerster and his team to start looking. That's when Paul Foerster met Dick Tukey. It was 1965.

"He was a superb salesman," Foerster remembered years later. "He had a way of making you feel comfortable and welcome." Indeed. Welcome *and* wanted. Tukey and his wife entertained Foerster and his team in their Spartanburg home. How he entertained was one of Dick Tukey's secrets of successful industrial recruiting. One of his sons, Pat Tukey, remembers well his family as an "internationally-flavored family unit."

To satisfy themselves that they had searched adequately for the best site, the Hoechst team visited several cities but quickly focused on the Spartanburg area because of its proximity to potential customers, especially along the I-85 corridor between Anderson and Charlotte. Team members liked how easily its products would be able to be delivered to customers' plants and how quickly equipment and supplies could be received from the port of Charleston. "The regional airport also played an important role in our decision," Foerster remembers. Of course, plenty of land was available right along I-85.

The search was soon over, the team's decision made. Back in Germany, Foerster delivered his team's recommendation. "Hoechst's American plant should be built in the Spartanburg area of Upstate South Carolina," he told the company's board. The members accepted the recommendation and asked him to head the operation. Foerster agreed.[22] It was a big job, but Foerster's newfound friend Dick Tukey was there to help. This was one of many European companies that Tukey would help to attract to Spartanburg County. He mobilized the Chamber of Commerce and industrial realtors in helping Hoechst acquire eight hundred acres near where I-85 crosses the Pacolet River. The project became a joint effort of Hoechst and the Hercules Corporation, which already owned land nearby. In just two years, the $24 million plant had been built. It opened at Thanksgiving 1967 under the name Hystron Fibers, Inc., with three hundred fifty employees. By 1970 a second phase had opened. The plant employed six hundred and continued to grow. Over the years, Foerster said the airport played a significant role serving his company's needs. "We transported millions of dollars worth of supplies, machinery and parts through GSP," he recalled. "We often needed help quickly and professional experts could reach us easily through GSP. The customs port also was a valuable asset."

Hoechst's success in Spartanburg became a source of great pride for Dick Tukey. He had been careful to develop close ties with many of South Carolina's leaders, especially its governors. He worked closely with Fritz Hollings in the late 1950s and early 1960s, then with Donald Russell and Bob McNair in the mid and late 1960s. He was a strong supporter of the governor's effort to establish a technical education system in South Carolina. He and Hollings believed that a well-trained workforce was needed to attract the kind of companies that could boost and broaden the area's economy.[23] That dream came true in 1961 when the first of what would soon become a statewide system of technical education colleges opened in Greenville. Another soon opened in Spartanburg.

As he increased his business efforts, Tukey kept repeating his slogan, "We don't sell South Carolina's magnolias and moonlight. We sell economic justification."[24] To him, economic justification was a well-trained workforce, a cooperative and encouraging business climate and a convenient transportation system. Tukey made sure any prospective business knew about the I-85 and I-26 interstates and the connections they provided—east and west, north and south—to a significant population of the United States. He promoted the availability of the port of Charleston and its proximity to the South Carolina Upstate via those interstates. He pointed to the air service for passengers and cargo that the new regional airport provided right along I-85 between Greenville and Spartanburg.[24]

Tukey's efforts had already achieved results. In 1965, Gerd Menzel opened his plant along I-85 in Spartanburg. Menzel Inc. became the first European firm to manufacture textile equipment in South Carolina. Two years later, Swiss native Kurt Zimmerli started his Zima Corporation, which provided supplies for the textile industry. Many other firms from Switzerland, Germany, Austria and other European countries followed the march to South Carolina's Upstate.[25] In the process, Dick Tukey's name became legendary not only in Spartanburg County but also in Columbia and especially at the offices of the State Development Board. Former governor Bob McNair and former State Development Board chairman George Dean Johnson Jr., when having difficulty convincing a business leader to look at the Upstate, would joke and say "Let's take him to the Upstate to be 'Tukeyed.'"[26] That was both a joke and a compliment. Dick Tukey had an ability to convince business people that they should settle in the Upstate. Many of the business firms, especially those from overseas, that settled in the Spartanburg area during the 1960s and 1970s had been "Tukeyed."

Dick Tukey developed a particularly close relationship with John West. A native of the historic midlands town of Camden, West was a lawyer who had served in the state senate for twelve years before being elected lieutenant governor in 1966. He would go on to serve as governor from 1971 to 1975 and then accept President Carter's appointment as ambassador to Saudi Arabia for four years. In 1967, Tukey and Lt. Governor West were flying to Basel, Switzerland, to attend an international textile machinery show. It was on that flight that Tukey shared with West his plan to promote what he called reverse economic investment.[27] His plan would encourage overseas companies to invest in South Carolina by building plants, buying equipment, providing jobs and making use of the state's trained workforce. Hoechst, Tukey reasoned, had decided its investment in the state would open new markets for the company here and across America. Why couldn't other international firms be convinced to invest here and reap the same benefits? he asked John West. The lieutenant governor liked the idea. He promoted it in his campaign for governor in 1970. After his election, he helped lead the state's efforts to recruit more international firms.

The decline of South Carolina's traditional textile industry had begun. The reverse economic investment efforts paid off by attracting not only textile related companies from overseas but also by recruiting other types of industry in order to diversify the Spartanburg area economy. During the 1970s, several overseas firms — most from Europe, some from Asia — moved or built new plants in South Carolina, many in the Upstate. By the late 1970s, almost one-third of South Carolina's new industrial investments were made by firms from other countries:[28] Germany, Switzerland, the United Kingdom, France, Italy and Spain among them. Dick Tukey's plan was working. His family and Paul Foerster knew why.

Dick Tukey and his wife were consummate hosts. Representatives of prospective overseas companies would spend hours at their home. "My parents' biggest success in entertaining foreign guests," said son Pat Tukey, "was their habit of making foreign guests feel comfortable by combining customs, food and social graces to which the guests were accustomed. Both worlds were at our family dinner table at the same time." He recalls spending many hours shucking bushels of fresh oysters, oysters on the half shell being a favorite delicacy of frequent visitor Gerd Menzel who had built his plant in Spartanburg.[29] Their hospitality was often returned. Dick Tukey and his wife made at least a couple of visits a year to Europe where they were entertained in the homes of the German business leaders whom they had met in Spartanburg. Paul Foerster remembers how thoughtful Mrs. Tukey was in attempting to acquaint her hosts and hostesses in Europe with American life. She would take copies of the Sears catalog to give to some of her hosts so they could learn more about American products. Tukey's stepson, Pinckney Spencer, of Spartanburg, says his father was "very driven to improve the economy and well-being of this area and the whole state."

Despite his focus on attracting international business and large firms from elsewhere in the United States to the Spartanburg area, Dick Tukey did not ignore small firms. That is how he met Hank Ramella, owner of a small manufacturing business in Amityville, New York. By 1970 he had decided to move his firm to the Midwest or to the South. To learn more about the I-85 corridor, he wrote the South Carolina Development Board requesting information. He soon received a call from Dick Tukey, who had received a copy of Ramella's inquiry. Tukey wanted to tell him all about Spartanburg and he extended an invitation to visit.

When Hank Ramella first flew his plane into GSP, he was impressed by the ample runway and the beauty of the airport. "It speaks well for the region," he thought. Then he met Tukey. If Ramella moved, he would be creating only a small number of jobs and initially he would be bringing only five young families. No matter. Tukey spent time with him and introduced him to other leaders. Ramella decided, "This is the place."[30] In July 1972, he opened Felt Parts Company off Highway 221, making industrial felt products, everything from lubricating wicks for electric motors to sealers for appliances, even blackboard erasers. He settled into the community and met lots of people, including county commissioner Liz Patterson. When she learned of Ramella's interest and experience in aviation, she suggested he might be interested in a position on the Airport Commission. He was, and in 1981 the Spartanburg County legislative delegation nominated him. Hank Ramella was appointed by Governor Riley on July 20, 1981, to replace Commissioner Jean Little.

On August 9, 1974, Dick Tukey had been appointed an airport commissioner. By that time, he was quietly battling cancer. On July 25, 1979, nine months before the end of his term as commissioner, and still serving as executive vice president of the Spartanburg Chamber of Commerce, Dick Tukey died at the age of sixty-one.

Andy Andrews

GSP Executive Director: 1962–1967

Airport manager immediately available; can take charge of field and ground work; knows mechanics and electricity, very capable.

—Ad in *Western Flyer* magazine, 1930

The skills needed to manage an airport in the last third of the twentieth century were much greater than in 1930. Through the almost forty-five years of Greenville-Spartanburg Airport's operation, only three men have carried the title of executive director. All three came to the job with long years of aviation and airport management experience.

Back in 1961, when the commissioners were ready to hire a person to plan for and then manage the new joint airport, they didn't have to look far. Andy Andrews had been managing the Greenville Downtown Airport for fifteen years. A native of Sumter County and graduate of the University of South Carolina, he had just retired from the navy with the rank of lieutenant commander when he first visited the airport in 1946. He took one look at the small terminal and single runway and decided the airport needed "direction."

Andrews was confident. He knew a lot about airplanes and airports. A pilot since 1938, he had directed the Memphis Naval Air Station's flight training school during World War II. In 1946, with thousands of pilots returning from the war, the economy picking up and airlines growing, he could foresee public interest continuing to grow in commercial flying and general aviation. He thought this little airport, just off two-lane Bypass 291 in Greenville, had a bright future. The airport needed a director, but the board had no money to pay him. No problem, Andrews took the job anyway. He knew how to make it successful. Within seven years, Andrews had a new terminal, a second runway and Eastern was providing daily service. Just as he had projected, general aviation had grown rapidly. Business was good. The airport was making money and the manager had a salary.

When it was time for the new airport commissioners to hire an executive director, their action was merely a formality. Senator Bradley Morrah, chairman of the Greenville County legislative delegation, had let it be known that he wanted Andy Andrews as the new airport's director.[31] Ottis LaVance Andrews had been named for an uncle who was a minister, but the commissioners, and just about everyone else, knew him as Andy. Until the regional airport was finished, Andrews held two jobs and continued to work out of his office at the Greenville Downtown Airport. That's where he conducted some of the job interviews just before the new airport opened.

Andrews was an outspoken champion for the joint airport. In the first four years after its October 1962 opening, the jetport—as it was known then—was the target of many passengers' frustration, doubt and taunting humor: the world's most expensive tree farm...a multimillion dollar jetless wonder...the jetless jetport...ten years too early. Ten years early, perhaps, but not ten years *too* early. "In the airport business," Andrews would explain, "you stay ahead or you never catch up. We need three to five years in the airport business to keep up with rapid development in the aviation field."[32] Sure, it was three years before the jetport had jet service, but Andrews would remind the critics in speeches and media interviews that when the jets did come the airport would be ready. He often credited the state legislators of Spartanburg and Greenville counties for their willingness "to overcome differences, forget petty political grievances and to ignore county lines to make the airport possible." The jets did come. Passenger traffic built steadily and on October 18, 1966—four years and three days after it opened—the airport had its biggest passenger day, with just over one thousand of them arriving or leaving.

Andrews had always insisted that his office be right near the passenger gates. "Andy really knew the airport business and he was a people person, good at public relations," Roger Milliken remembered. Andrews loved being among the people and he especially enjoyed greeting dignitaries. In late January of 1967, amid all his other duties, he and his staff were preparing for the arrival of Princess Irene of Greece. The Upstate already had a considerable Greek population and the princess was coming for an appearance at Converse College in Spartanburg on Thursday, January 26. The sociable airport executive director would not be there to greet her. Andy Andrews died suddenly at home three days before. On January 26, just six hours before the Greek princess arrived at the airport, several hundred gathered at Greenville's St. Francis Episcopal Church to pay their last respects to the man who had led the new airport through its first four years and three months of operation.

Dick Graham's Arrival
GSP Executive Director: 1967–1989

"If I get this job," Dick Graham said to his wife as they drove up the beautiful tree-lined entry road to the Greenville-Spartanburg Airport terminal in April of 1967, "we're never going to leave." Mary Graham agreed. They had already seen and heard enough. Graham had met with airport commissioner W.T. Adams a few days earlier in North Carolina. Now that he was here on site at the four-year-old airport in Greer, Graham was impressed. If he was offered the job of executive director, he would take it.[33]

At forty-seven, Dick Graham already had plenty of experience with airplanes and airports. Born and raised in the Philadelphia area, he entered the Marine Corps in 1940 and soon found himself in the heat of World War II, as a U.S. Marine paratrooper on Guadalcanal and other besieged Pacific islands in support of marine amphibious units. In the early 1950s, he was flying night-fighter intercept, intruder and ground support missions in the Korean War. He also participated in the historic Marine Corps battle at the Chosin Reservoir where one hundred twenty thousand Chinese troops had surrounded eighteen thousand U.S. Marines along with an army unit and a unit of British Marines. Winter weather found temperatures below -30° Fahrenheit. Some historians called it the most savage battle of modern warfare. Graham returned from his wartime experiences with sixteen military awards including the Distinguished Flying Cross.

His war years completed, Graham added to his aviation experience by completing airport management studies at the University of Tennessee. In 1960 he was hired as general manager of the Smith Reynolds Airport of Forsyth County in Winston-Salem, North Carolina. The airport was named after Smith Reynolds of the R. J. Reynolds tobacco family. He had been a well-known aviation figure in the 1920s. The airport was also the home base of rapidly growing Piedmont Airlines, which soon would become GSP's third airline. Graham had been at the Smith Reynolds Airport for about six years when the death of Andy Andrews left GSP without an executive director. Along with sixty-five others, Graham applied for the job. He was hired, began work May 1, 1967, and just as he had pledged, never left until retirement almost twenty-three years later.

Five years and growing

Passenger traffic grew steadily through 1966 and by June 1967, reached a record high of 23,447 arriving and departing passengers, a 25 percent increase over 1966. Dick Graham credited student and family travel for some of the increased passenger flow through the airport. GSP benefited then, as now, from being near several colleges and universities that increasingly attracted more students from across the United States and overseas. The University of South Carolina Upstate, Converse, Wofford and Spartanburg Methodist colleges in Spartanburg, along with Furman and Bob Jones universities in Greenville, are all within fifteen to twenty miles of the airport. Clemson University, with its large international population, is only forty miles away. Southern Airway's President Frank Hulse came to GSP in 1967 to inaugurate DC-9 jet service, a mid-morning flight to Memphis with an early evening return. The airline also added GSP to its route between Atlanta and Charlotte.

During the airport's first five years, passengers had grown accustomed to waiting for flights in the covered concourse at one end of the terminal because there were no passenger lounges in the original building. In mid-1967, Eastern passengers welcomed the convenience of a new enclosed lounge that could seat up to sixty people. It immediately became so popular that additional lounges were added.

By 1968, annual air cargo had doubled to 4.6 million pounds from five years before. Executive Director Dick Graham announced that construction would soon begin on an air cargo building and he predicted air cargo would exceed passenger traffic. "Air express is getting so big," said Graham, "we can't handle it in the terminal." The Greenville Chamber of Commerce was launching an effort to have GSP declared a Port of Entry to make receipt, inspection and sending of overseas shipments easier and quicker.

On May 14, Congressman Mann joined a delegation led by Greenville

Chamber of Commerce aviation chairman Ralph Schmidt for a meeting in Washington with Treasury Department officials to present the need for a customs port at GSP. They pointed out that North Carolina had eight such ports; Georgia six, but South Carolina had only one customs port and that was more than two hundred miles away at the port of Charleston on the coast. They also told the treasury officials that while Charlotte already had a port that in 1968 collected $2.9 million in customs duties, Greenville-Spartanburg area importers had paid $3.4 million in duties. The delegation sent a clear message to the Treasury Department staff that GSP needed, and in their opinion deserved, a customs port. Senators Thurmond and Hollings were also spreading the word that lack of a customs port was resulting in constant delays in the receipt of machinery and spare parts shipments for textile companies and other industries and creating difficulties for the hundreds of foreign exhibitors who came to Greenville each year for the large international textile shows. The chamber delegation, with the help of the state's senators and congressmen, apparently made a positive impression on the government officials.

By early 1969, everyone seemed to be enjoying success at the airport. When GSP was being designed, it was estimated that two hundred eighty thousand passengers would use the airport by 1970. That forecast was surpassed in 1968 when two hundred ninety-nine thousand passed through the airport. In 1969, Eastern offered nineteen daily flights, including nonstops to New York and Washington. Piedmont had eight; Southern had six. Air South ran several commuter flights to and from Atlanta, and South Atlantic offered commuter flights to Columbia; Charleston; Gainesville, Florida; Savannah; and Raleigh. On the general aviation side of the airport's operation, Stevens Aviation was handling twenty to thirty flights a day, 90 percent for business clients.

Those early years at GSP had been profitable ones for Stevens Aviation. That was good for Stevens and for the airport. One of the early pilots that president Ralph Cuthbertson had hired was Skip Shelton. He was a Furman University student when Pearl Harbor was bombed on December 7, 1941. Within two years he was flying bomber raids in

Europe. After World War II, Shelton returned to Greenville where he held several jobs, which included flying for Spartan Mills before being hired as chief pilot for Milliken & Company and then as a pilot for Stevens Aviation. As the airport's fixed-base operator, Stevens had developed a strong and respected role in corporate aviation. "We had about forty pilots," Shelton remembered years later. "Ralph Cuthbertson had a rule. All of us pilots had to be better dressed than any passenger we had on board." Image was important. Pilots had to wear white shirts, ties and dark suits. "Many times when I walked down the steps from the plane," recalls Shelton, "the person waiting would shake my hand, thinking I was the executive for whom he was waiting."[34]

Stevens Aviation planes were transporting corporate executives, entertainers, all sorts of famous people all around the country. Skip Shelton remembers flying famed TV night show host Johnny Carson across country to tape commercials for a clothing chain. He often flew Jim Nabors, star of the 1970s TV show *Gomer Pyle, USMC*, between GSP and his California home. Nabors was honorary president of and a major contributor to the Boys Home of the South in southern Greenville County.

One Fourth of July during the early years that Stevens was in its new facility at GSP, Shelton was assigned the task of organizing a big party and buffet for employees and their families. Before the party began in the company's large hangar, Shelton had hidden a surprise behind the large Milliken Gulfstream aircraft at one end of the hangar. Shortly after the party was underway and the buffet had opened, the Gulfstream was pulled out of the hangar revealing the famous Charlie Spivak band. Spivak was a nationally-known performer and band leader from the heyday of network radio and early television. In his later career he had moved to the Upstate where his big band played every night for several years at Ye Olde Fireplace on South Pleasantburg Drive in Greenville. Shelton had often flown Spivak to Miami, New York and other cities and the two of them had become good friends. He had a standing invitation to take his clarinet and play with Spivak's band anytime he wanted. On this July 4, Spivak helped his old friend by coming to play for lunch at the company party.

No fee, just lots of fun. Stevens employees loved the special treat.[35] Spivak and his band were not only famous, they were good.

Stevens Aviation had become a major dealer for Beechcraft planes. In May of 1969, president Ralph Cuthbertson invited popular *Greenville Piedmont* columnist Gill Rowland, Greenville photographer Bill Coxe and a dozen others to join him on a flight to Wichita, Kansas, to attend the introduction of a new Beechcraft model. Advertising manager Charlie Newman told Rowland about the growth of the civil aviation industry: ten million miles flown each day, most of them by general aviation planes, 70 percent on business flights. Indeed, general aviation was growing rapidly.[36] The future for Stevens Aviation and the Greenville-Spartanburg Airport, which it served as fixed-base operator, was bright.

The excitement of the Stevens Aviation business family was shattered on Easter Sunday of 1979. President Ralph Cuthbertson had delivered a Beechcraft Baron to a client in Miami. Before leaving, he went with the client as he flew his new plane for the first time, but the pilot lost control of the aircraft, it went into a spin and crashed. He, Cuthbertson and a passenger were killed.

On April 26, 1969, four years and one day after Greenville-Spartanburg had received its first regular jet service, the last Eastern propeller-driven planes left. The next day, Eastern began using jets on all its flights through GSP. With twenty arrivals and departures daily, Eastern would now be offering twenty-six thousand seats per month, including new service to Greensboro, Roanoke and Pittsburgh and improved or expanded service to Chicago, Jacksonville, Mobile and Birmingham. "These flights," said Eastern's GSP station manager Dick Spadafora, "are examples of Eastern's continuing interest in the rapidly growing Piedmont area." Some of that service was on the airline's new DC-9 Whisperjet II.

By June 30, 1969, the end of GSP's fiscal year, airplane movements (takeoffs and landings) had totaled seventy-two thousand. Passenger traffic was up 16 percent over the previous year, 2 percent better than the national passenger growth average of 14 percent. Airfreight had increased by 100 percent over fiscal year 1968, air express by 50 percent. GSP's growth experience was not unique. Many airports throughout the United States were experiencing increases in passenger and cargo traffic; however, the rapid and steady growth had its downside.

"The nation's airways are so crowded, the situation is reaching the danger point," warned National Transportation Safety Board chairman John Reed. He told the Senate Aviation Subcommittee on June 25, 1969, that more navigational aids and improved air traffic control systems were required to make existing and needed airports safer. Reed's well-publicized congressional testimony prompted an immediate answer from GSP's Dick Graham, who said he wanted to assure travelers in and out of his airport that they were safe. "We do not have any problem with overcrowding at this airport," Graham told reporters. He said the seven-year-old airport had all the latest safety features with the backup of several fire departments, ambulances and rescue units within a four to five minute response time.

Graham was always quick to remind the public of the safe record that GSP had established during its first years of operation. He realized that many people in the western Carolinas still had memories of what had occurred less than two years before. On July 19, 1967, a Piedmont Airlines jet took off from nearby Asheville, North Carolina, with seventy-nine on board heading for Roanoke, Virginia. Just a moment later, a small Cessna with three on board, perhaps not seeing the jet, flew into its underbelly. All aboard both planes died as they crashed alongside Interstate 26 just south of the Highway 64 interchange, near Hendersonville. Until that time, it was North Carolina's worst air accident.

As the decade of the 1960s closed, all GSP traffic—passenger, airfreight and mail—was increasing. Those increases were prompting predictions of growth. R. Dixon Speas Associates, in a report prepared for the Greenville-Pickens Regional Planning Board, calculated that passenger traffic would grow from a 1967 fiscal year total of almost 108,000 to 920,000 by 1990.[37] Chairman A.D. Asbury called that projection "one of the most astounding forecast figures" developed in local planning. Asbury said that kind of increase would require that area governments plan carefully in order to meet such demand. Cargo was also a concern. The Speas report projected airfreight and express cargo would increase at an annual rate of nearly 15 percent by 1990. Actual air traffic growth was much more than the consultant's estimates. By the end of fiscal year 1989, the Airport Commission reported more than 1.1 million enplaning and deplaning passengers at GSP. Passenger traffic grew 16 percent in that year alone.[38] Air freight that year was up 100 percent, air express up 50 percent.[39]

How to meet the growing demand for air service in the South Carolina Upstate would be a major challenge of the 1970s. Attempts to find answers to the dilemma were already prompting discussion about how GSP, the Spartanburg and Greenville airports, and the airport at Donaldson Center would fit into the area's aviation future.

The Dixon Speas 1989 report had some interesting recommendations. It suggested developing two new general aviation airports during the next twenty years, one in the Travelers Rest area of northern Greenville County and one in the Landrum area of northwestern Spartanburg County. It also suggested gradual separations so that Donaldson Center could be used for general aviation and cargo traffic, if needed, and it proposed improvements to Spartanburg Memorial and expansion of the Pickens County Airport. The report also recommended a three-county airport commission to plan and implement an airport system for Greenville, Spartanburg and Pickens counties. The report suggested that such a commission be given the power to finance airport expansion and to zone land around the airports.[40]

As the 1960s concluded and interest in and use of aviation increased, few could have imagined the challenges that lay ahead in the 1970s. An era of violence was about to grip the aviation industry. During the next decade, a southern president and the United States Congress would change the face of American commercial aviation. GSP—and every other airport in the nation—would feel the effects of both.

This aerial view on the eve of the airport's opening in October 1962 shows the wide open rural landscape. In the decades ahead, development of all types would extend toward the airport from Greenville, Spartanburg and Greer. Newly finished I-85 is just out of sight beyond the bottom of this photo. PHOTOGRAPH BY JOE F. JORDAN.

Finger building with open gate concourse, 1962. PHOTOGRAPH BY JOE F. JORDAN.

GSP Commission chairman Roger Milliken rides a Caterpillar tractor during groundbreaking ceremonies for the new airport on July 7, 1961. On the left is Senator Charles Moore, chairman of the Spartanburg County Legislative Delegation. On the right, behind the machine operator, is State Representative Belton O. (Tommy) Thomason of Greenville.

COURTESY OF THE SPARTANBURG COUNTY HISTORICAL ASSOCIATION MUSEUM.

From left: Airport cofounders Roger Milliken and Charlie Daniel, Col. Robert Stevens, CEO of J.P. Stevens textile company, who began Stevens Aviation as a division of his firm, and Greenville mayor David Traxler at a meeting of area leaders with Eastern Airlines president Eddie Rickenbacker at Greenville's Poinsett Club in 1961. PHOTOGRAPH BY JOE F. JORDAN.

Greer Mayor Lloyd Hunt was on the first official flight into GSP on the morning of October 15, 1962. Photographer Joe Jordan left the flight first in order to take this picture.

PHOTOGRAPH BY JOE F. JORDAN.

Donaldson Air Force Base "Air Lift Capital" sign. PHOTOGRAPH BY JOE F. JORDAN.

Eastern Airlines president Eddie Rickenbacker, standing alongside one of his planes at the Greenville Downtown Airport, signed this photo for Greenville photographer Joe Jordan in 1961. He was in the city for a luncheon meeting at the Poinsett Club with Charlie Daniel, Roger Milliken and other leaders as construction began on the new airport. PHOTOGRAPH BY JOE F. JORDAN.

A view from the control tower as thousands began gathering for the airport's November 4, 1962, dedication. Dignitaries spoke from the roof of the long gate concourse. The terminal is to the left and the runway garden is in the middle background with Eastern Airline's new DC-8 jet on display next to it. Jet service did not begin at GSP until 1965. PHOTOGRAPH BY JOE F. JORDAN.

On November 4, 1962, dignitaries and speakers gathered on the concourse building roof during dedication ceremonies for the new airport. In the foreground, third from right, is W.T. Adams, longtime airport commissioner, who was one of the first pilots recruited by the new Army Air Corps in 1916. PHOTOGRAPH BY JOE F. JORDAN.

CHAPTER 5

The 1970s

THE CUSTOMS PORT

As cargo business grew at GSP, the business community continued calling for a United States Customs Port. Chairman Ralph Schmidt and his Chamber of Commerce aviation committee were rallying business support and lobbying elected officials. Since opening six years earlier, GSP and the airlines serving it had been a major selling point in attracting new business and industry to the area. But it still took too long for deliveries of overseas goods to arrive. If they didn't have to be diverted or held up elsewhere, two or three days could be saved. Cargo, for example, could be off-loaded at the port of Charleston, trucked immediately to the Upstate and clear customs at GSP.

There were impressive statistics and reasons to bolster the request for a customs port. By the late 1960s, 45 percent of all South Carolina imports and exports originated in the Greenville-Spartanburg area. The region was served by three major airlines, four railroads, more than fifty trucking companies and six major highways. There were hundreds of firms in the Upstate that would benefit from a customs port. Many more firms could be attracted to the area if it had such a facility. But competition for customs ports was fierce. Not every area that wanted, or needed, a port would be granted one. There had to be compelling evidence and the person who would make the decision was the Commissioner of U.S. Customs.

The key to success would be arranging a visit by the region's top U.S. Customs official and selling him on the need. In late 1969, at the invitation of the local chambers of commerce, Everett DeBrand, the Southeast Regional Assistant Commissioner for Customs, paid his visit. He determined the need was valid and filed a favorable recommendation to the Commissioner of Customs in Washington, D.C. Two years of work paid off on July 3, 1970, when Senator Strom Thurmond cut the ribbon at dedication ceremonies for the new customs port that would be available to serve more than seven hundred manufacturing and distribution firms throughout the South Carolina Upstate. In its first eight months, by March of 1971, the port had collected $2 million in duties from sixteen hundred transactions. Director Gene Patterson said the main clients were textile machinery, fabric and apparel firms. Most of the overseas suppliers were European. Many were in the Orient. Clients included not only business and industrial firms but many individuals as well.

On the same day the customs port opened, the Airport Commission announced an air cargo building would be constructed just west of GSP's passenger terminal. When opened less than a year later, it would house the permanent location of the customs port, Eastern Airlines' cargo operation, customs brokerage firms and other facilities. Its four hundred fifty thousand dollar cost was covered by airport revenues and FAA funds. The need for a cargo building was critical. During 1968 and 1969, air cargo traffic in and out of GSP had risen 200 percent. In 1969, 933,357 pounds of air cargo moved through GSP. Of this, 737,854 pounds were airfreight, 136,673 pounds were airmail and 58,830 pounds were express.

Ironically, by the time the air cargo building opened in the spring of 1971, cargo shipments through GSP were down 32 percent from the year before. Eastern Airlines District Manager for Sales and Service Dick Spadafora credited the decline to the tight national economy and the resulting switch by many firms to cheaper means of transportation, resulting in a nationwide decline in airfreight. GSP's Dick Graham said the decline had begun in mid-1970. At the same time, he noted that passenger service at GSP remained strong in early 1971 and was up 7.5 percent from a year earlier.

The airport gained another major advantage in March of 1972 when Governor John West signed a law establishing, as a branch of the South

Carolina State Ports Authority, an inland port at GSP. That allowed goods arriving at the coastal ports but bound for the Upstate to be transported to GSP before being inspected. It also allowed international flights to come directly to GSP with cargo that could be inspected at the inland port of entry. On the airport's tenth anniversary, October 15, 1972, a Pan American B-707 landed at GSP on a flight from Stuttgart, Germany, with 84,000 pounds of cargo worth $600,000. On board were eleven knitting machines for the Sulzer-Morat firm in Spartanburg County. Governor John West greeted the flight and what he called "a new era of participation in international trade." West called GSP "the great link between the present and the future for much of our state which has put us (South Carolina) on the main line of economic growth in our nation."

Remembering Charlie Daniel

Had it not been for the vision and persistence of Charlie Daniel with his powerful business influence and his active commitment to the economic growth of South Carolina, GSP may never have been built. Except for Daniel's close relationship with Roger Milliken and his request that his old friend accept leadership of the airport project, Milliken might not have been involved in the airport project. Somewhere at the airport, Roger Milliken had always wanted to honor Charlie Daniel. One day as Milliken and executive director Dick Graham looked out at the terminal's front lawn, they realized that the lawn might some day be a parking lot. Neither liked the thought. To preserve the lawn and its beauty, the two men agreed a fountain was needed in the middle of it. It would make an attractive entrance for people driving into the airport. Milliken had found a special way to honor his old friend.

On July 3, 1970, the day that the customs port was dedicated, Roger Milliken's wish was fulfilled. During ceremonies attended by Senator Strom Thurmond and other dignitaries, business leaders and airport commissioners and staff, a plaque to Daniel's memory was unveiled and a beautiful fifty-foot fountain was turned on in front of GSP's passenger terminal. Designed by landscape architect Rick Webel, the fountain sits amidst a 140-foot-diameter pool with underwater lighting. The fountain and pool were a gift of Milliken and his firm, Daniel Construction Company and other area leaders. The small plaque at the water's edge reads simply: *This fountain erected in memory of Charles Ezra Daniel by his friends and admirers, 1970.* Charlie Daniel had died at the age of sixty-eight on September 13, 1964, just twenty-three months after GSP opened.

Ominous dangers difficult challenges

Atlantic Southeast Airlines Flight 2273 took off from Atlanta-Hartsfield Airport bound for Roanoke, Virginia, on August 2, 1986. On board the small propeller-driven commuter were just three passengers—a woman, a man and a child traveling alone. Forty minutes into the flight a twenty-nine-year-old man from Arkansas told the flight attendant he had a gun in his bag and he wanted to hijack the plane. That message was quickly relayed to the pilot, who was just twenty-five minutes away from the Greenville-Spartanburg Airport. The pilot notified GSP's control tower of the situation and his need to land the plane. By the time ASA 2273 touched down at 3:48, police and firemen, an ambulance crew and bomb squad were waiting. The man was handcuffed and removed from the plane to face an hour of questioning by three FBI agents. Meantime, the small commuter continued on to Roanoke.

After a weekend in the Greenville County jail, during which the passenger traded his white shirt, tie and slacks for a blue prison-issue jumpsuit, he appeared Monday morning for a hearing before a federal magistrate. He was answering to a charge of "making threats and allegations regarding aircraft piracy and possession of a dangerous weapon, causing the aircraft to be diverted to the Greenville-Spartanburg Airport." Court documents revealed that he told the attendant he couldn't believe authorities where he had boarded his flight in Birmingham, Alabama, had let him through with a gun in his bag. The would-be hijacker had no gun and he blamed his actions on drinking. He was required to post bond of fifty thousand dollars and to return to Arkansas, by car, with a federal probation officer.

Most air piracy cases have not ended so easily or so quickly. In GSP's forty-five-year history, that August 2, 1986, hijacking remains the airport's only brush with such a crime. Even by the time GSP had opened in 1962, crime and violence against airplane crews and passengers were nothing new. In fact, the hijacking of airplanes had reached a peak between 1959 and 1961 with Cubans trying to escape Fidel Castro's new communist regime and other hijackers forcing U.S. airliners to divert to Cuba. As far back as the 1930s, revolutionaries had taken control of an airmail plane over Peru. Then from 1947 to 1958 there were twenty-three hijackings, mostly overseas, by people seeking political asylum.

The first major violent act on an American passenger plane was on November 1, 1955, when a bomb hidden in luggage destroyed an airliner near Denver, killing forty-four. In January 1960, a National Airlines plane crashed after a bomb exploded. Those tragedies prompted calls for a device to inspect passenger baggage. Armed guards were first used on U.S. airliners in the summer of 1961 as part of President Kennedy's response to the hijacking of flights to Cuba. The guards, and a federal law imposing long prison terms and even the death penalty for air piracy, put a stop to hijackings for several years. Then the hijacking to Cuba of a DC-8 in February of 1968 launched a new era of aerial violence. In the next four years, through 1972, the U.S. Department of Transportation counted 364 hijackings worldwide. Many of them had become more violent, several resulting in crashes.[1]

Hijackings had often been viewed as political acts, perpetrated mainly by people seeking political asylum or wanting to make a political statement on some issue. That changed in 1971 when fifty nations signed an international agreement calling airplane hijacking a criminal act. Meanwhile, President Nixon in September of 1970 had authorized federal marshals to fly airliners as part of a comprehensive anti-hijack program. It wasn't enough. In March of 1972, bombs were discovered on three planes and Nixon ordered stricter airport and airline security. On November 10, 1972, a Southern Airways plane was hijacked over Alabama and forced to Havana. It was the first hijacking of a small U.S. airline plane.[2]

The Federal Aviation Administration ruled in December 1972 that all carry-on baggage must be inspected and all passengers scanned. In August 1974, Congress passed an anti-hijack bill making screening universal and permanent. It was three years before another hijacking occurred. In the meantime, however, a bomb on board a plane and one in a locker at LaGuardia Airport in New York killed a total of ninety-nine people in 1974 and 1975. Violence flared again in the mid and late 1980s with hijackings and bombings on flights particularly in Europe and the Middle East and with the 1983 shooting down of a South Korean airliner off Russia's east coast. In this country, crime against aircraft subsided and after February 1991 there were no hijackings in the United States...until September 2001.

The dilemma of snow and ice

Heavy snow is always a problem for airports. Seasoned fliers whose winter schedules have taken them to cities like Chicago, Denver, Detroit, Cleveland, New York and Boston have their stories about scary landings, deicing, flight delays and cancellations. Many have had the experience of restless overnight stays on airport benches and floors with thousands of others. For GSP, similar experiences are less frequent but snow sometimes does cause problems. As South Carolinians and visitors to the state know, it doesn't take much snow to create problems in a southern state where snow is rare. Thursday, March 25, 1971, for example. Forecasters at the GSP weather station had predicted rain. They were surprised when temperatures dipped just below freezing. The result was at least seven inches of snow, the area's heaviest one-day March snowfall on record. GSP remained open, thanks to employees who stayed overnight at the airport, and airlines continued flying. Many passengers could not reach the airport or were delayed getting home once they arrived by slippery roads made more dangerous by so many abandoned vehicles. By Friday, the area began returning to normal as temperatures reached more appropriate early spring levels.

The year 1971 was an unusual one for snowstorms in the Greenville-Spartanburg area. That March 25 storm was an unusually *late* winter storm, actually an *early* spring storm. Then in December, the area was hit with an *early* winter, actually a *late* fall storm. The snow began in the early morning hours of Friday, December 3. By five in the morning, plows were on the GSP runways trying to keep the airport open. By early afternoon, all flights had been canceled.

"We had eight inches or more and some drifts three feet high," airport executive director Dick Graham told reporters in the late afternoon. "It will probably take us all night to get the field open." Four plows would continue working all night. (Greenville's downtown airport, with no plows, had been closed all day.) Ultimately about a foot of snow fell, an unusual amount for the area, especially in early December. By Saturday, GSP had reopened and airline schedules were returning to normal.[3]

Ice is an enemy of aviation. January 13, 1982, was a tragic reminder of that fact. An Air Florida Boeing 737 crashed into a highway bridge seconds after taking off from Washington National Airport next to the Potomac River in Virginia. The jet had been deiced but ice had built up on its wings again while the plane awaited takeoff. Seventy-nine were on board. Five survived. Just ten days later, a World Airways DC-10 with more than two hundred on board landed in heavy fog on an icy runway at Logan Airport and skidded into Boston Harbor. Two passengers died.

Lightning, snow, pavement damage and ice are the usual reasons for closing a runway. It doesn't take much ice to cause problems. Three-eighths of an inch of ice or wet snow is too much for a large jet to land safely. While airport managers usually make the call to close a runway because of ice, control tower personnel decide when fog, rain or snow restrict pilot visibility.

The weekend paving job

It was early 1977. After almost fifteen years of use, GSP's 7600-foot runway needed strengthening to handle the heavier aircraft now serving the airport. Engineers estimated that to pave a 150-foot-wide 7600-foot runway with four inches of asphalt would require twenty-six thousand tons of asphalt. *That* is a big job! Such a job usually is accomplished by paving crews working only at night over a period of weeks or by actually shutting down an airport for several days.

GSP's Dick Graham had a better idea. Textiles were still the region's main industry in 1977. Most textile mills closed the week of July 4. GSP's business traffic would be lighter than usual over the holiday weekend and there were not as many holiday air travelers as there would be in future decades. Graham's idea? Pave the runway over the holiday weekend between early Saturday morning and Monday night. He wondered if it could be done that quickly. He had never heard of any other commercial airport doing it. Besides, could he find contractors willing and able to tackle such an enormous job on a holiday weekend? What if it rained? He checked Fourth of July weekend weather records for the previous twelve years. They looked hopeful. Graham was accustomed to taking risks. After all, he had faced plenty of risks as a fighter pilot; he was braver and more optimistic than others with less risk experience might have been. His engineering consultants were optimistic as well.[4]

It took months of preparation. First the Federal Aviation Administration had to grant permission. FAA officials confirmed there had never been a weekend runway paving job before, but they told Graham, "It's your money. If you want to do it, go ahead." With the FAA's concurrence and the airport commissioners' approval, he did. Airlines were notified. Sloan Construction Company of Greenville submitted the low bid of $1.25 million and was given the job. Ashmore Brothers paving from next door in Greer helped. In the months before July, two special roads had to be built from Highways 101 and 14 so that asphalt trucks could reach the runway.

As the holiday weekend approached, seven Upstate asphalt plants were working nonstop preparing to provide the estimated twenty-six thousand tons needed. The plan was to close the airport at midnight on Friday, July 2, and reopen for early morning flights on Tuesday, July 6. Then what Graham feared most happened. The weather station told him a thunderstorm was heading for GSP. It arrived at 4:00 p.m. Friday. The rain continued until midnight when the airport manager watched the clouds clear as the moon shone brightly on the runway. "Graham," said one of the paving company officials, "you must live right."

After a few hours of sleep, as he drove up to the airport at dawn on Saturday, Graham muttered to himself, "What have I done?" There in front of him, stretching as far as he could see, were more than one hundred asphalt trucks and eighteen huge rollers spaced down the runway ready to apply the additional two layers of asphalt, each two inches thick, on GSP's only runway. Everything has to go right, thought the airport's boss.[5]

"We paved and paved and paved," Graham remembers. There were 375 workers; 126 trucks moved constantly between their asphalt plants and the airport, from early Saturday morning until Monday afternoon. Then other machines had to apply the necessary markings and, right on schedule, GSP reopened for traffic early Tuesday morning. The weather had been perfect all weekend.

The National Asphalt Pavement Association, meeting in Los Angeles, presented its 1987 Proof of Quality Award to Sloan Construction. GSP Chairman Roger Milliken was delighted. "This is the proof of the pudding," he told reporters. "Ten years later a national award for performance against an almost impossible objective."

Airline rate and route deregulation before and after

The year 1978 was pivotal for America's airline industry. Congress deregulated the airlines' rate and route structure. In what some would call the "good old days" of our nation's airline industry, life for the airlines in many ways had been much easier and simpler than it is today. The CAB, forerunner of the FAA, granted airlines their routes and set fares. When their costs rose, the airlines simply asked the CAB to raise rates. It usually did. The CAB was a sort of barrier against competition. A fledgling airline, or an established airline wanting to enter new routes, had to seek agency approval. That approval rarely came quickly, sometimes not at all. As a result, on many routes competition was minimal or nonexistent. Add to all that, fuel was cheap.[6] Labor contracts were expensive. Employees were well cared for. Then on October 24, 1978, President Carter signed the deregulation bill. No more route protection. No almost-automatic price increases when costs rose. Competition increased. Fares decreased. Routes expanded. More people started flying. Air travel took off.[7]

One thing did not change...high costs. The major airlines were saddled with those expensive labor contracts, inefficient operations, too many cities to serve. No longer required, by regulation, to maintain unprofitable or low margin routes, the airlines dropped them or, at least, reduced service. Smaller airports like Greenville-Spartanburg lost airline service. After deregulation GSP had just two airlines: Eastern and a small commuter, Sunbird, which had only small airplanes going to the South Carolina coast. Executive director Dick Graham worried how he would meet payroll, but he cut expenses and GSP made it through a difficult time. The airline industry and the business of running airports was more complex and competitive.[8]

Within a short time, new and smaller airlines offering attractive low fares began popping up. People Express was one of the first. The big established airlines had to maintain and strengthen customer loyalty while looking for ways to attract new customers. In May 1981, American Airlines introduced its frequent flyer program.[9] Most of the other major airlines followed. Some of the airlines began switching to hubs. They could use smaller aircraft to service the small and medium-size market airports. Those planes would fly customers to major hub airports where they could catch long haul flights to other major cities throughout the country and overseas. The airlines also built in frustrating restrictions and special fees. They often charged business travelers, their best customers, more.

As complexity and competition increased, the more successful airlines searched for ways to increase their efficiency. The weaker airlines looked for ways to survive. Many of them, both the stronger and the weaker, found what they thought was their answer in consolidation. In the 1980s and 1990s, better and stronger airlines began buying up smaller airlines and their routes: Delta bought Western, TWA purchased Ozark, USAir bought Piedmont and Pacific Southwest.[10] For some airlines, it was too late. They couldn't compete. They were not able to cope with the constant industry changes and rising costs. One of the oldest, Eastern Airlines, shut down in 1991.[11] Its demise was a serious blow to GSP. Even fabled Pan-American World Airways, the airline that had pioneered overseas travel in the 1930s and '40s, succumbed in the 1990s to high costs and inefficiencies.[12] Other airlines sought refuge in international alliances. British Airways bought 22 percent of USAir in 1993, then sold its interest just two years later. KLM Royal Dutch Airlines bought part of Northwest. Continental struck deals with Air Canada and Scandinavian Air Service (SAS). In 2000, United Air Lines tried to buy USAir, by then renamed US Airways. However, the Justice Department refused, claiming the deal would be anti-competitive.

The decisions and actions, success or failure of airlines have always affected commercial airports. An airport can thrive or starve based on its ability to attract and keep profitable airlines. GSP, like almost any other small or medium-market regional airport, has had its share of challenges attracting and keeping airlines, as after the 1978 deregulation. In 1991 when Eastern failed, GSP struggled for a short time. In the months following the terrorist attacks of September 11, 2001, when passenger traffic nosedived and airlines faced their crisis, many airports suffered along with the airlines. In the last years of the twentieth century and the first years of the twenty-first century, one of the critical changes for major airlines has been one of the biggest boosts to airports: the growing number of commuter airlines. Most of the major air carriers have hooked up with one or more of the regional commuter airlines often under the umbrella of the big airline's name. More passengers flying into and out of small and medium-market airports like GSP found themselves aboard a propeller driven plane, or a regional jet, operated by the Delta Connection, United Express, American Eagle, Northwest Airlink, or some other commuter airline. Sometimes the commuter was owned by the major airline. In other cases, it was independently owned. Commuters could serve the smaller markets and provide the big airline more frequent service to those markets.

Not far in the future, smaller airports would have to begin shopping in a new kind of competitive aviation world populated by low-cost, no frills airlines. Attracting the right one—or ones—would prove difficult for many airports, including GSP.

CHAPTER 6

The 1980s

The PATCO Strike

Early on the morning of August 3, 1981, two air traffic controllers appeared in Dick Graham's office at GSP. They announced they were striking. Graham was unimpressed. He was well aware of the controllers union's dissatisfaction, but he thought that a strike was ill-advised and unlikely. "President Reagan," Graham warned them, "will not tolerate a strike. You might be out of a job."[1]

The two air traffic controllers should have heeded Graham's advice. They were among 12,300 of the 15,000 members of the Professional Air Traffic Controllers Organization (PATCO) who struck that morning at 7:00 Eastern time shortly after eleventh-hour contract negotiations had failed. As GSP's executive director had predicted, President Reagan was not pleased. He took firm and quick action.

At 11:00 a.m., just four hours after the strike began, Reagan addressed the air traffic controllers at an impromptu White House news conference. His ultimatum: return to work within forty-eight hours or face *permanent* dismissal. The president followed his announcement by ordering the federal government to move quickly on criminal, civil and administrative fronts to break the strike. Meantime, during its first day, the strike grounded 35 percent of the nation's 14,200 scheduled commercial flights. By the time the president's forty-eight-hour ultimatum period ended, only 875 controllers had returned to work. The president fired 11,350.[2] To keep as many flights operating as possible, several thousand supervisory personnel assumed air traffic control duties. Hundreds of military controllers were called in to help. Airlines had to cancel 50 percent of their flights at twenty-two major airports. To keep the schedules as uncrowded and safe as possible, the nation's general aviation system was placed under severe restrictions. President Reagan's firing had reduced from 16,375 to 4,200 the number of air traffic controllers. Most of those fired appealed the president's action but only a few hundred were eventually reinstated.

Recession and recovery

The lingering effects of airline rate and route deregulation, the Gulf War in which Kuwait was liberated from Iraqi occupation and a general economic downturn kept passenger levels at GSP and many other airports depressed during the first part of the 1980s. At GSP, recession began its surrender to recovery during the first half of 1983, when passenger traffic grew a total of almost 20 percent over 1982. The passenger level in the month of June alone was more than 40 percent ahead of the previous June. The growth was helped when USAir entered the market on June 1 and offered lower rates for several months that other carriers matched. The general economy was improving as well.

"The area is coming out of the recession," GSP's Dick Graham told reporters in July. "Business is getting better and better." He predicted 1983 would top 1982's passenger level of 513,450 by at least 10 percent. Eastern Airlines had a 17 percent gain over June of 1982. Piedmont had a record 2,864 passengers in June. "We're here to stay," Piedmont's station manager promised. "Things look very optimistic." The weak link was newcomer USAir, which had fallen well short of its three thousand passenger goal in its first month at GSP. Nevertheless, passenger traffic through GSP grew 20 percent in 1983 to 620,508; 80 percent of those passengers were business travelers.

Despite the comings and goings of several small airlines—New York Air, Freedom, Wheeler and Pinehurst—passenger traffic on the major carriers continued to increase into 1984. May traffic was almost 22 percent ahead of the previous year. April had the lowest monthly increase over 1983 and even then it was up almost 20 percent. Graham said much of the 1984 traffic, as in the previous year, was by business travelers and their number one destination was New York. By year's end, 1984 passenger traffic reached 735,961, 18.6 percent over the good year of 1983.

Never satisfied and always optimistic, Graham said, "I feel confident that there will be other airlines coming in here." Not that Graham was sitting on his hands just hoping and making bold predictions. Behind the scenes, he and his colleagues on the GSP staff and Airport Commission had been working hard, on the phone, meeting with airline officials, showing the statistics, selling the airport, promoting the Upstate as a dynamic and growing region good for even more industrial and residential development, telling everyone this was a perfect market for an airline. When Graham told reporters in mid-1984 that he was "confident" and that other airlines would be coming here he indeed was confident, for good reason. He was right.

January 25, 1985: American Airlines announces it will begin serving GSP on July 15 with three daily flights. January 28, 1985: Delta Airlines announces it will begin service to GSP on April 4 with four daily flights. The newspaper headlines told the story. "More airlines and more flights will keep the airport busier," said executive director Dick Graham. His and his team's hard work had paid off. American had been the first with the announcement. Yet Delta intended to be the first into GSP with service. Indeed, competition played a big part in Delta's decision. It already had GSP in its long-range planning, but when American announced it was coming to GSP in July, Delta decided to expedite its plans and be ready to come in April. "There's a lot of business here," Delta's vice president for marketing W. W. Hawkins told reporters, "and Delta wants to reach customers before American does." It turned out Delta would not enjoy that advantage.

The chambers of commerce in Greenville and Spartanburg were delighted with the Delta and American announcements. The Greenville chamber's economic development committee chair, Jim Talton, told Jenny Munro of *The Greenville News* that the two airlines "are going to make our job so much easier." With additional flights and competition pushing prices down, Talton said Greenville would have more to offer headquarters and industrial prospects. In their announcement three days before Delta's, American officials said the airline would offer its Ultimate Super Saver fares. The airline had a reputation for reducing fares in cities it served by as much as 70 percent. In response, Delta's marketing director promised, "Delta will be competitive."

The announcement from the two big airlines was a major recognition of the South Carolina Upstate as a growth area and a viable airline market. In January of 1985, Delta was already serving 103 U.S. and overseas cities. It flew 230 jets, had more than 38,000 employees and had concluded 1984 with a net income of more than $258 million. Once Delta's plans were announced, there was no way American was about to let its big competitor have a three and a half month advantage in service to GSP. So in mid-April, both airlines began their jet service to the Upstate at almost the same time, Delta on April 1, American on April 11.

By early summer of 1985, passenger business was booming. Delta was filling 58 percent of its seats in June, far more than it had anticipated. American's station manager said gradual growth had been expected "but it has been at a higher load factor." Eastern's load declined especially because of competition on its Atlanta route. So it started replacing 185-seat B-757s on the route with 120-seat DC-9s. USAir saw June growth up 72 percent over the year before, better than three times the airline's national growth. Piedmont Airlines had record months in May and June with 2,300 passengers more than the previous year. "It's strange, I can't explain it," said Piedmont's veteran GSP station manager Milt Ward. GSP assistant manager Hans Hess credited the reduced fares and heavy airline advertising, which he said had attracted more vacation travelers. Passenger traffic in 1985 reached 854,092, the most ever.

With the airport's successful year in 1985 still not completed, Clemson University released preliminary findings from an economic impact study it was conducting for the South Carolina Aeronautics Commission. It showed that with more than a month left in the year, GSP's estimated 1985 impact on the Greenville-Spartanburg area was already at $128 million. In 1970—fifteen years earlier—a similar study had estimated the airport's economic impact at $4.5 million.

Expansion!

Less than a month after American and Delta had announced in January 1985 their plans to launch service to GSP that spring, news reports began to circulate about the need to expand the airport. Indeed, the airport had started those discussions six months before. By February, executive director Dick Graham listed some of the needs: the ground floor of the terminal required expansion, a second baggage carousel was needed, and covered jetways were wanted so passengers would no longer have to board or leave flights in the rain. The reason expansion was needed, Graham said, was the significant increase in passenger traffic through the airport: 20 percent in 1983, another 18.6 percent in 1984. And now, two major airlines would soon start service. So during 1985, some limited upgrades were begun including an extension to the south concourse, improvements to the terminal, designing an addition to the fire and rescue building, improvement of emergency access roads, and construction of more security fencing.

With business continuing to grow, the Airport Commission in early 1986 ordered consultants Lott Parrish & Associates to conduct a study of the terminal to determine its future needs. By June, Ed Parrish gave his group's study results to the commission. They showed that more than two-thirds of GSP's passengers (68.2 percent) were business travelers. Parrish presented his analysis of likely terminal requirements to meet needs for the next twenty to twenty-five years and discussed development concepts, project financing and other details. The consultants were also told to include a proposed timetable for installation of one or more covered walkways.

By its next meeting, in November, the commission was looking for ways to make the airport more "user friendly." It wanted to hear ideas for curbside check-in stations, for adding a covered pickup area for taxis and limousines, for expansion of the restaurant and bar. "We're looking for the most superb user-friendly airport we can build," Chairman Roger Milliken told reporters. "Expansion should make the airport as convenient to travelers as possible so they'll use GSP and not drive to Charlotte." Richard Metskey presented Skidmore, Owings & Merrill's master plan. It proposed refurbishing and doubling the size of the terminal; lengthening the building to the south; expanding the restaurant, lounge and waiting areas; installing boarding bridges; and building a parking garage and two more parking lots. (Commissioners were always sensitive to the need for enough parking. Those who had known original commissioner L. A. Odom were still haunted by his advice. "Whatever you build," Odom would say, "the first thing you have to do is lick the parking problem.") Metskey told the commissioners the expansion plan would meet terminal needs through 2006. The architects' projected cost: $32.6 million. The commission had set mid-December as the target for tentative approval of the expansion design. Meanwhile mid-December came and went without any decisions. "We are taking time to review all the alternatives carefully," said the chairman.

Commissioners had many alternatives to consider. What should be simply improved and what needs to be expanded? What designs can be scaled back to save dollars? What should be built first? How should space be divided among the competing interests of airlines, concessions, public areas? And what would be the financial impact of delaying certain expenditures? The commissioners also had to consider how to minimize the inconvenience to construction crews and airport users of an expansion program that would likely last more than two years.

In addition to Roger Milliken, the other five commissioners facing these critical decisions as GSP entered its twenty-fifth year were Allen Lowdermilk, George Dean Johnson Jr., Leland Burch, Henry Ramella and Howard Suitt. Among them, they had years of experience in construction, development, insurance, finance and management. They were well suited to the task ahead, and by January 1987 they had some answers. Moreover, passenger traffic had continued to grow, by 20 percent in 1985, by 12 percent in 1986.

On January 26, 1987, the airport commissioners tentatively approved several of the proposed improvements: renovations to and expansion of the terminal, enclosing the existing southern gate concourse and its extension, improvements to the waiting and boarding areas, enlargement of the restaurant and bar, and relocation of the airport entrance along with the development of two parking lots and construction of a 1,558-car parking garage. The commission also approved bids for a new employee parking lot near the control tower. Deputy Director Gary Jackson said the expansion would make it easier to attract more airlines and "lots of glass will allow better viewing of our expanded garden" on the runway side of the terminal.

Executive director Dick Graham had hosted Roger Milliken's longtime assistant Ann Eversbach and a small group of her professional colleagues for a meeting and tour at the airport. It was a beautiful late afternoon in early 1987. Graham decided to give the ladies a unique view of the airport. He took them to the second floor of the control tower and out onto the roof of the concourse at dusk. The rays of the sun setting behind the distant mountains cast beautiful deep orange and red hues on the clouds while hundreds of lights came on along the darkening runway. Graham and his guests were struck with the beauty of that scene.[3] That view would soon influence an important decision in the design of the terminal expansion.

During the planning of the expansion, the Airport Commission usually met in the fire station assembly room next to the base of the control tower. Chairman Milliken had appointed his company's director of engineering, Wallace Storey, to consult with the commission and work closely with architect Mike Keselica to explore possible ways to board aircraft from the existing covered passenger wing in order to minimize cost. Alternatives such as ramps, scissor lifts and elevators were considered. Ultimately, the engineer and architect recommended a second floor on top of the open concourse building to accommodate boarding bridges, or jetways as they were often called.

Keselica was instructed to design a second-floor concourse and submit cost estimates. By the March 1987 commission meeting, Keselica had the design plans for building a second floor on the concourse building to accommodate new passenger lounges and ramps at each gate. Due to the higher cost of this revised plan, which included large windows on the runway side, there was some reluctance by the commissioners to agree to this proposal. To save cost and energy, one commissioner suggested omitting the large windows and just using small, slit windows as had been used in parts of the original terminal. Engineer Storey, an ex-Air Force pilot who loved airplanes, and architect Keselica, who also preferred windows, found themselves on the minority side of the discussion over large windows versus small windows. Executive director Dick Graham, remembering the sight of the runway lights and the setting sun the night he had taken his guests to the roof of the concourse building and aware of the chairman's preference to simulate concepts to aid in making a decision, suggested a visit to the roof to see the view. So Graham took the commissioners on a climb to the roof of the concourse. The beauty of the runway lights in the foreground with the setting sun as the background was exactly the same as it had been a few weeks before when Graham had taken his guests to the same vantage point. Allen Lowdermilk was sold. "We've got to do this and we must have windows!" he exclaimed. The rest of the commissioners agreed. The large windows would be used on the runway side; the slit windows on the opposite side overlooking the parking lot.[4]

The commission asked for a revised cost estimate if the second floor were added and the concourse were left open instead of being enclosed. Consultant Frank Newton had argued that the expansion would be easier to sell to the airlines if the now-traditional second-story passenger boarding method were used. "Overall the cost may be higher," Newton agreed, "but the airlines have more assurance of agreeing to the design." Newton was the person the commission retained to negotiate rates and fees for air carriers at GSP. His opinions and recommendations carried considerable weight with the commissioners. Persuaded by Newton's argument and Keselica's design, the commission decided to enclose

Two views of the ticketing area in the original terminal. The 1989 airport expansion doubled the size of the terminal, adding a large new baggage claim and rental car counter area and an attractive atrium. COURTESY GSP ARCHIVES.

Front of expanded terminal, 1989.

It was Airport Commission chairman Roger Milliken's idea to take prime space on the runway side of the terminal for a garden with water features and sculptures. COURTESY GSP ARCHIVES.

New garden and plane.

During the 1989 expansion, sculptures of children by renowned Utah sculptor Dennis Smith were added to the airport's popular runway-facing garden.

PHOTOGRAPHS © 1996 BY CYNTHIA BLAIR-MILLER.

Dennis Smith of Alpine, Utah, produced the sculpted dancers in the garden on the runway side of the terminal and the "Boy Aviator" statue in the terminal's atrium pool. COURTESY DENNIS SMITH.

Windows Restaurant and mural. PHOTOGRAPH © 1996 BY CYNTHIA BLAIR-MILLER.

Aerial of fountain and terminal. PHOTOGRAPH ©1996 BY CYNTHIA BLAIR-MILLER.

Airport Commission chairman Roger Milliken shows South Carolina Governor Carroll Campbell some of the features of GSP's expanded terminal at opening ceremonies on September 28, 1989. COURTESY GSP ARCHIVES.

Airport Commission chairman Roger Milliken and Spartanburg textile leader Walter Montgomery at the September 28, 1989, Celebration of Expansion. COURTESY GSP ARCHIVES.

Gates, lounges and boarding bridges were added in 1989 when the concourse building was enlarged and a second floor added. PHOTOGRAPH © 1996 BY CYNTHIA BLAIR-MILLER.

Planes at terminal—dawn. PHOTOGRAPH BY JOE F. JORDAN.

Both sides of an historical marker erected in 1999 by BMW and GSP at BMW's Flatwood Fields athletic complex. It honors the former Flatwood community on which both GSP and BMW were built. One side of the marker has names of former Flatwood families. The other side lists many Flatwood Peaches baseball team members. PHOTOGRAPHS BY GREG MOSS.

When GSP opened in October 1962, it was the first civilian airport to have a runway with centerline lighting. In 1989, the runway was lengthened. Along the runway's 11,001 feet are 218 lights and 465 sidelights. PHOTOGRAPH BY GREG MOSS.

Operations supervisor Nathan Garner checks a malfunctioning runway light. Lights along GSP's runway and taxiway are checked at dusk each evening and at any time when there are low-visibility conditions. PHOTOGRAPH BY GREG MOSS.

GSP's Larry Holcombe stands next to a huge earthmoving machine during the lengthening of the runway to 11,001 feet in the late 1990s.

Each year from Thanksgiving until New Year's Day, GSP's terminal atrium fountain is replaced by a colorful poinsettia "tree."
PHOTOGRAPH BY GREG MOSS.

only portions of the ground level passenger concourse for airline use, to build the second floor above and to order movable boarding bridges. At the same time, the commission shelved the idea for a pedestrian bridge between the terminal and the parking garage because of high cost.

When the commissioners reviewed the costs of the revised plans, they were pleased. "It's going to be an even swap," the chairman declared. "It's not going to cost any more." The expanded terminal would be double the size of the original twenty-five-year-old building and have an entirely new look. When the expansion was completed, it would have three levels, ticketing and baggage claim on the ground level, concessions on the second level and boarding on the third level.

At its March 23, 1987, meeting the Airport Commission made what had to be viewed as an unusual decision. It refused to seek a $387,000 federal government grant to pay for utilities to be extended to the new parking garage. Approval of the grant would have required an estimated nine months' wait and the garage project needed to be expedited to meet rapidly rising demand for more parking. "We feel it is incumbent upon us to move ahead as rapidly as possible," Chairman Roger Milliken explained.

The next commission meeting, on June 8, lasted for several hours. Commissioners, staff and designers thoroughly reviewed the details of the entire expansion plan. Even the parking garage design generated discussion about proposed locations of its ramps and the effect on traffic flow. The chairman kept emphasizing the need to cut costs, at one point telling the New York-based architects, "This is Greenville and Spartanburg, South Carolina, not New York City. We don't have the money to do everything they do in New York."[5] One point of contention was whether to have one security checkpoint on the upper concourse or two checkpoints. Architect Mike Keselica said the difference in cost could be five hundred thousand dollars. The commission opted for two checkpoints. By its meeting on July 14, some details still remained to be worked out but the commission gave its approval in principle to the expansion plan, which by then had increased to a cost of approximately $35 million.

Argo Construction of Greenville won the parking garage job on a bid of $7.5 million and started the project in August of 1987. In September, several of the commissioners and staff met informally with airline representatives and with construction companies interested in bidding on the terminal expansion project. While airline representatives said they wanted curbside baggage check-in and adequate room for security checkpoints, Chairman Milliken made clear he wanted conversational seating groupings in waiting areas. That was just another example of Milliken's penchant for details. Everyone from airport staff members to the architects who designed the original airport and this major late-1980s expansion always had to be prepared for the chairman's questions and for his insistence on controlling costs. But even architect Mike Keselica, the lead designer on both the original terminal and the new expansion project who had occasionally been the object of Milliken's barbs about design ideas that were too expensive, had kind words for the chairman. "Mr. Milliken was one of Skidmore Owings & Merrill's most interested and involved clients who challenged us for better ideas," Keselica remembered.[6]

Roger Milliken went beyond tough questions. He often loaned some of his company's executives to work with the airport on financial consulting, design, construction and other projects. For the expansion project just approved, he loaned his purchasing agent, Henry Laye. He traveled the country visiting other airports to ask questions, to see what materials they were using and to learn how GSP could save money on its purchases. To oversee the expansion that was about to begin, Milliken loaned his director of engineering, Wallace Storey, who had been responsible for designing and overseeing construction of more than forty-five Milliken plants and additions, to be the airport's construction representative to coordinate design and construction of the expansion project. It was just one of many airport projects on which he worked. The services were extended free of charge. They were a valuable help to a small airport that could not afford all of the specialized services that a bigger airport in a large market may have been able to pay. Years later, after the conclusion of the late-1980s expansion and following his retirement from Milliken & Company, Storey was appointed to the Airport Commission. Dick

Graham was always amazed at Milliken's commitment to the airport. "He has walked my legs off around here," Graham told Wayne Roper of *The Greenville News*. "He's been everywhere in this place. I think he even comes a lot of times when I'm not here and looks!"

"My interest in the airport stems from wanting to make it work and be attractive," Milliken told reporters. "You only have one chance to make a first impression."

The Airport Commission's final approval of the expansion plan came in September of 1987 just a month before the airport's twenty-fifth anniversary. In that quarter century, despite years filled with limited air service, new dangers to aviation, the unsettling effects of deregulation and a constantly changing marketplace, GSP had served more than ten million passengers. In just the first seven years of the 1980s, the airport had risen from recession to recovery; 1983 to 1987 had been good years. Fares were down, passengers were up, an average of 16 percent a year, according to consultant John Nommack. On November 14, 1987, Jean Reddy, a Ft. Lauderdale, Florida, resident visiting her brother in Fountain Inn, South Carolina, received two free Delta tickets to California. "Our one millionth passenger of the year is a winner," GSP's Dick Graham told reporters, "and so are all who live in this dynamic, growing area of western South Carolina. It was a happy and promising milestone. GSP was attracting more passengers and industry. President Chet Hoag of the Middle Tyger Area Council told *The Greenville News* in February of 1988 that the towns represented by his council—Greer, Lyman, Duncan and Wellford—planned to feature the airport as one of the towns' convenience factors. In the same February 18 article, airport chairman Roger Milliken promised that the major expansion already well underway would place priority on convenience. He noted the amount of nearby parking, the customs office and designation as a port of entry as conveniences GSP already offered. Reporter Wayne Roper said the airport's location near the fast growing Highway 290 corridor in western Spartanburg County was a reason that business executives were being attracted to the area.

The Siberian express, weathermen called it. The worst storm in GSP's twenty-five year history, the second worst snowstorm the area had experienced since 1930. It began falling at 2:40 a.m. on Thursday, January 7, 1988. By that evening, twelve inches were measured at GSP. Other areas of the Upstate had up to eighteen inches. Snowdrifts made it even worse. I-85 and many other highways were closed. "It is just absolutely terrible," said a veteran highway patrolman. Two days later, traffic was even worse, thanks to stalled and wrecked cars and ice. Viewing the scene from a helicopter, Governor Carroll Campbell observed, "South Carolina is ill-equipped for something like this."[7] Temperatures stayed below freezing for five days, many business firms and schools were closed for at least four days. The airport reopened after just twenty-four hours. However, there were no flights out for a couple more days and people couldn't reach the airport over the dangerous roads.

As architectural and engineering plans proceeded for the major expansion project, Roger Milliken suggested that the commissioners, along with engineer Storey and architect Keselica, visit a few new airports to look at and gain information about furnishings, ticketing, support areas and other ideas. One of the visits was to an expanded airport at Richmond, Virginia, where, rather than inspecting the facility, almost all the time was spent talking with the director in his conference room. He described difficulties his airport had faced during the construction of its expansion. There had been passenger disruptions, airline unhappiness, delays in aircraft operation. Ultimately, there were lawsuits between the contractor and the airport. On the return flight to GSP, Milliken and his colleagues on the commission asked how these problems could be prevented during the GSP expansion. There were legitimate concerns since the GSP project would involve building a second level over the existing concourse with columns on both sides and large fifty-foot concrete beams being erected over the passenger area. It was obvious that substantial protective passageways would be required through construction areas with probable changes in their locations as the work progressed. Storey suggested to Keselica that perhaps the work could be done at night—between midnight and 6:00 a.m.—when no flights were due. Besides avoiding initial interference, once the outside walls and roof of the second floor were complete, work could be accomplished inside without any conflicts. Commissioners were concerned that the idea of overnight work might be too costly. However, it was decided to solicit bids both ways: work during normal hours with protective passageways provided by the contractor and stop work as necessary for plane schedules or with the work accomplished during night hours. Storey remembers the surprise when the bids were received from several contractors. "Surprisingly, the alternate bid for nighttime work was about the same as for daytime work," Storey recalls. "It was interesting that on some later additional construction that could have been accomplished in normal working hours, the contractor, based on the ease of the main work, decided to do the work at night."[8]

By mid-1988, the final hurdle on the expansion project was cleared before construction could begin. The FAA, which had reviewed preliminary plans earlier, gave its final approval to the plans and to Fluor Daniel Construction Company's bid of $24.4 million. Meantime, Argo Construction was nearing completion on the parking garage. It opened in October 1988, almost doubling the airport's capacity to three thousand vehicles.

No taxes would be sought for the expansion construction. The airport would pay for the project from accrued reserve funds and by selling revenue bonds. On October 4, 1988, the commission approved a resolution for issuing $35 million of airport facilities revenue bonds. When those twenty-five-year bonds, with an overall average rate of 7.75 percent, went on sale in November 1988, investors were waiting.

"The bonds sold out in seven hours," said C&S Bank's Mike Bell, GSP's financial advisor. "Some sold to private and institutional investors elsewhere in the country." At the Spartanburg office of Shearson Lehman Hutton, broker Billy Blackford told the *Spartanburg Herald*, "There's a lot of interest in Spartanburg. It's a hometown story." At the Smith Barney Harris Upham office in Greenville, where $10 million worth of bonds sold, vice president Ron McGrath reported, "We sold multiple orders of $100,000 bonds. That indicates the strength and confidence people have in the Airport Commission and the airport bond issue." GSP spokesman Jack Norris was elated, telling reporters the bonds carried a AA rating. "Only six other airports in the nation have achieved a higher rating," he said. On December 1, 1988, the Airport Commission approved the bond sale and, just in case of unforeseen difficulties, approved buying a $279,000 insurance policy on bond repayment.

At the Airport Commission's April 10, 1989, meeting, architect Mike Keselica proposed expanding the south end of the terminal concourse by 525 more feet. That, he said, would provide five more gate positions, bringing the total to thirteen. The commission approved the proposal and added $3.3 million to the project, which now stood at close to $40 million.

Just before Greenville construction executive Howard Suitt joined the Airport Commission in 1985, his wife told him to be sure that boarding bridges—jetways as they have often been called—were added while he was on the commission. Years later, Suitt would not take much credit for them since the idea was already being discussed before he was elected a commissioner. Nevertheless, he could tell his wife that he voted for them. It was a serious decision. The bridges cost two hundred thousand dollars each. In August of 1989, those bridges were finally installed. "It will rain no more on travelers getting on and off planes at Greenville-Spartanburg Airport," *The Greenville News* reported. Mrs. Suitt, and thousands more passengers, were pleased with the news.

The airport expansion was on schedule. Some of it would continue into early 1990. The Airport Commission, however, thought that enough of it would be completed by late September. So at their August 7 meeting, commissioners set Thursday, September 28, 1989, as the date for what they decided to call A Celebration of Expansion. It would begin at 6:00 p.m.

The six hundred guests began gathering before five thirty on September 28. Many parked in the new five-level garage across from the new wing of the terminal. They were directed first into the football-field-length baggage claim and rental car counter area of the lower level. This new wing doubled the length of the original terminal. Governor Carroll Campbell told the crowd, "This airport has been the core of growth and prosperity for this entire Upstate region." Campbell said capital investment was growing rapidly along the Interstate 85 business corridor and the importance of the airport would only grow. Newly-crowned Miss America Debbye Turner joined the governor in leading the big crowd in a champagne toast. Airport Commission Chairman Roger Milliken paid tribute to all the people who had worked so hard on the expansion project. "Unless you were on the inside," Milliken told the crowd, "you couldn't possibly imagine the building accomplishments of the last two months, and of the last two weeks, of the last two days, of the last two hours." Indeed, administrative assistant Louise Nelson remembered years later how workmen were still polishing floors and making other last minute preparations upstairs in the terminal while the governor was speaking downstairs at the beginning of the celebration evening.[9] Much of the original terminal building was still being expanded and renovated and would not be complete until early the next year.

Before guests began their tour of the expanded airport, Roger Milliken's Airport Commission colleagues announced the naming of the new garden between the terminal and the runway in his honor. Following the ceremonies, the guests were taken on guided tours. On the next level they were introduced to a spectacular change: the new Windows restaurant. Through the twenty-six-foot-high glass window they had a spectacular view of the airfield and the beautiful expanded formal garden with pools, fountains and sculpture. (See Chapter 7.) The enlarged restaurant, bar area, and upper lobby were beautifully designed with comfortable furnishings. Opening off the corridor leading from the upper lobby, guests found the short-order counter of the restaurant, which was operated by a division of Spartanburg-based T. W. Services, Inc. On the new gate level, the guests found spacious departure lounges for each of the airlines. They also had a close-up look at those new passenger loading bridges.

For the past twenty-seven years, passengers had to walk outside and climb movable metal stairs. They would still have to do that for smaller planes, but for boarding and leaving the larger jets, they would be dry no matter what the weather. Ticket counters would have more space and be more convenient, there were more gates, baggage claim would be faster and more convenient, and the gift shop had been expanded. "Everything is going to be bigger and better," said the airport's deputy director, Gary Jackson. In fact, one hundred forty thousand square feet had been added to the terminal. It was virtually twice its original size.

Area leaders were pleased with the expansion, many of them feeling that it would help economic development in the Upstate. However, the expansion did not mean that there would be any immediate increase in the number of direct and nonstop flights to major cities. Nevertheless, the executive director of the Greenville Convention and Visitors Bureau, Mike Carrier, noted that the airport has "better service here than many of the other cities around us." The expansion pleased Jim Morton, director of public relations for Michelin Tire Corporation. He told *Greenville News* reporter Tamara Aldus that the airport had been a "critical" factor in Michelin's decision to establish headquarters near the airport on Greenville's east side in the mid-1970s. "Service," said Morton, "has been improving significantly year to year in most respects."

Executive Director Dick Graham was optimistic regarding air service. "There is no doubt service is going to grow and grow," said Graham. "But you are never going to have it to the point where everybody can go where they want to go when they want to go. That's impossible."

Sena Black, associate director of research and information resources for the South Carolina Development Board, said, "An airport is the number one or number two factor considered when corporate headquarters look for a place to build." Greater Greenville Chamber of Commerce President Harvey Schmitt told reporters, "I think the airport has proven to be a model for a lot of regional communities to look at. It's there to say the ability of Greenville or any of the Upstate communities to compete effectively would have been severely limited had we not gone to a regional concept." Schmitt said he thought the expansion had likely increased the area's opportunities for future growth and development. "I think it makes a very clear statement that the community is on the move, it's aggressive, things are going in the right direction. This is a good place to be. From our perspective," said the chamber president, "it has a tremendous marketing appeal."[10]

Roger Milliken was pleased with the reaction of the Airport Commission's guests on that Celebration of Expansion evening. He was glad they liked the plan of the larger terminal, the convenience of the new features and services and those new bridges at the gates. He was most gratified, however, by their reaction to the aesthetics—the furnishings, the artwork, Windows restaurant and that expansive view toward the mountains, across the runway and down at the garden. That garden; it was his favorite along with the landscaping that lined the roads of the airport and enhanced the terminal. Since planning had begun for the airport thirty years earlier, he had always envisioned a garden in the airport and the airport in a garden. The old garden was nice, but the new one was even better. The old landscaping was attractive. Now the trees were more mature and Rick Webel, son and protégé of the man who had designed the master plan for the airport's layout and landscaping thirty years ago, had again put the magic Webel touch on the airport's exterior appearance.

Leadership change
graham to jackson

In addition to celebrating the spectacular new expansion at the airport that last week of September 1989, a changing of the guard was also being observed. Longtime airport executive director Dick Graham was retiring and his deputy director, Gary Jackson, was assuming the executive director's position.

"How things have changed," Graham told *Greenville News* reporter Tamara Aldus on the eve of his retirement. When he arrived on the job at

GSP on May 1, 1967, there were just two gates, no bridges, no departure rooms, no air cargo building. There were four hundred parking spaces, one fireman and a makeshift fire truck, one security guard, and only limited jet service. Now, almost twenty-three years later, his September 28, 1989, retirement ceremony was being combined with a preview for area leaders of the new expansion. Now there were eight gates, and room for five more along a sprawling departure concourse, large cargo facilities, a customs port, thirty-two hundred parking spaces, firemen with sophisticated trucks and rescue units, round-the-clock airport police protection and several airlines providing dozens of flights a day in and out of GSP.

Dick Graham had wanted to leave when he was sixty-five. That was four years ago. The airport commissioners had asked him in 1985 to stay on a little longer until the expansion was finished. "A little longer" had stretched into four years. Now the time had come and the staff and commissioners threw a party for him. They praised him for his leadership, his integrity, for the way he had treated them and the airport's customers, everyone. The people who couldn't come—and many of those who did—wrote him letters. The staff collected pictures and many of them mentioned his competitive spirit, exemplified by the way he operated the airport and by the manner in which he whipped most of his opponents on the tennis court.

Graham's administrative assistant, Louise Nelson, put all the letters into a handsome hardcover book. The tributes came from members of Congress, state legislators, mayors, airport commissioners, employees, business and community leaders, heads of federal and state agencies, airline officials and consultants. And Louise Nelson included her own note: "I have always been proud to say I work for Arthur R. Graham, believing he would try to do what is right and fair."

Perhaps the most clever and funny letter came from Doug Smith, one of Graham's tennis buddies and longtime general manager at WYFF-TV. One of the questions Dick Graham had been asked the most during his long tenure at the airport was, "When will you build the *second* runway at GSP?" Teasing him about those frequent inquiries, Smith wrote in his letter with tongue in cheek: "As a personal token of my appreciation I am passing along a rather historic note that I recently found in a Kitty Hawk antique shop. I am well aware of your contributions to our area, but was surprised and happy to learn that you were also involved in such an historic occasion. The Smithsonian has been badgering me for this valuable and historic document, but I feel it should rightfully be in your possession." Attached to Smith's letter was a note allegedly dated December 17, 1903, that said simply, "Orville: Dick Graham says we should hold up until we have a second runway. Wilbur." In 2007, the airport's forty-fifth year, the second runway still had not been built. Nor would it be for at least several more years. The FAA requires a certain level of takeoff and landing activity. GSP's traffic still is not enough for the FAA to approve initiating preparations for a second runway.

After years of retirement, the man with the delightful sense of humor and who laughed often still had a good chuckle whenever he looked at that note from Doug Smith, alias Wilbur Wright, in his book of memories. Dick Graham had enjoyed twenty-three good years as executive director. Now he was ready to turn airport operations over to the man he had prepared for the job.

J. GARRETT JACKSON

Dick Graham had been planning to retire as soon as the terminal expansion project was finished. He was looking for someone who could replace him at that time and he kept hearing the name Gary Jackson. Entering airport management in Louisville, Kentucky, and later managing the Texarkana, Arkansas Municipal Airport for nine years and the Columbus, Georgia Metropolitan Airport for eight years, Jackson had established a good reputation. The two men met at a professional meeting in Florida in 1986. Jackson liked what he heard about Greenville-Spartanburg Airport. Graham liked Jackson's operating ideas and offered him the job of deputy director. When Dick Graham retired three years later, Jackson was ready for the airport's top job. On October 2, 1989, Gary Jackson became GSP's executive director.

Jackson had been in his new post only a year when BMW began its quiet search for a North American plant location and started focusing on the South Carolina Upstate. His first years as executive director were filled with the challenges of the BMW move, lengthening of the runway, and the need to protect the airport's environs by acquiring more land and developing zoning restrictions. In the process of meeting those challenges, Jackson developed a reputation for a quiet, fair, deliberate and thoughtful management style. He also pleased his former boss. "I made a great choice," Dick Graham claimed years later. "The best thing I did for the airport was have Gary replace me."[11] If one sign of good management is a smooth transition from one chief executive to another, GSP's 1989 leadership change had been successful.

Jackson's move to executive director presented a new opportunity for a longtime airport employee. Larry Holcombe had worked in the New Mexico oil fields before serving four years in the navy including two tours in Vietnam. Then he returned to his hometown of Greenville and worked odd jobs until he was hired as GSP's second fireman in 1973. Later he was appointed fire chief while at the same time working to earn a business management degree at Limestone College.

By the time his longtime boss Dick Graham retired, Holcombe had been operations manager for several years. When Gary Jackson moved up to executive director, Holcombe replaced him as deputy director. Seventeen years later as the job of executive director grew more demanding, Larry Holcombe would be promoted in March of 2007 to airport manager, assuming full control of day-to-day airport operations and leaving Jackson with more time for his executive responsibilities as GSP continued to grow.

CHAPTER 7

The Art and Beauty of GSP

When GSP's fixed-base operator, Stevens Aviation, decided in 2006 to refurbish its original hangar and move its Turboprop Center back to GSP, the company's vice president for operations, Larry Baker, was delighted. He had moved from Orlando in 1994 to join Stevens. His office is at company headquarters in Donaldson Industrial Center, less than twenty miles from GSP. Baker also spends time at Stevens FBO sites in other cities. "But coming here to GSP is like going to a state park," said Baker. "I've been to a lot of airports and there's not a more beautiful airport in the country."[1]

The Garden

From his earliest days of overseeing the design and planning of the new airport, Roger Milliken had decided he wanted it to be a place of beauty, a place that people would enjoy visiting. He often reflected on that night in Germany, relaxing in the biergarten at the Frankfurt airport. That was the experience that had sparked his idea to have a garden at this airport. He thought it was such a good idea, he insisted on it. Unlike any other airport in the world, Greenville-Spartanburg has a formal garden between the terminal and the runway, gates and planes on either side of it. The garden has proved to be a welcome idea, a popular place for fliers and visitors to relax, a beautiful view for the diners in Windows restaurant to enjoy.

The original garden was 220 by 168 feet with a 60 by 25-foot reflecting pool in the center. Several beds of plants and flowers—three of them elevated—were adjacent to the pool. Around the garden were an English ivy groundcover and a border of Japanese holly along with azaleas, crepe myrtles, Chinese red berry holly and magnolia trees. Five thousand plantings left no room for grass.

The placement of the runway-facing garden has surprised many people over the years, especially visiting airline and airport officials. After he became GSP's executive director in 1967, Dick Graham was hosting a group of leaders from the Knoxville, Tennessee airport when one of them asked, "How did you convince the airlines to let you make prime airplane space into a garden?" "It's easy," Graham responded. "You just get a chairman and a commission like mine who say that's where it's going to be."[2] Indeed, from the day Roger Milliken shared his unusual idea for a garden facing the runway, he never retreated from that desire. Neither has he ever regretted it. He has always believed it is one of the best features of the airport, certainly the most unique and special.

The airport chairman, however, was not satisfied having simply a garden. He wanted the whole airport to be as pleasant to the senses as a facility laden with concrete could be. Most of the concrete, though, is on the runway side of the terminal, the side with the garden. Along the entryway and interior roads and sidewalks, next to the parking garages and lots and other buildings, that's where Milliken wanted trees, flowers, lawns. That's how the master landscaper he chose, Richard K. Webel, and in later years his son, Rick Webel, could use their creativity and experience to oblige Milliken's desire to have, as he liked to say, "an airport within a garden."

When GSP opened in 1962, it looked much different from the way it appeared in 2007, its forty-fifth year. There were no parking garages. All of the ground parking was adjacent to the terminal, which was just half its eventual size. In that era of much less concern about security, automobiles were accommodated on the curb directly in front of the terminal at parking meters! There were no waiting lounges. Passengers and visitors waited in the open concourse of the so-called finger building. Across the road in front of the terminal there was an expansive lawn. It's still there, graced now by the tall fountain that was added in 1970 in tribute to the airport's cofounder, Charlie Daniel.

By the mid-1980s, the airport was almost twenty-five years old. Passenger and cargo traffic demanded expansion. The terminal had to be enlarged; a parking garage and more ground parking were needed. More cargo facilities and room for support services was required. The airport had to prepare for its next twenty-five years. While some of the facilities were growing inadequate, the airport's beauty was increasing. Trees were maturing; flower beds and lawns were well-tended. Artwork had long ago begun to appear on terminal walls and the display of community art, which had been a feature of the opening and dedication ceremonies in 1962, had proved so popular it was made a permanent terminal feature. Most GSP users didn't want the airport's beauty to be diminished by expansion. Some, however, were nervous.

It was early December 1988. Construction had begun on the $40 million terminal expansion and renovation project. As his plane taxied onto the apron, the passenger couldn't believe his eyes. There it sat. A huge bulldozer...right in the middle of that garden in front of the terminal. That garden that he and just about everybody else liked so much. The bulldozer was tearing it to pieces. He was shocked. As soon as he was able, the distressed passenger called the Airport Commission office. "You couldn't have done anything worse," he complained firmly. "That garden made the airport."

Deputy Director Gary Jackson was pleased with the man's complaint. "Wait and see what takes its place," he told the unhappy passenger.[3] That was the favorite response of GSP officials when they received calls about the dismantling of the airport's unique trademark garden. Jackson and his colleagues enjoyed telling people about plans for that area of the airport: a glass-enclosed restaurant—with skylights and palm trees, twice the size of the old one—right in the middle of the terminal...and looking out on an even bigger and better garden. Everyone would just have to wait until the fall of 1989. Then the garden would be back. It would be beautiful. Jackson was sure that the unhappy flier would like it, and everyone else too.

Gary Jackson was right. The upset passenger with whom he had talked early in the expansion project would have been just as pleased with the new garden as were the six hundred guests who first saw it on Celebration of Expansion night, September 28, 1989. The garden was approximately the same size and in the same place—right in the middle of the terminal's gates overlooking the runway. It still had varieties of flowers and hedges, bushes and trees. It had more water than the original. In the big pool was a waterfall and large fountain with several small ones around it. In a smaller pool there was another waterfall and a couple of small water spouts. Surrounded by a variety of trees, the garden then and now offers places to sit and enjoy the beauty of it. An intriguing new feature had been added to the garden: sculpture...special, custom-designed sculpture...with a message.

Roger Milliken had been in Vail, Colorado, the night that President Gerald Ford dedicated the new town center. It included a fountain with sculptures of young people. The magic of that night never left Milliken's mind. Years later, when plans for the terminal expansion began, it became obvious that the garden the airport's chairman loved so much would have to be removed to make room for the construction that was to double the size of the terminal. He ordered a new and better garden to replace it. The next garden, he decided, would have sculptures of young people.

Milliken called his friend Dean Knox, owner of the prestigious Knox Galleries in Colorado and northern Michigan. Knox represented an artist whose work Milliken had bought before. He agreed that Dennis Smith could produce the kind of sculptures that Milliken wanted.[4] For years, Smith had been specializing in sculptures of children. He had always been inspired by the innocence of childhood. He wanted to preserve those childhood memories and hopes, expressions and gestures. To Smith, the child is a metaphor for life. During his long career, Smith had been capturing the essence of children in many media—metal, glass, oil paint, pen and ink, bronze. He loved sculpting, especially when he was sculpting children. Milliken invited Smith and Knox to fly to South Carolina for a visit.

Roger Milliken and Dennis Smith understood each other. The order was placed and the sculptor went to work. What he created can still be enjoyed in the runway garden at GSP: boys and girls dancing, displaying the vibrancy and freedom, the passion and energy of youth.

After graduating from Brigham Young University, Dennis Smith attended the Royal Academy of Art in Copenhagen. Then in 1968, he set up a studio in his father's old chicken coop not far from where he grew up near Provo, Utah. Soon he began to exhibit professionally. His reputation spread across America and overseas. His works are displayed at U.S. embassies in London, Prague and Moscow, and in several countries, including Denmark, the country of his heritage and where he received some of his training. They can be found in many American cities, at a children's hospital in New Orleans, at the American Academy of Pediatrics in Chicago, even at other airports. Several of his air ships, which he fashions from welded steel, hang in the airports at Salt Lake City and Yuma, Arizona.[5]

"I absolutely love my work," says Dennis Smith. It shows, in his sculptures, his paintings, his etchings, even in his poetry and prose. He is a thoughtful and talented man. Writes Smith: "It is only through using their imagination that children are able to understand what it might be like to be grown up. We're all children in a sense, with limited perspective of a broader universe. Through our imagination we are able to envision the potential of our own eternal nature."[6]

Smith's studio, foundry and gallery are in his hometown, the beautiful mountain community of Alpine, Utah. In 2004, Smith was called upon again by GSP. The airport commissioned the statue of a young boy fascinated with the progress of flight. It now stands in the pool at GSP's terminal atrium in honor of the airport's cofounder. (See Chapter 15.)

Murals

Roger Milliken loved the newly expanded airport. But even before the late September 1989 dedication, while work was continuing on the multimillion dollar expansion, there was still something that bothered the airport chairman. He knew just the person who could do something about it. With a few weeks remaining before the scheduled Celebration of Expansion, Milliken placed a call to his friend Carl Tait in LaGrange, Georgia. A native of New England, Tait for years had designed for the American Greeting Card Company and had often been commissioned to paint murals. For the past several years he had consulted for Milliken's Interior Furnishings Division.

Tait answered the phone in his studio and immediately recognized the familiar voice. "Carl," said Milliken, "there's this horrible blank wall in the beautiful new restaurant in our renovated airport. What do you think we should put on it?" Milliken gave the artist all the details about location and the restaurant's furnishings. "I think you should put on that wall a piece of art that would cover the entire space," Tait replied, "one that would make a statement. A mural." Milliken asked for his ideas. He needed a mural quickly.[7]

Just five days later, Tait had a detailed drawing to show. The airport chairman liked it, but he was concerned that the mural might be a departure from the conservative nature of the terminal and he thought some might question the Airport Commission's use of funds for the mural. "So," said Milliken, "I'll donate it to the airport."[8] Tait admitted his mural design was avant garde. It showed Marilyn Monroe sticking her tongue out, Batman and trapeze artists, a New York streetwalker and a skateboarder. Tait was pleased with Milliken's approval. He wanted to show what he called "this marvelous country" from a youthful perspective. They are the ones who will inherit this, he would say. Youth was his theme. That would be the statement of his mural, and, thought Tait, what better place for such a mural, a statement, than an airport where travelers are leaving to see so many of these sights.[9]

The colorful mural begins on the West Coast and takes the viewer's eyes eastward with sights recognizable to almost everyone—Disneyland, the Grand Canyon, deserts and mountains, windmills, alligators and Indians, famous performers, cities and countryside. There is even a little boy in a Coke bottle. "Where did you get that idea?" asked *Greenville*

Piedmont writer Jimmy Cornelison. Tait explained that he served part of his World War II duty in Louisiana where he observed that many of the children would rather drink Coke than milk. "All day long," said Tait, "I would see them going back and forth to the store to get a little bottle of Coke, never milk. There was one child I noticed all the time and I told him once, 'one day you are going to end up in a Coke bottle.'" Tait never forgot the image.

Only a few weeks after he had received the request from Roger Milliken, Tait's mural—twelve feet tall, one hundred sixty feet long—was complete. It still graces the high wall overlooking Windows restaurant in the airport terminal where it is studied and enjoyed by thousands who pass through GSP each year. Harold Krisel, an art consultant for Skidmore, Owings & Merrill, the airport's architect, conceived, and Carl Tait painted, several of the wall murals in the terminal and concourses.

The airport had received its first major piece of permanent art on July 16, 1981. *Right Bank View*—a ten- by eighteen-foot fiber art mural by Spartanburg artist Robert Bove and New York artist Randee Silverman—was hung opposite the ground floor ticket counters. Bove had attended Converse College. The two artists, assisted by Michael McDunn Jr., resident woodworker at the Greenville County Museum of Art, installed the mural. It was designed to create dimensional relief areas using a stuffing technique known as trapunto. The stuffing was of cotton and polyester fiberfill and the backing fiber of cotton muslin. Woven areas were woven by hand directly onto the canvas. The Arts Council of Spartanburg and the Metropolitan Arts Council of Greenville bought the mural with help from the South Carolina Arts Commission.

Birds in the terminal!

A few years after GSP's 1989 expansion, Chairman Roger Milliken and landscape architect Rick Webel were walking through the new baggage claim area of the terminal looking up at the high ceiling and the small windows. Milliken was extolling its beauty and inviting Webel's comment. "It reminds me of a barn," Webel replied. "I expect to see barn swallows come swooping down over us."[10]

"Why not?" Milliken thought. The two men discussed the possibility. Why not have some birds in the terminal? Milliken asked Webel if he knew anyone who sculpted large birds. Webel immediately recommended an artist who had sculpted several animals for his father's ranch in Montana; he also sculpted birds.

Jim Dolan is a California native who moved to Montana as a young man to work on a family member's ranch. He also studied agriculture at Montana State University in Bozeman, but something kept nagging at him. As a child, Dolan had always enjoyed art but he had never taken a course. In high school he toyed with sculpture and in college signed on for a course in welding. That's when it clicked. He could sculpt with welded metal. Since 1973, Jim Dolan has been creating at his studio in Belgrade, Montana. Today, more than one hundred thirty public pieces of his sculpture are on display in hospitals, business parks, civic plazas and other places throughout America. He sculpted forty-foot tall teepees for an Indian tribe out West. He has eleven works on display in Japan and several in South America. His specialties are big game animals, horses and birds.[11]

Birds, that's just what Roger Milliken wanted. So in 1996 Jim Dolan began sculpting nine snow geese, each about six feet long with an eight-foot wing span. Dolan estimates each bird likely took him at least one hundred hours to sculpt. In the spring of 1997, Dolan, Rick Webel and GSP workers hung the birds in the GSP terminal. Each weighs about seventy pounds and is suspended on a steel rod attached to the terminal's cement ceiling. They are difficult to miss, flying over the atrium fountain and pool and on into the baggage claim area. They add to the ambience Roger Milliken, his colleagues on the Airport Commission and the staff wanted to create in the terminal, especially in December. That's when the snow geese are decked out in their bright red hats and scarves. That was the idea of GSP's Larry Holcombe, who found hats and scarves in a local store. Along with the tall red poinsettia tree that stands in the fountain area of the terminal's atrium, the snow geese add to the happy seasonal atmosphere at GSP every year between Thanksgiving and New Year's Day.

The beauty and art of GSP have generated not only many compliments during the airport's forty-five years, but also several recognitions from the Spartanburg Chamber of Commerce, a number of men's and women's garden clubs and the Federal Aviation Administration. The airport was one of only five in the United States in 1968 to receive an FAA Certificate of Commendation for promoting airport beautification. In 1985, the FAA's southern region presented the airport a Certificate of Commendation calling it a "showcase of beauty and efficiency."

Local nurseryman Ray Bracken accepted one of only five National Environment Improvement Merit Awards given by the Associated Landscape Contractors of America. In the mid-1960s, Bracken planted more than one million pine seedlings on several hundred acres of airport property under the federal government's reforesting program. Bracken also maintained for several years trees along the airport's access roads and its parking lots. "The trees," said Bracken, "hide much of the concrete and asphalt and you get a wonderful feeling of driving through cool shade."

Trees and landscaping

Thank Richard K. Webel's design for that. Webel used trees to structure physical space, trees in rows, closely spaced, often repeating into the distance. He placed dozens of Darlington and willow oaks in GSP's parking areas and planted American sweet gums along the approach roads to the terminal. Richard C. Webel says his father and Umberto Innocenti believed, "that beauty in the world could be achieved through the overlapping of a strong visual order on the ground plane with the enriching effect of living, changing and at times uncontrolled vegetative cover." Richard K. Webel described it simply, "If the ground plan guides one's feet and the planting leads one's eyes, the scene can be infinitely rich."[12] All who have enjoyed the Webel landscape designs at GSP, Furman

University, Wofford College, Milliken & Company, the GE plant and elsewhere could agree.

Innocenti, the planter, died in 1968; R. K. Webel, the designer, in 2000. Richard C. Webel has been the CEO of Innocenti and Webel since the 1980s. With degrees in architecture, landscape architecture and business from the University of Pennsylvania, and after years of experience working with his father, he has definite design philosophies. "We should set the stage rather than decorate the solution," said Webel. That is why he appreciates, as did his father, Roger Milliken involving his firm continuously from the beginning of the design for the original airport and for the 1989 expansion through the 2006 design of the new entry off I-85. "GSP is efficient in land use and the spending of money," Webel observes. "The green curtain (of landscaping) is less expensive than at most airports." He likes the fact that Milliken insists designers build flexibility into their design to allow for future change. "If you simply throw on a blanket of beauty, it gets washed away," Webel claims.[13]

Seeing the beauty and effectiveness of R.K. and R.C. Webel's landscape design using trees, Roger Milliken several years ago, with Rick Webel's help, started the Noble Tree Foundation. The effort has attracted the interest and commitment of numerous Spartanburg area residents and organizations. Every year Milliken hosts a dinner on his company's property for foundation members. The work of the foundation has developed a new appreciation for the value and beauty of trees and the planting of thousands throughout the Spartanburg area.

CHAPTER 8

The Airlines That Have Served GSP

During its forty-five-year history, GSP has been served by many passenger airlines. Some have served only a short time. Others have come and gone and come again as market forces closed or created opportunities. In the spring of 2007, airlines serving GSP were providing more than sixty daily, nonstop flights to airports serving fifteen major cities. A few have had long histories with GSP. Eastern, Delta, American, US Airways, Continental, United, and Northwest—along with their partner airlines—have been the stalwarts in length of service, flights provided and numbers of passengers carried.

Eastern Airlines

Eastern Airlines for more than twenty-eight years was GSP's major carrier. The first commercial flight into the airport on its opening day—October 15, 1962—was an Eastern Lockheed Electra, Flight 580 from Atlanta.

Eastern's last flight out of GSP was in January of 1991, when the airline ceased all flight operations. It was running out of cash and faced more than $200 million in debt. The *New York Times* called Eastern "by far the largest casualty of the pressure brought about by deregulation of the airline industry thirteen years ago." It had also been a casualty of high operational costs, investing and management policies, severe labor unrest that led to a crippling strike and the economic effects of the 1990 Gulf War. Eastern was one of many airlines that began as an airmail carrier. As Pitcairn Aviation, and then as Eastern Air Transport, it flew the Mailwing single engine plane on one of the first airmail routes—New York to Atlanta. Spartanburg joined that route in 1928. A stop in Greenville was added in 1930. World War I ace Eddie Rickenbacker bought Eastern in 1938 and led the airline through its most prosperous decades. Later, another famous pilot, astronaut Frank Borman, was its president. In 1983, Eastern was the launch customer for Boeing's new 757. The first official flight of the B-757 was from Atlanta to GSP that year.[1]

Before GSP opened, Eastern had served the South Carolina Upstate for years. Its planes flew into airports in Greenville, Spartanburg, Anderson and Greenwood.

Delta airlines

For several years, Delta had flown into local Upstate airports, but when GSP opened in 1962 it canceled Upstate service. The airline resumed service to the area in April of 1985 and has been GSP's biggest airline most years since.

Delta's predecessor began as a crop dusting operation. In 1927, it began flying mail between Ecuador and Peru. After a Monroe, Louisiana, businessman bought it, Delta Air introduced passenger service between Dallas and Jackson, Mississippi. In 1941 it moved its headquarters from Monroe to Atlanta. Over the next five decades it grew by acquiring other airlines and in 1991, bought the assets of bankrupt Pan American World Airways and its European routes.[2]

As one of the so-called legacy airlines, Delta struggled in the early years of the new century in the wake of the 2001 terrorist attacks, competition from new low-cost carriers and rising fuel costs. It entered bankruptcy in late 2005 and on April 30, 2007, emerged from bankruptcy with potentially profitable new overseas routes in its possession.

In the spring of 2007, Delta along with its partners: Comair, Atlantic

Southeast, Chautauqua, Skywest and Freedom operated fourteen flights a day out of GSP to Atlanta, Cincinnati, New York's LaGuardia, and Orlando.

US AIRWAYS

Piedmont Airlines began service to GSP in 1967. Twenty years later it was acquired by USAir. In 1987, the USAir/Piedmont merger was the largest in American airline history. The airline changed its name in 1997 to US Airways. It filed for bankruptcy protection in August of 2002, emerged six months later after reorganizing and cutting labor costs, and then re-entered bankruptcy protection in 2004.

Its predecessor was founded in 1931 by chemical company heir Richard Dupont as All American Aviation, delivering airmail in Pennsylvania and Ohio. It became All American Airways in 1949 and Allegheny Airlines in 1953 when it expanded further into the Midwest and to the East Coast. The name changed to USAir in 1959 when the airline entered markets in California and the south, then to US Airways in 1997.[3]

In the spring of 2007, US Airways, through its partners PSA, Air Wisconsin and Piedmont, was operating seventeen flights a day out of GSP to Charlotte, Philadelphia, New York's LaGuardia and Washington's Reagan National.

AMERICAN AIRLINES

As is the experience of so many airlines, American had its roots in the early days of airmail delivery. Robertson Aircraft Corporation was the second aviation company to gain a U.S. mail contract. Its chief pilot was Charles Lindbergh. On April 15, 1926, Lindbergh flew his small DH-4 biplane from Chicago to St. Louis and back with bags of mail. Three years later, Robertson was one of several new aviation companies acquired by The Aviation Corporation. The consolidation morphed into American Airways and, in 1934, into American Airlines, Inc. By 1940, American had reported more revenue passenger miles than any other domestic airline. It pioneered nonstop transcontinental service in 1952 with a DC-7. In 1959, it introduced the Lockheed Electra, the first U.S.-designed turboprop plane. American placed the first DC-10 order in 1968 and flew it first in August 1971.

The airline was the first to offer frequent flyer marketing when it introduced its AAdvantage Travel Awards program in 1981. The airline's American Eagle system began in 1984, a network of regional airlines operating under the American umbrella.[4]

In the spring of 2007, American Eagle was operating seven flights a day out of GSP to Chicago's O'Hare and Dallas-Ft. Worth.

United airlines

In 1930 one of United's predecessors—Boeing Air Transport—took the suggestion of a nurse, Ellen Church, that nurses be hired to serve coffee and sandwiches to passengers. She became aviation's first stewardess. That is the reason that for the first decades of air passenger travel in America most airlines hired only nurses as stewardesses, later known as flight attendants.

In 1990, United took major steps in its goal of becoming a global airline. It launched service to Paris, Madrid and Tokyo from various U.S. airports, bought Pan Am's routes to London and during nine days in October of that year placed the largest airplane order in commercial aviation history: $22 billion. Within a year it was flying to cities in South America as well. Late in the 1990s, it partnered with four other international airlines to form the Star Alliance. During the early years of the new century United faced many financial challenges and was a victim of the September 2001 terrorist attacks. It remains one of the world's largest airlines.[5]

United—through its partner United Express—in the spring of 2007 had seven flights a day out of GSP to Dulles and O'Hare.

Continental airlines

Varney Speed Lines began service in July of 1934 flying a five hundred-mile route from Pueblo, Colorado to El Paso, Texas. Robert Six bought

40 percent of the company, became its leader and in 1937 changed its name to Continental Airlines and moved headquarters to Denver. Its first jet flight was by a Boeing 707 on June 8, 1959. During the decades of the 1960s and 1970s, it established itself as a major trans-Pacific airline flying Boeing 747s and DC-10s to faraway countries like Japan, New Zealand and Australia. It entered bankruptcy protection in 1983 and a little more than a year later had reorganized, emerged from bankruptcy protection and had begun nonstop service to several European cities. As a long-established global airline, Continental in 2001 launched the first-ever nonstop air service between New York and Hong Kong. Following the September 2001 terrorist attacks, the airline reduced its long-term flight schedule by 20 percent and furloughed twelve thousand employees. Most other major airlines took similar steps. In 2004 it joined SkyTeam, a major airline alliance with eight other international carriers.[6]

Continental Airlines in the spring of 2007 had eight daily flights out of GSP to Houston, Newark and Cleveland.

Northwest Airlines

Northwest Airlines started flying airmail on September 1, 1926, from Speedway Flying Field in Minneapolis, site of today's international airport. Its first paying passenger paid forty dollars on July 5, 1927, for a twelve-hour, one-way flight from Minneapolis to Chicago with two stops in between. In all of 1927, Northwest carried 106 passengers. The next year, it became an international airline with weekly flights between Minneapolis and Winnipeg, Canada. In 1947, it became a true international airline with service to Japan, Korea, China and the Philippines, and in 1950 it was selected as the federal government's prime contractor for the Korean airlift during the war in that country. The airline made history when in 1956 it leased an island in the Aleutians from the federal government for use as a fuel stop on its north Pacific route, becoming the first airline to operate its own airport. Northwest inaugurated service from New York to Tokyo over the North Pole in 1959, and the next year the airline began what it called "the fastest U.S. jet service to Asia" with the Douglas DC-8, its first "pure jet."

In 1984, the airline signed its first regional marketing partnership—the Northwest Airlink agreement—with Mesaba Airlines. In 1989, it was the launch customer for the world's largest commercial airliner, the Boeing 747-400, which Northwest would use on its trans-Pacific routes. Later that year, it received its first European-made Airbus A-320.[7]

Northwest—through its Pinnacle regional airline partner—in the spring of 2007 was serving GSP with seven daily flights to Detroit and Memphis.

Allegiant Air, a new, small, low-cost airline began service to Greenville-Spartanburg in November of 2006. In the spring of 2007 it was offering four-day-a-week flights to Orlando and three-day-a-week flights to Tampa using the 150-passenger MD-83 aircraft.

Pleased with its acceptance in the market, Allegiant Air announced in late June that it would begin nonstop service twice a week between GSP and Las Vegas in August 2007.

CHAPTER 9

The Aviation Cluster

The Greenville-Spartanburg area has a major economic advantage: a unique and efficient aviation cluster. It is a group of airports that provide complementary aviation services along with a growing number of aviation-related companies. While the airports compete in some ways, the philosophy of the boards and managers at those facilities is that they—and the region they serve—will benefit more from cooperation than competition. Michael O'Donnell, executive director of the South Carolina Aeronautics Commission, says the Greenville-Spartanburg aviation cluster provides valuable support, especially to the business corridor that has developed along Interstate 85 through the South Carolina Upstate.[1] Before the value of an aviation cluster was ever envisioned or recognized, there were debates that could have prevented it from developing. As GSP was being designed in the early 1960s, proposals were considered to close the local airports in Greenville and Spartanburg; but enough leaders recognized their potential as general aviation airports and they remained open.

Greenville businessman Neel Hipp Jr. is chairman of the South Carolina Aeronautics Commission. A longtime general aviation pilot, Hipp says South Carolina's fifty-four general aviation airports contribute significantly to the state's economy. "Many of our cities and counties," Hipp wrote in *The Greenville News* on May 15, 2007, "consider their local airport the 'front door' of their community and a powerful economic engine."

Spartanburg Downtown Memorial Airport

Spartanburg Memorial, as it was dedicated in 1927, later had the name Downtown added as the southwest side of Spartanburg grew closer. It was the state's first commercial airport. Owned by the city, it has a 5200-foot runway where more than 42,000 general aviation visitors arrive each year. In 2005, the airport generated an estimated economic impact of $15.4 million. It hosts "an increasing number of corporate flight departments" and is home to several aviation enterprises and a Civil Air Patrol squadron.[2]

Greenville Downtown Airport

Opened and dedicated in 1928 as Greenville Municipal Airport, its name was later changed to Greenville Downtown as the city's east side moved out to, around and beyond it. It is the busiest general aviation airport in the state with more than 75,000 annual takeoffs and landings. Operated by the Greenville Airport Commission, it has 5400-foot and 4000-foot runways and in 2005 had an estimated economic impact of $35 million. Today it provides "a full range of aviation services" to support corporate flight departments and other business and community needs.[3]

During World War II, the Greenville airport served as a training base for glider pilots.

Donaldson Center

Donaldson Air Force Base was built eight miles southeast of Greenville in 1942 as a World War II B-25 training base. When its value to the military declined two decades later, it was deactivated, turned back to Greenville city and county, and reborn as a 2,600 acre industrial center and air park with an 8000-foot runway, dozens of business firms, many of them aviation-related, and a 2005 estimated economic impact of $222 million. It has two rail spurs and is nearby Interstate 85.[4]

Greenville-Spartanburg International Airport

GSP opened in 1962 as the regional jet-age airport. By 2005, it had an 11,001-foot runway, a customs port, immigration office and agricultural inspection station, two major cargo terminals, service by several airlines, more than sixty daily flights, including nonstop service to sixteen major cities, and a National Weather Service forecasting office. A study by Wilbur Smith Associates estimated its 2002 economic impact at $405 million.[5] Stevens Aviation is the fixed-base operator serving the growing corporate aviation community at the airport. It also has a large turboprop maintenance facility.

The airports are only part of the aviation cluster. The placement and varied services of the four airports have offered advantages that continue to impact positively the region's economy. Corporations with aircraft of any size that need landing and parking space, maintenance and repair, fuel and other services have a choice. Companies like General Electric and BMW that require a long runway for heavy cargo shipments can use GSP or Donaldson. Exhibitors looking for a show location near an airport find the Carolina First Center convenient because it sits next to Greenville Downtown. Corporations and individuals with their own airplanes can use any of the airports depending on the size and type of the aircraft and the services needed. Firms that have regular air shipments have Fed Ex, UPS or DHL available at Greenville-Spartanburg Airport. Among them, they have planes leaving every evening and arriving every morning, so shipping anywhere in the world is fast and easy. The uniqueness of Donaldson Center, with its airport and multimodal facilities, is valuable to the Upstate. It is home to more than sixty firms including the headquarters of Stevens Aviation and others related to the aviation industry. The largest and most visible, Lockheed Martin, has major maintenance and repair contracts with the federal government to work on military aircraft. By late 2006, more than forty-six hundred were employed at Donaldson Center and it had become one of the largest industrial air parks in the South. Longtime executive director Vardry Ramseur, who died suddenly in early 2007, often called Donaldson "the industrial heartland" of Greenville County.[6]

Aviation-related business and education

Aviation-related firms are spread throughout the Upstate and they are the fifth component of this aviation cluster. A brochure prepared by the Greenville Area Development Corporation (GADC), a major business recruiting agency, showed the value of the aviation cluster. Entitled *Greenville, South Carolina: A Growing Aviation Center*, the brochure credited Lockheed Martin along with Honeywell, GE, Michelin Aircraft Tires and Champion Aerospace as leaders in positioning the area as "a growing aviation cluster." The GADC said that by 2007 more than one hundred aviation-related companies were located in South Carolina, many of the largest in the ten-county Upstate region. It also noted that the area is "well known as an automotive hub, and the Greenville-based Clemson University International Center for Automotive Research (ICAR) is focused on advanced technologies and the testing of products that are applicable to the aviation industry." The GADC suggested that "there is a solid platform set for applied research and development in the aviation industry."

Supplying a workforce trained for aviation-related jobs requires specific education. Through its engineering department and the aviation research and development advantages of its ICAR campus and curriculum, Clemson University is a part of that education component. Greenville Technical College and Spartanburg Community College offer related courses. Greenville Tech has also partnered with Florida-based Embry-Riddle Aeronautical University to provide aviation-related courses at its Greenville campus. Bob Jones University offers an aviation administration degree and has a flight school at Greenville Downtown Airport. The University of South Carolina, with an Upstate campus in Spartanburg and a presence at Greenville's University Center, also has an engineering school and one of the top-rated business schools in the nation. Both USC and Clemson are rated among the nation's leading one hundred research universities.

By 2007, the cluster of airports, aviation-related business firms and educational institutions had become a major force in the developing economy of the South Carolina Upstate. Statewide, "aviation-related business in South Carolina represented a $4.3 billion investment for the state in 2005," said Michael O' Donnell of the South Carolina Aeronautics Commission. "That included sixty-five thousand jobs and a $74.5 million tax benefit. The potential," predicted O'Donnell, "is huge."[7] As Greenville Downtown Airport's 2005 economic impact brochure claimed, "there is a strong relationship between South Carolina's economy and aviation."

CHAPTER 10

The 1990s

The BMW Story

Paul Foerster was the German who in the mid-1960s had recommended Spartanburg County as the site for the Hoechst plant. He had then directed the plant's construction and managed it. Now it was the summer of 1989. Foerster was retired and living in Spartanburg when he received a call from South Carolina Governor Carroll Campbell. With his German heritage and contacts and with his long and successful career heading a European company in the United States, Foerster was the person whom Campbell wanted to represent the interests of the State Development Board (later renamed the State Department of Commerce) in Europe through the board's reopened office in Frankfurt. It would mean frequent trips back to Europe, but Foerster did have some contacts that might be helpful to the state. He accepted the governor's invitation.[1]

Not long after he began spending time back in his native country, Foerster learned that German automaker BMW was quietly looking globally for a place to build a plant outside of Germany. Several locations were being considered, including in the United States. Foerster alerted the governor. Indeed, in late September of 1989, the *Spartanburg Herald-Journal* had reported that representatives for BMW were conducting a site search in Anderson and Laurens counties.[2] Through some old friends, Paul Foerster received an invitation to attend a large global seminar that the BMW Foundation was sponsoring in Berlin. BMW Chairman Eberhard von Kuhnheim would be there. Foerster wrote a brief note to give to the BMW chairman, if he would be fortunate enough to meet him. He was.

Foerster told von Kuhnheim about his years of positive business experience in South Carolina and that the governor of the state would appreciate an opportunity to meet with him and confirm South Carolina's interest in being considered for a plant site. Before the two men parted, Foerster gave von Kuhnheim the fifteen-line note he had written weeks before. Then he called Governor Campbell with his report on the brief meeting. Several weeks later, Foerster received a call from Campbell's office. An aide explained that the governor was overseas, could be in Munich in about ten days and wanted to meet Chairman von Kuhnheim, if Foerster could make the arrangements.[3]

The July 1990 meeting in Munich was short and successful. Just four men were there: Chairman von Kuhnheim, Governor Campbell, Bernd Pischetsrieder, BMW's director of manufacturing, and Foerster. Campbell assured the BMW chairman that South Carolina was a pro-business state and that if the company selected the state as its site for a plant he would, as governor, do his best to make all economic development means available for the project. "The hour-long meeting," Foerster recalls, "was a confidence building session and the governor was great at it." Foerster was optimistic and he stayed in contact with Pischetsrieder, whom von Kuhnheim had charged with the responsibility of finding a site. Foerster soon learned that the BMW officials were interested in building a plant adjacent to, perhaps even on, airport property. That turned out to be one of the attractive points about the competing Nebraska proposal where officials were offering land on airport property in Omaha. That is when Foerster began talking to Pischetsrieder about Greenville-Spartanburg.[4] Meanwhile, the focus was on Anderson County and by autumn of 1991, a consulting group had identified for BMW a possible site in northern Anderson County. For several months, engineers and other representatives of the company studied the site carefully. On January 31, 1992, the *Anderson Independent* reported that the site was at Clemson University's Simpson Agricultural Station. That focus changed quickly, however, when Chairman von Kuhnheim and director of manufacturing Pischetsrieder flew into Greenville-Spartanburg in early March, looked at the open area around the airport and liked what they saw.[5] Before they left a couple of days later, BMW's top officials had switched the company's focus from Anderson County to the airport area.

Governor Campbell had to work quickly. He needed to assure the BMW officials that property would be available near the airport. He and Chairman John Warren of the State Development Board called George Dean Johnson Jr., a former airport commissioner and owner of Johnson Development in Spartanburg, and asked for his help. The governor said they had a potential big project and needed his assistance in tying up a large tract of land. He needed options on at least two hundred acres adjacent to the airport. Johnson said he would help and assigned his colleague Foster Chapman to the task. It was Thursday and the governor needed the land optioned by Tuesday. Chapman enlisted the help of realtor Doug Lancaster and they began contacting the half dozen or so landowners on the property that they wanted to option. By Monday, they had ninety-day options in hand. If the unnamed client decided within ninety days it wanted the land, property owners would receive their money and have to move. Otherwise, the deal would be void.[6] By this time, only a few people knew that BMW had shifted its attention from Anderson County to the airport area.

With the initial land option information from Foster Chapman in hand, Governor Campbell flew to Spartanburg on March 25, 1992, to deliver an address about education to the annual meeting of the Chamber of Commerce.[7] Following that meeting, he and chamber president Lane Fowler drove to nearby Wofford College to meet with Airport Commission chairman Roger Milliken. The governor pressed Milliken to sell BMW some of the airport property. Milliken told Campbell, "No, but I'll help you find a solution."[8] He told the governor that he wanted to help attract BMW, but even if the Airport Commission could sell three hundred acres of the airport's property, it wouldn't be big enough for BMW. It would be surrounded by a runway, I-85 and residential housing. "You're jumping into a box, spending $1 billion and you can't get out of the box," Milliken told Campbell and Fowler.[9] The textile executive had a long-standing philosophy of buying plenty of property for his plants so that there was always adequate room for expansion. He thought that BMW might want to do the same and suggested that there was adequate land that he thought could be available immediately east of the airport toward Highway 101. The three men also discussed BMW's need for a runway longer than GSP's 7600-foot runway. Milliken said the commission would begin studying immediately how that could be accomplished.

The next morning, Milliken and commissioner Wallace Storey met with state officials. Milliken told them the airport was in a difficult position. He said the Airport Commission wanted to help the governor secure BMW's decision to build the plant but releasing airport land that the company wanted would preclude future growth of the airport. He explained that, as he understood the situation, BMW wanted to be able to taxi B-747 aircraft directly from the airport's runway to the manufacturing plant that the company was considering building. Storey, at Milliken's request, had already been assessing potential building sites adjoining the GSP property and with frontage on I-85. East of the airport he had found a sparsely inhabited plateau fronting on I-85. He suggested this site could more practically connect to a possible road from BMW to the northeast end of the runway.[10]

Milliken, Storey, and airport executive director Gary Jackson met the next day with State Development Board chairman John Warren, board director Wayne Sterling and Spartanburg Chamber of Commerce executive Ben Haskew. BMW's desires for the airport site were discussed and chairman Milliken asked Storey to present his findings and thoughts. The group agreed to accept the recommendation and carry it back to BMW.[11] With the group's support of Storey's recommendations and the initial land options already secured by Johnson Development Associates, Governor Campbell thought he had enough to meet with BMW officials and try to convince them to continue considering the Upstate for their North American plant. He was taking a big risk. He knew the Airport Commission did not want to sell property that was BMW's preferred site. But he had a reasonable suggestion for a site next to the airport and he thought prospects of obtaining the land were good. Meanwhile, airport commissioners met the next day and discussed preliminary ideas of how the airport's only runway could be expanded.

The year 1991 had been a difficult one for GSP. Passenger traffic had dropped to 140,000, down 11 percent from the year before, due largely to the January 1991 closing of Eastern Airlines. Overall in that year, 1,050,000 passengers had used GSP. Air cargo had declined 31 percent, primarily because Emery Air Freight had moved off airport property during the year. As 1992 began, newspaper stories were still discussing GSP's business declines. They also noted that January traffic was off 2 percent and that unrented space in the terminal and cargo buildings would contribute to an estimated $400,000 income decline in 1992.[12] Business was also down 25 percent at Stevens, GSP's general aviation operator. By March, however, Stevens officials said business was rebounding and GSP's executive director Gary Jackson estimated the airport's 1992 income should almost double expenses.[13] Nevertheless, the trend was worrisome. Passenger traffic had peaked in 1990, but Eastern's demise, the Persian Gulf War and a depressed national economy had reduced air travel. During some months in early 1991, passenger traffic at GSP had been off by almost 15 percent. By mid-1992, passenger and cargo traffic was picking up and a decision was nearing that would have a profound and lasting impact on GSP and the entire Upstate.

Witty Davis wasn't exactly surprised when he opened his mail that day in March of 1992. He had mixed emotions as he read the letter from Foster Chapman of Johnson Development: "We have been approached by representatives of the state and local chambers of commerce to assemble a tract of land for presentation to a large industrial prospect. Before expensive engineering studies are undertaken, it is imperative that there be no doubt about the availability and price of the property." The letter went on to describe the prospect as "an industrial manufacturer with an international reputation for excellence."[14] Davis didn't want to leave the home and twenty-three acres along Brockman-McClimon Road that he and his family had enjoyed for decades. The property sat just beyond the edge of the land the airport had needed back in 1962. He didn't have to move then, but life in what used to be Flatwood had changed since the airport opened thirty years ago. Back then, Davis's brother had led an unsuccessful effort to block development of the airport. Now, although he didn't want to leave, Davis might accept an offer, if the price was right.

Davis, and many of his neighbors who received that same letter, already knew the identity of the international manufacturing prospect. The word had been out for some time that German automaker BMW had been considering a South Carolina site for its first facility outside of Germany. Until Davis and his neighbors just south of GSP began receiving letters urging them to sell their property, they thought the focus of BMW's interest had been on those sites in Anderson County.

Fifteen hundred miles northwest of Upstate South Carolina, Omaha, Nebraska, was the other site on which BMW had been focusing much of its attention. Omaha, it turned out, was South Carolina's strongest competition in the effort to attract BMW. Governor Ben Nelson had offered BMW some space at Omaha's Eppley Airport. Next door was a large industrial tract of available land with rail and highways adjacent. Nevertheless, Eppley's executive director, Don Smithey, told GSP manager Gary Jackson, "We routinely handle 747s and we have twelve acres of concrete for handling cargo planes."[15] Jackson and GSP commissioners Wallace Storey and Hank Ramella had flown to Omaha the last week in March to do what Jackson called some "scouting around." They inspected the proposed site and evaluated its potential and shortcomings. "It had many disadvantages," Storey remembered. The trio's report was forwarded to Governor Campbell.[16]

Each state had many similarities to offer BMW but Nebraska was promising bigger financial incentives. This was high-stakes competition. A BMW plant would bring a huge capital investment and up to four thousand jobs eventually to the winning state, not to mention the additional millions of dollars invested in jobs created by the dozens of suppliers who would be likely to follow BMW. Nebraska was working hard to gain BMW's commitment and South Carolina's governor had no intention of losing this huge industrial plum to Nebraska or any other state. Campbell had already talked with chairman von Kuhnheim. He knew BMW's needs and demands. As late as mid-May, Governor Nelson, Omaha's mayor and a group of Nebraska leaders would fly to Munich in a Union Pacific plane to pledge support for their $160 million incentive package.[17] An empty Union Pacific railroad facility in Omaha was also being mentioned as a possible plant site. Nebraska was serious about attracting BMW, but maybe too late.

By spring 1992, it had been almost two years since South Carolina's governor had first met with BMW's top executives at that meeting arranged by Paul Foerster in Munich. So in late March of 1992, when he was back in Munich presenting his incentive package, Campbell was not talking to strangers. Nevertheless, as one source who was at those talks told *The Greenville News*, "It was two days of very tough negotiations. The competition is fierce."

Undaunted, Governor Campbell returned from those meetings with optimistic, albeit cautious, words. So cautious, he still would not use the BMW name, referring only to "the industrial prospect" even though reporters at the governor's April 1 news conference knew he had been in Munich at BMW. Campbell was not about to embarrass or appear to upstage BMW's chairman.

The pressure was on the governor and he had pressure on everyone else. He worked with leaders on both sides of the Senate and House aisles to forge a legislative package of additional incentives. Within a month of his return from negotiations in Munich, Campbell signed legislation on April 29 for an additional $35 million package, bringing the state's total ten-year incentive package to $115.5 million if BMW created one thousand new jobs and to $145 million if it created four thousand jobs with a new plant.[18] That incentive package included state funds to go with FAA money for lengthening the GSP runway to accommodate BMW cargo flights.

Before Governor Campbell had left for Munich at the end of March, Johnson Development Associates president Foster Chapman, along with real estate agents Doug Lancaster, Jim Bright and Jim Mayo, were already organizing an effort to contact dozens of landowners whose property stretched all the way from the eastern boundary of the airport to Highway 101. The land they wanted to option included plants, one subdivision, cattle farms, a peach orchard, a mobile home park and several individual homes. Within a few weeks, they had ninety-day option agreements with 180 separate landowners on 156 parcels of property covering almost 1,200 acres at a potential cost of $39 million.[19] Most of it would be bought ultimately by the South Carolina Ports Authority and Spartanburg County, then leased to the client. A limited amount would be bought directly by BMW. After ninety days, if BMW agreed to move to the site and all of the options were exercised, there would be no need for any airport property. However, BMW's land would adjoin the airport.

Ruby Davis didn't know the man at her door. "I'm Douglas Lancaster from Lancaster Realty." He had come to explain that he wanted to buy her house to make way for an industrial prospect that was considering locating in the area. She and her late husband had lived in their one-story brick house on Brockman-McClimon Road most of their married life. "If I had my choice," the seventy-two-year-old widow replied, "I'd stay here."[20] She and her neighbors quickly realized, however, that they didn't have a choice. They might have to move in ninety days. Meantime, Ruby Davis's brother-in-law and nephew were facing the same decision. They lived nearby on property that had been owned by generations of Davis families for more than a hundred years. During the past three decades, G.W. Davis had already sold some of his two hundred acres along

Brockman-McClimon Road and Highway 101 to GSP, to Tungsten Industries and to the state highway department. Where he had once grown peaches, he now grew soybeans, millet and fescue on his last twenty-three acres. Now, he would have to sell the rest of his property and move the seed business he and his son owned.

"We just always felt we were way out in the country," explained Phil Davis. Of course, they hadn't been for the last thirty years since the airport had opened right next to their remaining property. Even now, Davis said, "We felt we were on the edge of everything, but growth is inevitable. You can't stand in the way of progress."[21] Most of Davis's neighbors understood that. They also realized that prices being offered for homes and acreage were better than they could have hoped to receive under normal circumstances. They just didn't like feeling as if they were being rushed into a decision. Once BMW officials turned their interest and attention to the property next to GSP, Governor Campbell had to act quickly if he had any hope of keeping BMW interested in moving to the Upstate. He knew the only way he could maintain the interest that he had generated in Munich was to assure BMW that adequate land would be available. So he gave local realtors less than a month to contact the residents and obtain the options on their land. It was a tough sell. The people who were the most difficult to convince were some of those longtime Flatwood residents to whom *home* was more important than *money* and to whom *staying put* was more attractive than *moving on*. If they had their way, they would be happy to stay right where they were. If those landowners could not be convinced to sell, the governor knew the BMW deal would collapse. He needed someone to convince them to sell and he knew just the man.

Senator J. Verne Smith was a folksy, affable native from just up the road in Greer. He also happened to be a respected and effective legislator, persuasive on behalf of any cause he appreciated. He felt strongly about the potential of BMW and the economic help it could be for his native area and its people. So when Governor Campbell called asking for Verne Smith's help, the influential senator said yes. As Campbell's then-chief of staff Bob McAlister recalled in a March 2006 *Greenville News* column (just months before Smith's death), "He visited the families one by one in their homes. He identified with their reluctance to sell. He explained the stakes—thousands of jobs that would feed families, educate children and improve the quality of life for generations to come." Verne Smith always called himself "just an old tire salesman." He was a good tire salesman for the same reason that he was able to persuade many of those landowners to sell. With that bright smile and positive spirit, almost mischievous chuckle and folksy way of expressing himself, he was difficult to resist. Most people, he could convince. As McAlister noted, "While influential business leaders like John Warren and Francis Hipp, Buck Mickel and Roger Milliken were using their prestige behind the scenes to help the governor land BMW, Verne Smith was able to convince many of the people who were most personally affected to say yes to selling their property and leaving the land they loved."[22]

The governor's deadlines were met. By the end of April, he had legislative approval for the entire incentive package. In all, local real estate agents contacted more than two dozen landowners and had obtained options on approximately twelve hundred acres east of GSP. Those options would start expiring the last week in June. Now all the governor, and local and state officials who helped him, could do was wait. Selecting and committing to a location for a project of this size was an immense and sensitive task for BMW. Competitors were still making overtures. Nebraska had enlisted support from neighboring states. Not to be outdone, Governor Campbell—in mid-May—asked neighboring Governor Jim Martin, whose state of North Carolina had ceased its lobbying for BMW, to write a letter supporting South Carolina's bid.[23]

North Carolina's governor addressed his letter urging BMW to select South Carolina to Bernd Pischetsrieder, deputy chairman and one of nine members of BMW's management board. Days later, on May 22, 1992, Pischetsrieder told reporters in Germany that Upstate South Carolina's labor costs and location had advantages over Omaha, Nebraska.[24] A week later, a major Munich newspaper reported, "The cat is out of the bag." It claimed BMW had decided to build a plant in the U.S. and that the South Carolina site next to Greenville-Spartanburg Airport is "probably" the location.[25] "That's news to me," said Governor Campbell's spokesman Tucker Eskew.[26] "Absolutely wrong," said BMW spokesman Richard Gaul.[27]

"The world is big," Eberhard von Kuhnheim told a reporter who tried to pin the chairman down about where BMW might build. As late as May 12, at BMW's annual meeting in Munich, von Kuhnheim told an inquiring stockholder, "It is our job and our duty to look at possibilities outside of Germany and to do serious research. We are thinking of additional places in Europe, Asia and America."[28] Nevertheless, indications were that BMW was nearing a decision. Public affairs director Richard Gaul had told reporters in Munich as early as April 3 that the list of potential sites had been reduced to "a handful."

Responding to escalating media reports, on June 3, Governor Campbell said, "I have every reason to believe we have put forth a competitive package and that we stand a chance to get it."[29] Campbell had reason to be confident. A few days before, unknown to reporters, top BMW officials had spent two days at the governor's mansion in Columbia negotiating final details of an agreement to build the plant in Spartanburg County.[30] Just a week after the governor's June 3 statement, a small group of attorneys and South Carolina officials were in New York City meeting with BMW representatives on final details of the BMW-South Carolina package.[31] While in Munich, a high-ranking BMW official told reporters on June 11 that the company's management board was only one meeting away from the final decision. Meantime a team of Spartanburg real estate agents prepared to start making calls to landowners to set up appointments for closings. Their phones would start ringing as soon as BMW made its decision official.

Governor Campbell spent much of Friday and Saturday, June 19 and 20 on the phone to Munich. He and other state officials were busy gathering answers to BMW officials' final questions. That last Saturday was a pressure-packed day. At the governor's mansion in Columbia, a small group of officials and support staff discussed final details of an agreement and talked by phone several times with BMW staff in Munich. By mid-afternoon the governor confirmed "we have a deal."[32]

Reporters began calling the governor's office in Columbia. Obviously determined not to upstage BMW, Campbell's chief of staff, Bob McAlister, told reporters there would be no response from the governor until official notification had been received.[33] The official word came Monday morning. By that time, German and North American media had been notified and a room at GSP was being prepared for the official announcement the next morning. Governor Campbell flew to GSP Monday afternoon for a private dinner that evening at Spartanburg's Piedmont Club with BMW officials and local and state officials who had worked with him.[34]

Tuesday, June 23, 1992; 7:30 a.m. BMW's Bernd Pischetsrieder made the long-awaited announcement along with the company's planning director, Helmut Panke. Joining them on the platform in a room at the Greenville-Spartanburg Airport were an obviously happy and relieved Governor Campbell and Senator Verne Smith of Greer.[35] BMW chairman Eberhard von Kuhnheim was back at the Munich headquarters making the same announcement to company employees and media from across Europe. His announcement was carried during the local news conference for the dozens of regional and national media at Greenville-Spartanburg International Airport.

The company's announcement was conservative but welcomed. In his televised statement from Munich, von Kuhnheim revealed BMW's criteria for its selection of South Carolina: the quality of life—housing, education, culture and recreation—to attract, retain and motivate its employees; a positive business-government relationship; ample air, sea, rail and land transportation; and the availability of "reliable utilities and support for the communications technology required to integrate the new facility into our international production, supply and distribution network." The BMW chairman told his American and European media audience, "the site on Interstate 85, the Greenville-Spartanburg area and South Carolina completely fulfill our requirements."

In response, Governor Campbell welcomed BMW. "Today," he said, "we celebrate. Tomorrow, we set about the work of producing the world's finest automobile right here in South Carolina."

Pischetsrieder announced an investment of up to $300 million and two thousand workers by 2000. Hiring would start soon and construction would begin in the fall. The goal was to have the plant in operation by 1995. Pischetsrieder also told the reporters that at least twenty of BMW's suppliers could be expected to locate here to be near the new plant. The plant would cover 1.9 million square feet.[36]

Governor Campbell welcomed BMW, unveiled an oversized South Carolina license tag bearing the number BMW 1 and predicted the plant would be a "tremendous boost for the economy" and especially for Greer. Roger Milliken liked the emphasis on quality. "One thing I have heard over and over is the talk of importance that BMW places on quality and I am pleased that our area is so connected to quality worldwide." The GSP chairman said, "I think it is safe to say that the airport will benefit from the need to extend the runway to handle loaded 747s. This will open up new possibilities for air cargo and travel and will further develop the airport."[37]

Ruby Davis's phone rang early that Tuesday morning. Mrs. Davis knew who it would be. She had just watched the BMW announcement and news conference on television. When she picked up the phone, Douglas Lancaster, the real estate agent who had knocked on her door in late March, told her he was ready to exercise the option on her land if she was willing to meet with the lawyer as soon as possible, preferably today. Anticipating the BMW decision and Lancaster's call, Mrs. Davis had already found another house. The next day she had a check for her home and one acre and was ready to close on her new house.[38]

When she watched the noon news on television that day, Dixie Turner had mixed feelings. She was glad the suspense was over but she was sad that she and her husband would soon have to move. Fred and Dixie Turner had built their dream home just eight years before on three acres where they intended to live the rest of their lives, enjoying the peacefulness of the area. To Luci Williams, the announcement that BMW was coming after all these months of uncertainty was a relief. "It's good for the community and for the state," Mrs. Williams said. "If it puts people in our state to work, I think it's well worth it." For Martha Boling parting with the land would be difficult. Having to move for BMW would uproot her from land that had been in her family for two hundred years. She, her parents, two brothers and an aunt would all be moving. "The family is going to be scattered now," she told a reporter.[39]

For those who would not have to move from the land that had been their home, BMW's coming was easier and happier news to hear. "It will have a tremendous economic impact on this region," said former Spartanburg Chamber of Commerce chairman Dr. G. B. Hodge. Mayfair Mills president and former U.S. Secretary of Commerce Frederick Dent Jr. said, "This announcement brings with it international recognition." Mayor Robert Rowell saw it as a "chance to sell Spartanburg County." Roger Milliken told reporters at the news conference that it was terrific news for the community. "I think the airport facility played a key role in attracting the plant to the site."

Two weeks after the June 23 BMW announcement at GSP, Governor Campbell was back in Munich for dinner at chairman von Kuhnheim's home. The next day the two men signed a document formally declaring BMW's intention to build their South Carolina plant. "Strictly protocol," the governor told reporters. "This is what they'll do and we'll do. It's not a contract."[40] Campbell also used the signing ceremony as an opportunity to introduce von Kuhnheim and the other BMW officials to his friend, President George Herbert Walker Bush, who was in Munich to attend the annual economic summit of the world's richest nations. The governor also made what he called "initial contacts" with executives of some BMW suppliers who could potentially locate in South Carolina.[41]

Governor Campbell returned to GSP on Wednesday, September 30, 1992. He and BMW's chairman Eberhard von Kuhnheim presided over the groundbreaking ceremony for the new plant. BMW's decision to build next to GSP thrust the thirty-year-old airport into its next expansion. Planning for the runway extension had already begun.

The plant to be built next to GSP was not BMW's first entry into the United States. It employed several hundred at its North American headquarters in New Jersey. The company also had four hundred dealerships across the United States that had sold fifty-four thousand cars in this country during 1991.[42] Neither would BMW feel strange in Spartanburg County. Thanks in large measure to the legacy of former Spartanburg Chamber of Commerce executive Dick Tukey, who had died thirteen years before, at least forty German plants had already located in the county, many of them along I-85 not far from where BMW would be located.

In an interesting irony, BMW was founded in 1916 during World War I to make airplane engines.[43] Now, eighty years later, its first North American plant would be making automobiles next to an airport. BMW would be a boost for South Carolina's economy and for efforts to attract more overseas investment to the area.

Greer: changed forever

Greer will be changed forever, a local official told the media after BMW announced it was coming. Fact is, many people believed the same thing. Greer *would* never be the same.

By the time BMW decided in 1992 to move almost next door, Greer was already more than a century old. Timberman James Manning Greer had bought 190 acres in 1872 and conveyed right of way to the Atlanta and Richmond Air Line Railroad. Another area resident, Alfred Taylor, also gave the railroad some right of way. The next year, the railroad built its first depot. The post office department soon rented an office there and designated it Greer's Depot. During the next three years, several parcels of land were sold and in March of 1876 the state legislature incorporated the community as the town of Greer's and extended its boundaries one-half mile around the railroad depot. Within three years the new town had two hundred fifty residents. In 1901, the post office department officially dropped the 's' from the town's name but the 's' remained in people's conversation until the 1920s.[44]

Greer has always been linked to transportation. It began around a railroad depot in the 1870s. About 1920, a new "national highway"—number 29—was built along its northern border. In the early 1960s, an interstate highway and a regional airport were built next to Greer. Now, in the 1990s, one of the world's great automobile manufacturers had decided to build its first and only American plant next door. BMW would attract people, create traffic, develop business opportunities, present challenges. BMW would be big. Greer was still small. The town would change. As far as Don Wall was concerned, that was all right with him. A graduate of Greer High School and the University of South Carolina, Wall owned several pharmacies in Greer and elsewhere in the Upstate. He was elected mayor in 1992, the same year that BMW announced it would be moving next door. Wall welcomed BMW's decision. "Greer was in bad shape. Downtown was depressed. Our population had grown by only two hundred in ten years. The tax base was inadequate," he remembered. "Our only way to provide the services needed was to raise taxes to an unacceptable level or reduce services." Wall thought BMW's large workforce would help to change that. There would be a demand for more houses, prospects for new business firms, a boost in retailing. There should finally be a strong enough tax base, he thought, to provide the services needed, especially if Greer could annex some property.

When Wall began his eight years as mayor, Greer covered just six-and-a-half square miles; by 2000, the city had twenty-seven square miles. It was bursting with new subdivisions. Downtown was being restored and revitalized. The major hospitals in Spartanburg and Greenville were planning new facilities in the city. Wall admits the growth had presented challenges and increased traffic, but the feared major increase in crime had not materialized. For two prime reasons, he believes: the type of people attracted by BMW and a good police force.[45]

Traffic was one of Greer's problems, especially when frequent major accidents closed lanes and disrupted traffic on nearby I-85. Many times each year, interstate traffic would be rerouted right through the center of town. City officials devised a solution for that problem. Wall took the idea to Governor Carroll Campbell, who won legislative approval and funding.[46] The result was construction of a new, six-mile stretch from Highway 29 to Highway 14 on the northwest side of the airport. Named for state senator Verne Smith, and opened in the early 2000s, the parkway not only accommodated diverted interstate traffic away from downtown, it also provided access to land on one side of the parkway that could be used for future industrial development. That, in turn, would help boost the tax base.

By 2000 when Wall retired as mayor, BMW had been in operation four years. "BMW has been the most positive thing that has happened to the economy of this area and South Carolina in my lifetime," Wall claimed. "We saw a window for a growth opportunity. Fifty years from now, Greer will be the largest city in the state." Indeed, Greer had come a long way. Wall remembered as a young man hearing people predict that Greer would eventually be swallowed up and there would be one large city stretching from Spartanburg to Greenville. He was determined that would not happen. Now, in 2000, Greer's future seemed assured.[47]

Greer had two services many outlying areas wanted: water and sewer. Mayor Wall's successor, Rick Danner, continued pursuing annexation especially down Highway 29 on the city's west side and further south beyond Interstate 85. It was in that direction where, beginning in the mid-1990s, the leaders of Greer had run into a necessary clash of wills and oversight with officials of the GSP airport commission. Some targeted areas bucked annexation. Others begged for it, but to the south Greer hit a proverbial wall. Standing in the path of the city's push for annexation was GSP and an Airport Commission as determined to preserve and protect the airport as Greer officials were to preserve and enlarge their city. It was a scenario set for conflict. In November of 1995, the annexation conflict went public. The two conscientious public entities eventually found a way to accommodate each other's concerns and goals regarding both annexation attempts and environs protection. Finding the solutions took time, patience and some help from the state legislature.

Protecting the airport's future

The Airport Commission had two challenges in its effort to protect the airport's future. In the short term, it had to work with Greer in finding a solution for the city's annexation attempts, which could threaten the airport. In the long term, the commission had to find a way to permanently and adequately protect the airport's environs.

In late November of 1994, Greer City Council voted tentatively to annex twelve hundred acres south and west of the city. Included in that area was a thirty-foot-wide strip surrounding the airport. The Airport Commission was facing its short-term challenge. The strip would allow the city to extend its water and sewer services and also permit it to meet requirements that annexed areas be contiguous to the city. Greer had found a way to forge past the airport to reach land it wanted and many property owners who, in turn, wanted Greer's services. Greer had already asked the Airport Commission's permission to annex the thirty-foot strip. Commissioners, however, had asked for time to study how giving up that strip might affect the airport's future. Meanwhile, a bill was ready to be introduced in the legislature that would prevent annexation of any multi-county airport property without prior written permission of the airport's authority. "We felt we needed to go ahead and act," Mayor Don Wall explained. Airport officials asked Greer's City Council to delay their final vote until the airport study was completed in January. Nevertheless, on December 6, the council gave final approval to annexing the twelve hundred acres.[48]

"Nothing is going to happen to that thirty-foot strip," city administrator Ken Westmoreland told reporters. He said the city had no plans to put anything on land in the strip. No matter how narrow, it was land the airport owned and that was FAA regulated. In late January 1995, the

Airport Commission notified Greer it would challenge the annexation move in court.[49] "We're ready to defend it," Mayor Don Wall replied. Airport commissioner Leland Burch of Greer opposed his colleagues' decision. "I think," said Burch, "we're about to start an adversarial relationship with the city of Greer." No one was interested in a conflict between the airport and the city, but the airport chairman was thinking of the future and how Greer's annexation plans and GSP's zoning needs had to be reconciled. "We've got to open our eyes to what the economic expansion has been and can be," said Roger Milliken.[50]

On February 28, 1995, the Airport Commission made good on its intention and filed suit against the city of Greer over its twelve-hundred-acre annexation attempt. Developers were concerned that progress on projects planned or already beginning in the areas Greer had voted to annex would be harmed. "Uncertainty will slow down or stop just about everything," a major Greer developer told *The Greenville News*. "It's like driving a stake in the heart of development."[51]

Determined to find a solution to the annexation impasse, Representative Lewis Vaughn of Greer met with the legislature's legal staff in Columbia. He described the situation and asked for ideas. That's when the model used by coastal cities was proposed. They are allowed to annex land across the intracoastal waterway as if the waterway did not exist. Legally, that makes the land on the other side of the water, in effect, contiguous to the community wanting to annex. The legal counsel suggested applying that principle to the airport. Land on the opposite side of the airport would be considered contiguous to Greer. So the city could legally seek to annex property on the other side of the airport simply by "leap frogging" the airport as coastal communities leap frog the intracoastal waterway to annex land they want on the other side.

"Draft the legislation," said a relieved Representative Vaughn when he was told the same principle could apply to the Greer annexation proposal. Then Vaughn discussed it with House Speaker David Wilkins and other key legislators. The proposed legislation was drafted.[52]

In early 2007, after he had been elected to the state senate to replace

Senator Verne Smith, who died in late 2006, Lewis Vaughn was still pleased with that solution and the growth and economic opportunities it made available to Greer and the property owners and developers on the south side of the airport. Many of them had wanted to be annexed because of water and other services that Greer could provide. "The relationship between Greer and the airport," Vaughn said, "is great."

Shortly after the Greer twelve-hundred-acre annexation issue was resolved, airport commissioner Wallace Storey saw on television a documentary about the problems that the Dallas-Ft. Worth Airport was experiencing in its attempts to expand. He secured a copy of the documentary for showing at a GSP airport commissioners meeting. Built in the 1970s, the airport, along with the cities surrounding it, had grown so much that the airport's future growth was being restricted and lawsuits had multiplied. "We on the Airport Commission realized," said Storey "that we must be more proactive in protecting the Upstate's investment in GSP" in order to avoid the kind of time-consuming and costly legal wranglings that had plagued the Dallas-Ft. Worth airport and its neighboring communities.[53]

In an effort to prevent future conflicts regarding land use around the airport, a long-term solution to protecting the airport's future was suggested by consultant Frank Newton of Newton & Associates in Charlotte. He cited the Dallas-Ft. Worth experience and that of Charlotte and other airports that had faced the issue of incompatible development because not enough land had been set aside for buffer zones and future uses. Newton proposed establishment of an environs zone that would place restrictions on use of land in a prescribed area around the airport.[54] (Spartanburg County in 1993 had passed an environs ordinance to protect airport land. Greenville County had one as well, but it was limited mostly to height and noise concerns. As Greer annexed more county land, Spartanburg County's ordinance no longer applied to the annexed property.)

In mid-February of 1995, Rep. David Wilkins of Greenville introduced legislation that would restrict development from the center of the airport's runway six miles to the southwest, seven miles to the northeast, one mile to the northwest and 1.8 miles to the southeast. Senator Verne Smith of Greer dubbed the proposed restricted area "the big box." A smaller area within that box—closest to the runway—would be restricted to industrial, commercial and agricultural use only. Wilkins' legislation also proposed setting up a twelve-member commission to oversee future development in the area.

Several Greenville and Spartanburg county legislators quickly voiced their support for Wilkins' bill, but debate continued for several weeks over the makeup of the proposed new zoning commission and how much influence the two appointees of the Airport Commission would have. Finally, two months after the bill was introduced, the South Carolina House of Representatives on April 19, 1995, passed the environs bill calling for the protected zone and for a *nine*-member zoning commission with two each from Spartanburg and Greenville counties and Greer, one from Duncan and two to be appointed by the Airport Commission.[55]

"We are a long way apart right now," Senator Verne Smith said a month after the House of Representatives gave its approval to the bill. He and other senators had concerns, especially after hearing from residents in the outer limits, zone two, of the proposed "big box" area. The matter of liability was troubling to several legislators. Which government entity would be financially liable for legal judgments arising from any law suits challenging the environs area plan? Residents in zone two, the outer limits of the "big box," had questions about how restrictions on homes and other buildings would apply.

The Senate debate continued until the last day of the 1995 General Assembly session when all parties came to agreement and the legislation creating the environs zone and the Airport Environs Planning Commission was passed. Under terms of the final legislation, zone two, the outer area of the initial "big box," was dropped from the environs area. The smaller zone one, land nearest the airport, would be restricted to industrial, commercial and agricultural uses, with one exception. If land had already been platted for a subdivision and/or infrastructure was already in place, that land would be "grandfathered" even if it did not conform entirely to the new restrictions. Any new development would have to conform. The legislation approved by the Senate on June 1 also required the new Airport Environs Planning Commission to conduct public hearings and to adopt rules for the environs area no later than January 31, 1996.[56]

The original appointees to the nine-member Airport Environs Planning Commission were: Danny Allen and Robert Hitt, appointed by Spartanburg County; Bob Leach and Eddie Harbin, appointed by Greenville County; E. M. Compton and John McManus, appointed by the city of Greer; Jacqueline Moore, appointed by the city of Duncan; and Robert Coleman and Wallace Storey, appointed by the Greenville-Spartanburg Airport Commission.

During the last half of 1995, the new commission held several public hearings under the leadership of its chairman, retired textile executive Robert E. Coleman. Some attendees used the hearings to air their concerns about, and in some cases outright opposition to, the proposed restrictions in the environs zone. At the final hearing, environs commission member Wallace Storey proposed that a larger "small" box be adopted. Its size, he argued, should be similar to the size required by the U.S. Air Force at its newer major bases. With consultants Newton & Associates and the LPA Group working out details, the final size of the environs area—with restrictions—was adopted by the commission.[57]

Senator Verne Smith of Greer, who had struggled with some of the bill's proposals, was pleased with the final version. "We worked hard to protect the rights of our people and to protect one of our most valuable assets, the airport," the veteran senator told reporters.[58] Representative Lewis Vaughn of Greer also liked the results of the effort to control growth around the airport. "I believe everyone understands the need for the airport to have adequate space," Vaughn said in 2007 after he had been elected to the state senate. The veteran legislator thought the environs zone and the oversight of the Airport Environs Planning Commission was working well. "I've had no complaints in recent years," said the former chairman of the Greenville County legislative delegation.[59]

Although the final legislation was considerably different from the bill he had originally introduced, House Speaker David Wilkins was pleased. A decade later, by then serving as U.S. ambassador to Canada, Wilkins said he still considered the ordinance, including the oversight of the Airport Environs Planning Commission, a wise step toward ensuring continued protection of the airport. “The point is that, even in disputes,” said Wilkins, “the Airport Commission has proved time and time again that it can solve problems and reach solutions that work.” The former longtime state representative from Greenville said, “GSP is the huge catalyst for driving the economy in the Upstate and many business firms would not have located here without it.”[60]

After having watched the effect of the environs ordinance and the actions of the Airport Environs Planning Commission for several years, GSP’s Larry Holcombe, the designated compliance coordinator for the commission, said “I think the environs area and the commission have been good for the county, for the communities and the airport.”[61] As the new century dawned and development continued to crowd into the east side of Greenville County and the west side of Spartanburg County, the airport and its neighbors were benefiting from the careful, long-range planning, the community input and the legislative action that produced the airport environs zone and the new planning commission. “Working together,” said airport executive director Gary Jackson, “we did something great for the future of the airport. It’s good for everybody.”[62] Airport Commission legal counsel Larry Estridge agreed. “We are in better shape than most airports,” he said.[63]

The Environs Zoning Ordinance, adopted by the new planning commission in January of 1996, was amended in 1997 and again in 1999. In the years following its passage, it was the object of scrutiny by governments and airport commissions elsewhere seeking to find effective ways to protect the future of their airports.

Les McCraw in 2007 assumed chairmanship of the Airport Environs Planning Commission. The retired chairman and CEO of Fluor Corporation has developed an appreciation for the environs area around GSP and the ordinance, which sets the terms of restrictions within the protected area. He said he has observed at several airports throughout the country the difficult problems and expensive lawsuits that develop when airports and communities fail to plan ahead and work together to protect airport boundaries. McCraw calls the GSP environs zone and the planning commission to oversee it "a visionary and brilliant concept." He says the commissioners have considered a number of proposals and projects. "Developers have been cooperative and reasonable," he says. "We ask a lot of questions and they understand the reasons for the environs area." McCraw points to a multi-use development being planned at the Highway 14 and I-85 interchange. A portion of that property is within GSP's environs zone. That required the developer to make a number of modifications to his plans and design. "Over several months," said McCraw, "all of the regulations were complied with and it worked out great. The environs commission approved the developer's plans."[64]

Regional solutions

The natural tensions between the city of Greer and the airport next door, and the way in which those tensions were addressed, illustrate the importance of creative and constant regional planning. The South Carolina Upstate is a dynamic area. The growth of an entity as large and vital as the regional airport impacts the communities around it. For the first forty-five years of GSP's existence, except for the farming area of Flatwood that disappeared in the wake of GSP's and BMW's arrivals, no community had been impacted more than Greer.

In 2007, nearing the end of his second four-year term, Mayor Rick Danner allowed, "Greer has an excellent working relationship with GSP. We realize," said the mayor, "that the airport is vital to our continued growth and I think the airport's leaders realize that a thriving city next door is good for the airport." The mayor agreed that the Airport Environs Planning Commission has been beneficial in planning for the future. "We still must work closely with the airport," said Danner. "We understand that the airport is growing and must protect its environs, but Greer wants to be able to develop and grow as well." The mayor suggested that the results of those goals "may cause us to be more creative. It doesn't prohibit growth," he explained, "but it calls for carefully planned growth for those areas near the airport."[65]

How Greer's annexation plans develop—especially across I-85 to the south—will dramatically alter GSP's setting. In the decades ahead, the airport that began in 1962 in a wide-open rural setting could find itself an urban airport, surrounded by a city still growing. If so, that will add credence to the 1990s wisdom of establishing the Environs Zoning ordinance and the Airport Environs Planning Commission to be sure that land planning and use around the airport are compatible for both the airport and the communities around it.

Safety and Security

Airports are generally safe places, but every airport has to be on constant guard to ensure safety and to be prepared for an emergency or even a disaster, just in case it ever happens. A major part of an airport's safety operation is its fire department. It is a department that has to be ready with skilled firefighters and adequate equipment when an aircraft accident occurs.

Alan Sistare has been chief of GSP's fire department since 1985. By 2007, his department had twenty certified aircraft rescue and fire-fighting personnel, more than half of them emergency medical technicians. His department's equipment included three crash trucks, a custom pumper truck and a rescue/mini pumper. The crash trucks can apply dry chemical to a fire as well as foam and water. Airport fire and rescue equipment is funded mostly or entirely by the FAA. A fifty-eight-thousand-pound "first out" crash truck delivered in 2004 cost seven hundred thousand dollars. The fire department is licensed as an emergency medical first responder by the South Carolina Department of Health and Environmental Control, and as a hazardous materials first responder. In addition the department provides confined-space rescue, auto extrication, structural firefighting as well as its primary job of aircraft firefighting and rescue.

Looking at Chief Sistare's sophisticated and powerful fire-fighting equipment in 2007, it is difficult to imagine how limited resources were in GSP's early days. There were not as many planes in those days and they were not as big. Flight traffic was only a fraction of today's. Large, sophisticated fire and rescue equipment like that of today did not even exist. GSP, like many airports of the 1960s, depended largely on local fire departments for help in an emergency.

When Dick Graham took over as executive director in 1967, GSP was less than five years old. It had one fireman and one truck. Graham's deputy director, Harold Boiter, was an excellent, creative handyman who designed and built several tools and facilities for the airport. In those early years, Graham and Boiter had the philosophy: "We will obtain what we can from government surplus and use all our ingenuity to convert it to the airport's benefit." It is a philosophy and practice that continues to this day.

In 1973, Dick Graham hired Larry Holcombe, a jack-of-all-trades who would later be promoted to deputy director in charge of airport operations and, in 2007, to airport manager. Holcombe started as a fireman, one of six. The airport also had nine maintenance men but still only one policeman. Once Graham discovered all of Holcombe's technical skills and insights, Holcombe realized his job was more than a fireman. In fact, over the years, GSP's firemen have been handymen too. They and employees of the maintenance department adapted an old military surplus fire truck cab and chassis by building a one-thousand-gallon water tank on it and mounting a pump and hose. They overhauled engines, painted vehicles and built equipment trailers. Some of the work was accomplished in the department's facilities, much of it outside next to the terminal. "I had no experience in hydraulics," Larry Holcombe admitted. Sure enough, his first job at GSP was preparing hydraulics for the turret on an old fire truck. That was 1973, but all the modern equipment of 2007 has not spoiled GSP's firemen and maintenance workers. They still adapt and build some of their own equipment and tools.

Each year the department answers hundreds of calls for medical treatment, fires, hazardous material spills and other emergencies. Not only does the department respond to situations anywhere in the five square miles of airport property, it also answers calls to surrounding highways and property. The department works closely with several dozen area fire departments, EMS and rescue squad units that help each other in serious emergencies. Through almost forty-five years of operation, there has not been an accident at GSP involving any large aircraft.

The airport and all of its supporting agencies in surrounding counties conduct a disaster drill every year. One year it is a "tabletop" drill where a scenario is described and emergency preparedness representatives discuss how they would respond. The next year it is a simulation of the real thing, a full disaster drill with all emergency agencies and hundreds of staff and volunteers enacting a scenario. It is a serious effort to prepare everyone for the real thing. It is also a valuable operation to test communications procedures.

Air Traffic Controllers are a vital part of air travel safety. At GSP all the controllers have two jobs. They take turns atop the seven-story control tower clearing planes for takeoffs and landings and directing ground traffic in and around the ramps and taxiways. They also spend part of every shift on a lower floor of the tower in the radar room. That is where, for periods of about seventy-five to ninety minutes each, they concentrate on a radar scope, responsible for any planes flying through GSP air space under ten thousand feet. All planes above that level are tracked by controllers in Atlanta and Charlotte. Most of the planes under ten thousand feet being tracked by GSP controllers are civilian aircraft over-flying the area or aircraft of any type approaching or leaving one of the airports within about a sixty-mile radius of GSP while they are under ten thousand feet.

There are eleven airports in the GSP radar coverage area. Only three—GSP, Greenville Downtown and Donaldson Center—have control towers. The other airports are at Spartanburg, Anderson, Clemson, Pickens, Union, Greenwood, Laurens, and Rutherfordton, North Carolina.

Air traffic control must be a cooperative, precise effort. Consider the large number of planes in the air. They are flying at various altitudes and directions, cruising at different speeds, some taking off, some landing; some are small private planes, others fast corporate jets or airliners, some helicopters or military aircraft. All of these must be kept at a safe distance from each other and someone must know where all of them are at any time. That's the job of air traffic control.

When a pilot tells the passengers that their plane is waiting to take off until it is released by Atlanta, for example, that is because each plane must be spaced properly in a queue where it is assigned by controllers. So the pilot is told when to leave and the exact route to follow to fit into that queue for landing in Atlanta. Controllers in the Atlanta flight control center—located several miles south of Atlanta's Hartsfield-Jackson Airport—have been told how far apart they may space planes depending on weather, the number of incoming and outgoing flights that all the airlines serving the airport have estimated and scheduled, and other variables. For GSP, with its comparatively light schedule of takeoffs and landings, that is not difficult. For an airport like Atlanta, with dozens of takeoffs and landings an hour, the job of keeping all the planes spaced safely and as close to schedule as possible is challenging. In order to meet that challenge at a feeder airport—as GSP is for a hub airport like Atlanta—a plane may have to wait on the ground at GSP or Asheville, Columbia or Augusta before departing for Atlanta.

The FAA's flight safety director at GSP is Lamar Foster. A graduate of South Carolina State University and a long time FAA controller, trainer and administrator, he has been at GSP since 2000. "This is the smallest airport with a radar room that I have worked at," says Foster, "but it is one of the most complex. Greenville Downtown and Donaldson are so close," he explains, "that the approaches parallel and even overlap each other." So coordination between the GSP tower and those at Donaldson and Greenville Downtown must be precise. Not only that, Foster points out that GSP is between two of the nation's busiest airports—number one Atlanta and number ten Charlotte.[66] So there is always lots of air traffic through the area, both above ten thousand feet in Atlanta or Charlotte-controlled air space and under ten thousand feet in GSP-controlled air space. Foster likes GSP's layout. "There are no runway crossings and all of the planes' gates are on one side of the airport," Foster observes. He says that helps to eliminate problems with ground traffic movement.

While air traffic control maintains safe skies and safe runways and taxiways, policemen work to maintain safety in the airport and for the thousands who pass through it each day. Chief Tommy Watson says keeping people safe and happy at the same time is a balancing act. After four years in the U.S. Air Force, Watson had been police chief at nearby Lyman for ten years when he took the chief's job at GSP in 1990. There were just two officers and twenty-five contract security guards. In 2007 there are eighteen full-time state-certified police officers, two part-time ones, four dispatchers and an administrative assistant. Officers patrol the terminal and five square miles in addition to helping Greer city and highway patrol officers when necessary on the bordering highways. There is little crime, but there are those who disobey speed limits and disregard post-9-11 parking regulations. "Some people have grown more intolerant of the stricter airport rules required by the FAA," says Watson.

Another vital component of the airport complex to help keep fliers safe and comfortable—and to provide weather forecasting for all people in the area—is the regional weather station. For several years in the early 1990s before it moved to its new location at the GSP airport, the future of the weather station was uncertain.

Forecasting the Weather

"The odds are sixty to forty that weather forecasting will be the same or better under the plan to close the weather station at GSP." That troubling prediction sounded alarm bells throughout the Upstate, not only because it forecast the possibility of losing the area weather station but especially because of who was making the prediction.

It was August 7, 1989. The speaker was none other than the director of the National Weather Service, Albert Friday Jr. He was speaking in Spartanburg to about a hundred people attending a congressional subcommittee hearing that had been arranged by South Carolina's 4th District Congresswoman Liz Patterson. It was the first such hearing to gain response to the proposed modernization of the National Weather Service that had been announced five months earlier. By the plan's projected 1996 completion date, 126 weather stations would be closed across the country, including the longtime Greer weather station—at GSP—and the one in Charlotte. The plan called for them to be closed as early as 1993 and in fact they had already been cut from projected budgets. Charlotte's station would be absorbed into the one at Raleigh, North Carolina. The station at Columbia would provide weather forecasting for South Carolina's Upstate after the station in GSP's control tower closed.

The National Weather Service faced a dilemma. Like most federal government agencies in 1989, it was under congressional pressure to cut costs. Weather stations were expensive to build and operate. Every new station cost an average of about five million dollars. So if it could close 126 of its stations, the Weather Service could reduce its operating budget substantially, but only after an initial capital investment of about one billion dollars over the next ten years.

The Weather Service director said at that August 1989 hearing in Spartanburg that the agency's plan included placing 114 "next generation" radar systems at select weather stations around the country. And Friday said the station at Columbia, South Carolina, would have one of those new radars. That plan did not satisfy many people at the Spartanburg hearing. Several questioned whether even a "next generation" system at Columbia could accurately track weather eighty-four miles away in Spartanburg or ninety-seven miles north in Greenville. Skeptics pointed out that radar cannot see small tornadoes outside a thirty- or fifty-mile range. In 1989, that was a top-of-the-mind concern since parts of Spartanburg County had recently been struck and severely damaged by small tornadoes. A radar system at Columbia, said the critics, would be too far away for accurate forecasting on which to base adequate warnings. Director Friday even admitted it might be "borderline" whether the Columbia weather station could provide better coverage than the station

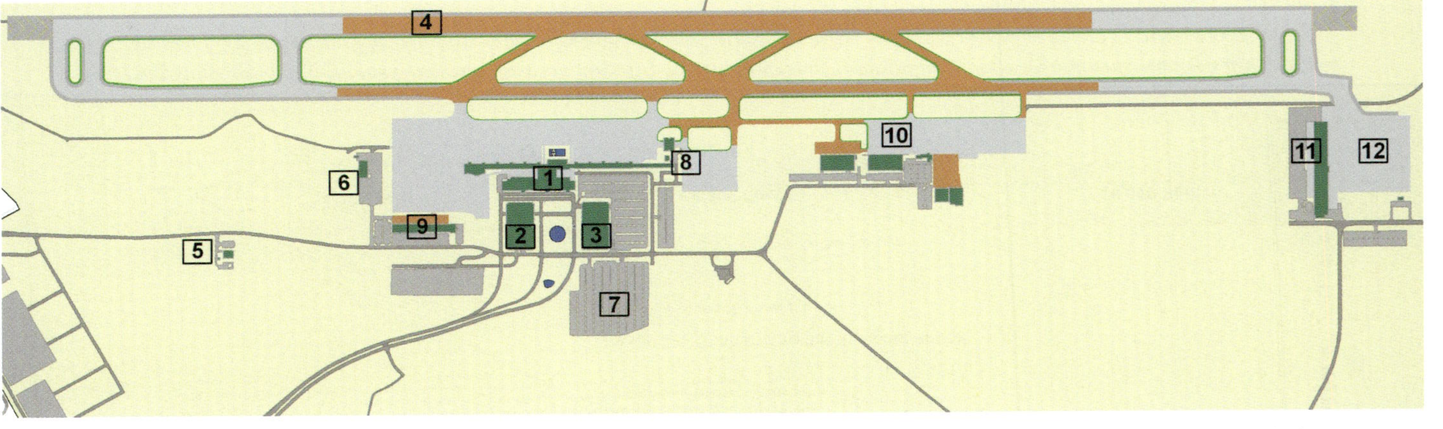

1 – Terminal
2 – Garage A
3 – Garage B
4 – Runway
5 – Weather Bureau
6 – Maintenance Facility
7 – Economy Parking
8 – Air Traffic Control
9 – South Cargo Facility
10 – General Aviation Hangars and Terminal
11 – Federal Express "3K" Facility
12 – North Cargo Apron

A locator map of GSP. Parking garages (2 & 3) are located close to the terminal (1). Rental cars are conveniently located in garage A(2). Remote parking (7) is a short walk from the terminal. Stevens Aviation's general aviation terminal and hangars are 10. Cargo facilities are at 9, 11 and 12.

COURTESY JACK MURRIN AND NATHAN GARNER, GSP.

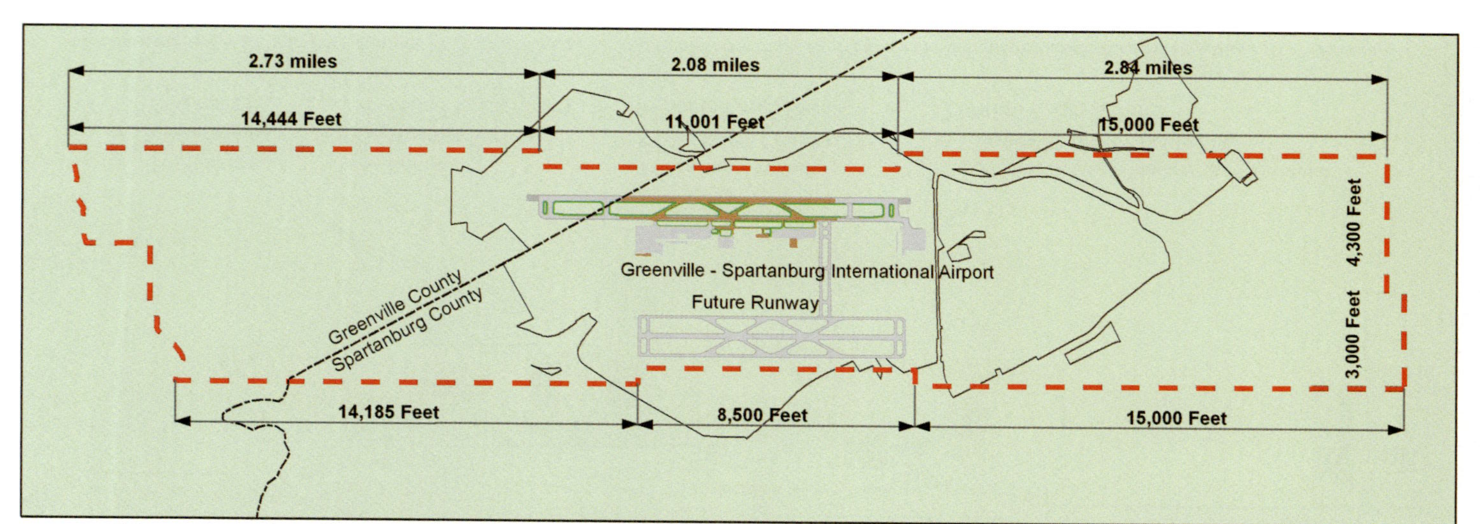

This map shows the outline of the Greenville-Spartanburg Airport's environs zone (broken line) where an ordinance controls development around GSP's property. The light, irregular solid line indicates airport property. COURTESY JACK MURRIN AND NATHAN GARNER, GSP.

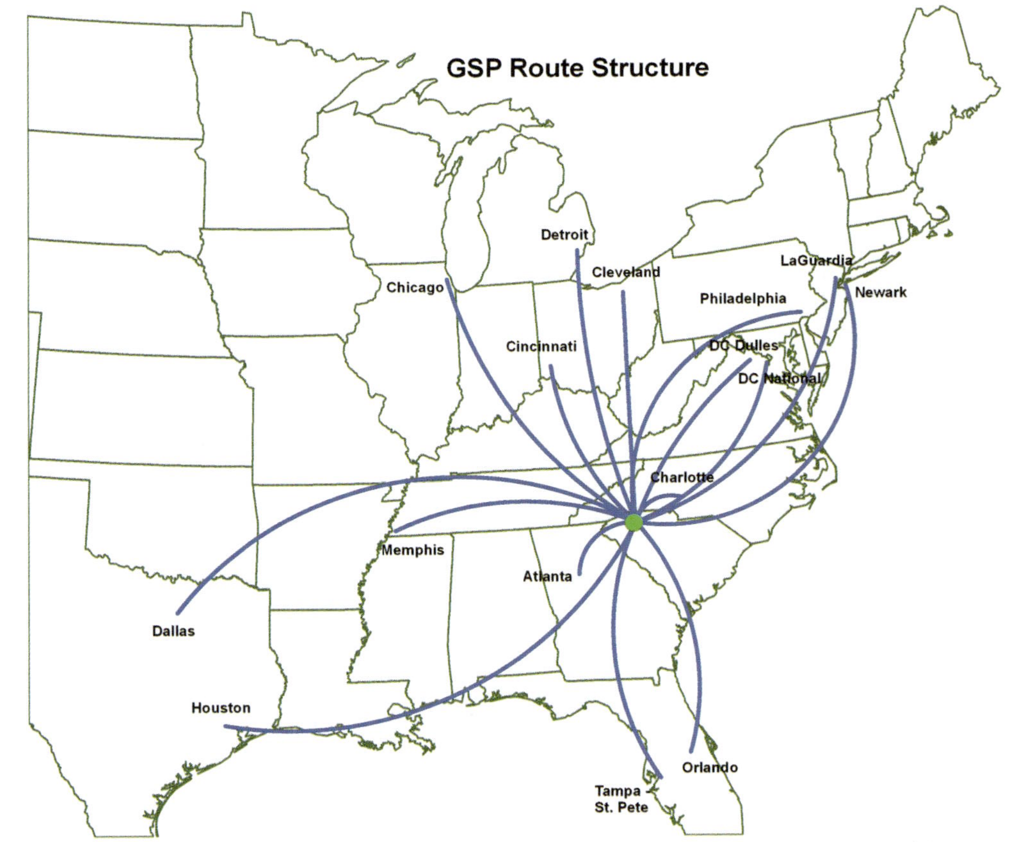

In May of 2007, GSP offered nonstop service with more than sixty flights a day to fifteen major cities. Twice a week nonstop flights to Las Vegas were added in August 2007. COURTESY JACK MURRIN AND NATHAN GARNER, GSP.

One of GSP's several sophisticated fire and rescue units. PHOTOGRAPH BY CINDY HOSEA.

Jim Dolan of Belgrade, Montana, sculpted the snow geese which "fly" above the terminal's atrium pool and into the baggage claim area.

PHOTOGRAPH BY GREG MOSS.

Air Force One at its usual remote parking place at the Greenville-Spartanburg International Airport. Inset: President Bush prepares to greet waiting dignitaries. COURTESY GSP ARCHIVES.

A huge Russian-built Antonov 124 lands several times a year at GSP to load heavy cargo. COURTESY GSP ARCHIVES.

Two huge cranes lift a large piece of cargo made at the General Electric plant in Greenville into a waiting cargo plane at GSP for an overseas delivery. COURTESY GSP ARCHIVES.

A fifty-tire truck arrives at GSP from the nearby General Electric plant carrying part of a gas turbine bound for a flight overseas. COURTESY GSP ARCHIVES.

An average of 22,000 packages are received, sorted and shipped daily by truck and plane from the FedEx 3K facility at GSP. UPS and DHL also provide daily air and ground shipments at GSP. Inset: Don Starling tracks each FedEx shipment. PHOTOGRAPHS BY GREG MOSS.

Stevens Aviation's Turboprop Center. It is located in an original football-field-size hangar at GSP which was refurbished in 2006. A next-door tenant hangar houses the aviation offices and aircraft of several area companies. PHOTOGRAPH BY CINDY HOSEA.

Stevens Aviation is GSP's fixed-base operator (FBO). It serves general aviation fliers. PHOTOGRAPH BY CINDY HOSEA.

The "Boy Aviator" statue by noted Utah sculptor Dennis Smith was presented in 2004 in honor of Roger Milliken's longtime service as Airport Commission chairman. It stands in the terminal's atrium pool. COURTESY GSP ARCHIVES.

Widened to four lanes in 2006, GSP's main entry road from I-85 retained its "Blue Ridge Parkway" feeling. PHOTOGRAPH BY CINDY HOSEA.

The front entrance drive between the airport's terminal and I-85 is designed to provide a pleasant welcome to the Upstate. The waterfall was added in 2006 when the road was widened to four lanes. PHOTOGRAPH BY CINDY HOSEA.

The 162-foot-long Carl Tait mural above Windows Restaurant in the GSP terminal with fountains of the runway garden in the foreground. COURTESY GSP ARCHIVES.

Interstate 85 runs past the Greenville-Spartanburg Airport, seen at top of photo, and BMW's North American plant on the right. A road connects BMW with the airport's large cargo apron in the upper right of the photo. The Brockman-McClimon road interchange on I-85 (Exit 58) is in the center left. The main road to the airport off I-85 is out of the left top corner of the photo. COURTESY GSP ARCHIVES.

The Greenville-Spartanburg Airport with its 11,001-foot runway sits between I-85 and the city of Greer. The Highway 14 interchange is in the lower left and the new entrance to the airport is to the right. COURTESY GSP ARCHIVES.

at GSP already provided. Critics in the audience worried coverage might not be as good.

The issue of radar range was critical to the Weather Service's ultimate decision on what to do with the Greer station at GSP. By Weather Service rules and congressional mandate, Friday would have to prove that there would be no "degradation of service" if the local station were closed and merged with Columbia's. During the three-hour public hearing, the Weather Service director heard plenty of support for keeping the local weather station open. Meteorologists from three area television stations complimented the quality of service provided by local forecasters. Emergency preparedness directors from several Upstate counties urged that the station not be closed.

For more than a year, Representative Patterson, whose 4th district included both Greenville and Spartanburg counties, and Senator Ernest Hollings continued their efforts to keep the Greer station open. Patterson explained the situation to Representative Robert Roe, chair of the House Committee on Science, Space and Technology, the committee with oversight of the National Weather Service. In early October, 1990, fourteen months after the public hearing in Spartanburg, Representative Patterson received a letter from Chairman Roe. It cited the provision she already knew well and gave hope for the future of the Greer station. "A federal law," Roe wrote to Patterson, "prohibits closing of weather offices without proof that forecasting will not be hurt. This certification process will assure the continued operation of the Weather Service office in Greer." Roe obviously agreed with Patterson's objections. Meantime, Senator Hollings had been working on his side of the Congress to assure that the Greer station continued in operation.[67]

Ironically, it was legislation coauthored by Hollings that threatened the Weather Station with another challenge. Congress had passed the Gramm-Rudman-Hollings Deficit Reduction Act that was to take effect October 1, 1990. In fiscal year 1991, it would require federal agencies to reduce their budgets by a combined total of $70 billion. One way the National Weather Service decided to cut its cost was by ordering several of its weather stations throughout the country to close overnight, beginning at nightfall. Again, the Greer station at GSP was targeted. Nightfall closings would create a major problem. Since pilots were required to have weather forecasts no older than one hour before their takeoff, if the weather station had to close in some winter months by 6:00 p.m., there would be no commercial flights allowed out of GSP after 7:00 p.m. That would severely disrupt the schedules of airlines and the travel needs of their passengers. The resulting reduction in flights would be a financial blow to the airport and to the airlines that served it, to say nothing of the severe inconvenience to travelers.

The National Weather Service proposal stunned GSP spokesman Jack Norris. "I can't imagine the government would allow this to happen," Norris told reporters. "It would be terrible." If the possibility of having to close the weather station at nightfall stunned Norris and other airport officials, the thought of possible consequences angered Congressman Liz Patterson. "I am upset now but if there was a threat to lives and welfare of people in my area, I would get downright angry," she declared.[68] She promised to strive to correct the problem. The prospect of nightfall closings also concerned Wayne Jones, chief meteorologist at the weather station. "If we had to close," said Jones, "there would be very serious consequences. Our whole system operates on the assumption of twenty-four-hour service. If we had a tornado or a severe thunderstorm threat, we would have no way to alert the public."

By the spring of 1991, the National Weather Service had enough of its own challenges. Radar and satellite problems were delaying its plans to modernize and streamline its system. Announcements that weather stations like the one at GSP would be closed or merged with others were resulting in political and civic opposition. Finally, the Weather Service said no weather office would be closed until at least 1996.

In July of 1991, Senator Ernest Hollings of South Carolina had become convinced that the weather station at GSP should not only remain open, but as a staffed facility not an automated one. "It covers terrain that just can't be monitored by equipment alone," said Hollings. "We need those personnel."[69] As chairman of the Senate committee on Commerce, Science and Transportation, Hollings' actions and influence were vital to the long-term future of the weather station at GSP. On July 9, he moved in a Senate subcommittee meeting to cancel government plans to convert the GSP station to an automated facility. Fourth District Representative Liz Patterson said she would lobby House conferees to support Hollings' amendment.[70] Eventually, Congress approved a new National Weather Service plan that included keeping the weather station at GSP open.

By May of 1995, the weather station had survived the threats of the past six years and was ready to move from the control tower at GSP to a custom-built 5800-square-foot facility near the airport terminal. Not only had the station survived, its forecast area had grown. Equipped with a new Doppler radar system and other modern equipment it was now charged with forecasting severe weather across forty-six counties. The new radar would be a major improvement over an older radar system that did not detect tornadoes well. By May of 2000, the Weather Forecast Office Greenville-Spartanburg, its new official name, had completed modernization and was responsible for all weather forecasting for a three-state area stretching from six northeast Georgia counties to the counties around Charlotte, North Carolina, and from the high mountain counties along the North Carolina-Tennessee border to counties bordering South Carolina's Midlands.

By 2007, the office had a staff of twenty-five including ten forecasters, other specialists and support personnel. They generated and issued local forecasts and storm warnings twenty-four hours a day, seven days a week. It is one of 122 WFOs that blanket the United States. The closest ones to GSP are those at Columbia; Charleston; Atlanta; Raleigh; Morristown, Tennessee; and Blacksburg, Virginia. Most weather stations used to be located at airports. By 2007, the GSP Weather Forecast Office was one of only a few still at an airport.[71]

Larry Gabric moved from Caribou, Maine, in 2005 to be Meteorologist in Charge at the GSP WFO. He and his staff cover vast differences in weather. The most challenging to forecast is in the mountains of North

Carolina where there is more precipitation, greater fluctuation in temperatures and more severe thunderstorms, often with torrential rain that can quickly cause creeks and rivers to rise within an hour.

What does a meteorologist in charge of a regional weather office wake up in the night worrying about? For Gabric, it can be tornadoes that develop quickly from severe storms and follow unpredictable paths. For his predecessor in Greenville, Joseph Pelissier, the concern over mountain floods could keep him awake at night. Pelissier directed forecasting for the weather office at GSP for ten years until 1995. He worried about the narrow mountain valleys, especially in western North Carolina, that can be the victim of deadly flash flooding during sudden torrential rains.

The Weather Forecast Office uses every communication means available to alert people to severe weather. The media can receive computerized alerts directly from the WFO. Regular forecasts and warnings are posted online at the local WFO's website: weather.gov/gsp. Some counties, like Spartanburg, have community sirens. The WFO also supplies frequent aviation updates with information pilots need: clouds and their heights, wind speed and direction, visibility, and forecast preparation. Larry Gabric recommends that families buy a NOAA weather radio. They sell for twenty to forty dollars at electronics stores. Weather radios can be programmed to receive only the WFO warnings for a particular county. Especially at night during stormy weather, a weather radio can be a lifesaver. Gabric would say, don't be home without one.

The 11,001-foot runway

As soon as BMW decided to build its North American plant next to GSP, airport officials faced a big job. They had to begin making plans to extend their runway. Its 7,600 feet had served the airport and its airlines adequately. The automaker, however, said it needed a longer runway. Governor Campbell had committed to a runway long enough for a "fully loaded" Boeing 747 to take off. A company spokesman did not specify a length but the governor had the impression that 10,000 feet was required.

That would have been possible on airport property. Airport leaders wanted to be sure they did not extend the runway any longer than absolutely necessary. However, an early decision was needed. Already, thirty to forty representatives of affected agencies, utilities and firms were meeting each Monday at the airport to coordinate the details of preparing, building and operating the new BMW plant.

On July 13, 1992, the Airport Commission retained the LPA Group of Columbia, South Carolina, to study environmental issues and recommend the most cost-effective way of extending the runway. The group's consultants were already familiar with the airport and its property. They were accustomed to working with Wallace Storey. He had been the longtime Director of Engineering at Milliken & Company. Roger Milliken had often donated Storey's services on airport needs and projects. Now retired, he had been elected to the Airport Commission in 1989.

Storey asked the LPA Group to study weather records available from past years to determine the impact of temperatures at GSP's altitude. Since the term "fully loaded" had not been explained by the company in detail, for purposes of this study the consultants were to assume that only BMW automobiles and accessory parts would fill the cargo holds. Those were critical statistics to determine because load effects range. The LPA engineers did not have much time to find those answers. The Airport Commission wanted to know the answers and Governor Carroll Campbell needed to know. The governor had to assure both BMW and the Airport Commission that the state could deliver on the promises it had made to BMW a few weeks before.

Just nine days after their firm had been hired, President Ed Parrish and CEO Glenn Lott were with Roger Milliken, Wallace Storey and airport executive director Gary Jackson in the governor's office presenting the report and recommendations from his LPA Group regarding the proposed runway extension. Parrish and his staff had compiled a thirty-year history of daily temperatures at GSP during various day and night hours. Parrish displayed that chart showing the runway altitude—960 feet above sea level—and the operational characteristics of a Boeing 747-200F aircraft at different payload weights as applied to various runway lengths. After carefully explaining the chart and his calculations, Parrish concluded with his recommendations that a runway of 11,000 feet would provide adequate length for safe takeoff on virtually any day of the year. If, indeed, there was an occasional day when temperatures were too high, a cargo flight could be delayed a few hours until cooler temperatures allowed for an adequate takeoff. Parrish also recommended that the 11,000-foot length would be the most cost-effective if the runway could be extended on both ends—by 1,400 feet on the northeast end toward Highway 101 and by 2,000 feet on the southwest end next to Highway 14. Roger Milliken and other airport commissioners present at the meeting endorsed Parrish's recommendations. Milliken told the governor that this solution would preserve the integrity of the airport and eliminate the need to spend a tremendous amount of money to relocate Highway 101. He said the extension plan, as presented, would cost about $46 million. Of that, the FAA would pay 90 percent, the state 10 percent.[72]

Governor Campbell accepted the proposal and suggested that the Airport Commission call BMW officials. The next morning, July 23, Roger Milliken explained the runway extension decision to chairman Eberhard von Kuhnheim and manufacturing chief Bernd Pischetsrieder. He also told them that the governor concurred. BMW's two leaders were satisfied with the information.[73]

Later that day back in Greenville, airport commissioner Bob Coleman moved that GSP's executive director Gary Jackson be authorized to submit to the FAA a preapplication for the estimated $46 million project. The airport commissioners approved unanimously and gave Parrish a standing ovation for what Commissioner Storey called the consultants' "fine work in a remarkably short period of time."[74]

Even though Senator Ernest Hollings would have preferred to have the BMW plant built in his hometown of Charleston, where the large navy base had just been closed, he worked hard to obtain the necessary federal funding for the runway extension at GSP. It helped that he was the powerful chairman of the Senate Commerce Committee, which oversees the FAA. "If Hollings were not the chair of this committee," a committee aide told the *Spartanburg Herald-Journal* as reported on October 4, 1994, "my guess is it would have taken a lot longer to get the money, if ever." The funding gradually was received, and by the time the required environmental impact hearing was held, land cleared, and the runway strengthened and extended 3,400 feet, it was May of 1999 before the full 11,001-foot runway was ready. The initial 1,400-foot extension on the northeast end near Highway 101 had been completed in January of 1997. The entire project had taken almost seven years and had required the moving of more than seven million cubic yards of soil.

While the runway was being built, BMW spokesman Bobby Hitt was still predicting frequent BMW use of the runway once the automobile plant was fully operational. Donaldson Center executive director Phil Southerland, however, wasn't convinced. "They're spending money on what-if's," he told *The Greenville News*. "If that money goes to GSP like it's doing, we are going to be hard pressed to attract money from the FAA for an airport just eight miles away."[75] Southerland was referring to Donaldson's difficulty in its attempts to gain federal money to upgrade the center's aging airport runway and other facilities.

In its first decade of operation, BMW made little use of the lengthened runway. However, it was not a wasted investment. Occasional big planes for industrial clients—like the Antonov 124 for General Electric—needed the longer runway. GSP still had the potential as a major distribution center for cargo. Bechtel Infrastructure consultant Omran Assa, who prepared the airport's fifty-year plan in 2003, told the Airport Commission as early as 1997 that "there is a great opportunity for GSP to serve the community and state in this capacity." Indeed, just two years after the runway was extended, the airport opened a cargo facility for FedEx near the north end of the runway.

To be precise, the GSP runway was lengthened to 11,001 feet. The reason for the extra foot was bragging rights. Several other airports in the United States already had a runway of 11,000 feet. At 11,001 feet, GSP's is the nineteenth longest east of the Mississippi River.

Flatwood remembered

Just as they had in the early 1960s when acres of rolling farmland were being transformed into a modern-day jet airport, the former residents of Flatwood for the past several years had kept their eye on their old home area. It was now the late 1990s. Virtually all of what the former Flatwood residents remembered about their old home place had disappeared: the peach orchards, grain fields, pasture lands, the spacious home sites, the old school house, the corner grocery stores. Even some of the gently rolling ridges had been flattened by the large machines that helped transform the once pastoral land into acres of buildings and parking lots, runways and taxiways, highways and roads. GSP had expanded again and already more than a thousand people reported to work every day at BMW's huge new plant. Flatwood was merely a memory, but a strong one. When F. E. Hendrix saw BMW's athletic fields being built—right on the site of the old Flatwood baseball diamond—he wondered if the company would consider naming those fields in honor of the Flatwood community. He called Bobby Hitt at BMW. The company granted the request and its athletics complex today is known as Flatwood Fields.

Frances Earle (F. E.) Hendrix, Witty Davis and Clyde Dobson had played for the Flatwood Peaches. They wanted to have an historical marker that would enshrine the names of former Flatwood families and baseball players. On September 22, 1998, Hendrix wrote a letter to airport chairman Roger Milliken asking if the GSP Airport Commission "could assist us in establishing some type of historical marker for the people of Flatwood."[76] Milliken and the commission approved the request. So did BMW. Today, the attractive marble marker stands conveniently for all to see near the Flatwood Fields sign alongside Brockman-McClimon Road, half a mile west of Highway 101 and just opposite the Stevens Road entrance to GSP.

Sunday, October 10, 1999. Rain soaked the region all day but it failed to dampen the enthusiasm of Flatwood's former residents. They gathered at 4:00 p.m. in Abner Creek Baptist Church just off Highway 101 southeast of the airport for the dedication of the new historical marker that stood four miles away in the rain. More than a hundred of them and their guests looked instead at pictures on a big screen as they were reminded of the good old days in their beloved community.

Master of ceremonies F. E. Hendrix recalled the Flatwood Grammar School, nestled among the big oak trees, and the school's two outhouses where long balls sometimes had to be chased down during the Saturday afternoon baseball games. He introduced some of the players on the Flatwood Peaches team who had thrilled the big crowds decades before with their skill and exciting plays. He recalled how foul balls would bounce into the cotton fields where BMW employee teams now play. He reminded the audience that home plate at the old ball field was right at the corner of Brockman-McClimon Road and what is now Stevens Road—the "back entrance" to GSP. "Memories," said Hendrix, "are wonderful and no one can take them away from us."

Vivian Leonard Langford grew up near the grammar school and recalled the Flatwood lifestyle of the 1930s, '40s and '50s—the love neighbors shared, the willingness to help each other. "We'd gather on the porch or in the yard to talk," she remembered. "Now we gather around the TV, but in those days we would eat fatback one day and work it off the next day." Then in the late 1950s, Mrs. Langford recalled, Interstate 85 came through "and gave our whole community a different look." Then the airport came and years later BMW. "But it's like your children," she suggested, "you don't want them to grow up but you wouldn't stop them growing if you could."

Emcee Hendrix thanked GSP's executive director Gary Jackson and BMW's Lennie Beamon for GSP's and BMW's gift of the historical marker and for BMW naming its new athletic complex alongside Brockman-McClimon Road Flatwood Fields. "BMW is proud to honor Flatwood," replied Beman. GSP's Jackson said, "It's sad to see things change, especially a place with such good memories." Thinking of the airport and the BMW plant that had spelled the end of Flatwood, Jackson suggested, "Flatwood got caught between fast planes and fast cars."

Representative Rita Allison, chairman of the Spartanburg County legislative delegation, thanked GSP and BMW "for looking beyond the progress of today to remember the Flatwood community." State Senator Verne Smith recalled his first boyhood visit to Flatwood sixty-five years earlier for a "watermelon slicing." He had ridden with his "mama" and other family members in a 1925 Franklin automobile. "It was a rainy day like this," Smith remembered, "but much worse. It was a real frog strangler." Smith remembered how difficult the journey back the few miles to Greer was over roads the rain had turned to slick mud. "I'm so happy," said the senator, "that we are keeping the Flatwood memory alive."[77]

It was left to Vivian Langford to suggest the lasting value of this special day and the permanent historical marker that GSP and BMW had erected with the names of dozens of Flatwood families and ball players. Mrs. Langford promised, "Because of this day and this marker, we'll never lose sight of our little Flatwood community. Every time we travel past this marker and the Flatwood Fields sign, we'll pull the memories of Flatwood from our hearts for a minute and then place them back where they belong." By those who had once lived on the land that GSP and BMW now occupied, Flatwood would always be remembered.

CHAPTER 11

The Transportation Network

Railroads

In the 1800s, railroads changed America. By the 1850s, rail lines stretched from the South Carolina coast to the state's Midlands, then began penetrating from Columbia north a hundred miles to the Upstate cities of Greenville and Spartanburg. Now those residents of Charleston and other coastal communities who could afford it had a way to escape the summer's sweltering heat by taking the train to the higher and cooler elevations of the Upstate. The visitors—and those who moved north—were an economic boon to the still relatively remote communities of the Upstate. While railroads were extending the opportunities of short distance travel, they were also making possible long distance journeys. On May 10, 1869, in the high ranges of the Great Basin Desert in far northwest Utah, officials of the Central Pacific and Union Pacific railroads met to drive the last spike into the ground near the village of Promontory. The first transcontinental railroad was complete, an accomplishment that would have monumental economic, social and political consequences for the nation. Cross-country rail travel could begin. The rails had penetrated the western frontier.

For almost a century, railroads ruled America's travel habits. Automobiles, trucks and highways gradually changed those habits. Railroads remained a vital part of moving cargo across America and they still transported passengers; but the decision that really moved Americans from rails to roads was made by an old soldier turned politician.

Cars, trucks and highways

By 1919, Harvey Firestone was already a longtime advocate of a national highway system, for two good reasons. More than six million passenger cars and almost a million trucks were registered. Automobile factories would soon be building two million units a year. There were already two million miles of highways in the United States, only 12 percent were paved.[1] That didn't bother Firestone's good friend Thomas Edison. The two men, along with automaker Henry Ford, vacationed together for several years. They often escaped to quiet rural areas where Edison preferred the two-lane, unpaved roads.[2] Most people, however, craved smoother, easier and faster travel. Firestone correctly believed that if highways were better organized, marked and paved, more people would travel. More cars would be sold. More travel meant more tires would be sold. Firestone also saw a future in trucks. He even created a slogan, "The 100-mile radius belongs to the truck," Firestone claimed. Even the wartime railroad administration agreed. During World War I, it had tried to convince shippers to turn from trains to trucks for short hauls. Railroads agreed.[3] Their yards were overcrowded and their profits were small on short haul loads. Firestone was convinced that trucks could create new growth opportunities for communities not served by railroads. His "ship by truck" slogan became a nationwide campaign, complete with civic festivals, parades, speeches, advertising and news stories. The campaign brought results. Some states began using vehicle license fees and gas taxes for road construction and paving.[4] And the federal government decided to organize a transcontinental convoy to promote the need for a better system of roads.

In the summer of 1919, twenty-eight-year-old Lt. Col. Dwight David Eisenhower volunteered to participate as an observer on the first transcontinental motor convoy. Designed to test the nation's fledgling—and in some places nonexistent—road network and the military's travel durability, the convoy left Washington, D.C. on July 7 with seventy-three army vehicles of all types, including trucks loaded with equipment and supplies. They soon hooked up with the partially completed, and still largely unpaved, Lincoln Highway and headed west toward San Francisco.[5] The route took the convoy past Harvey Firestone's Columbiana home and farm near Akron, Ohio. Firestone had donated some of his new, softer pneumatic tires for some of the convoy's trucks. Firestone invited the convoy to stop for rest and dinner. That's the evening that the fifty-year-old tire baron met twenty-eight-year-old Dwight Eisenhower and shared with him his ideas about the future of America's roads.[6]

From Firestone's Ohio home, the convoy struggled on for seven more weeks across the plains, over mountain trails, crossing farmers' fields where no roads existed. Vehicles were often mired in mud or stuck in sand. Interestingly, those with Firestone's new and softer pneumatic tires fared better than those vehicles with hard, solid tires.[7] Tires had to be changed frequently and where roads were nonexistent cattle fences often had to be removed and provisions sometimes ran dangerously low. Sixty-two days after leaving Washington, the travel weary military convoy reached San Francisco. Including all the delays, the nationwide journey had averaged a mere six miles an hour. The arduous trip had illustrated a need for a better and more organized system of roads and the potential for long haul freight travel by truck.[8] The convoy's experiences and the conversation in Ohio with Harvey Firestone had left an indelible impression on Lt. Col. Dwight Eisenhower. He was still carrying the memories of that conversation with him when he entered the White House thirty-four years later.

Strange as it may seem today, in the early years of the twentieth century there were many people who thought the automobile would never catch on. The horse and buggy were still popular. Railroads were fine for long- and short-distance travel. Streetcars served many large cities.[9] Who needed a car? It was a luxury for the rich, many middle Americans believed. To them, the automobile was simply a novelty. Henry Ford disagreed. He thought everyone—no matter income—should own an automobile. In 1913 he began producing his Model T on the industry's first assembly line. His cars were now less costly to make and more affordable to buy.

Americans responded. By 1927, nineteen years after Ford had introduced the Model T in 1908, he had sold more than sixteen million of them.[10] Several other companies were selling cars as well. So by the mid-1920s, there were an estimated twenty-five million cars on America's streets and roads. Trouble was, the nation's roads were not ready for all of them.

Many main roads followed the routes of old trails. Most were unpaved. Some were cobblestone. Road markings were haphazard and confusing. So Congress passed the Federal Highway Aid Act of 1925, which created the "U.S. Highway System" and provided standardized routes and signs nationwide. Many of those highways remain today. Others were replaced by a new road system that Congress would create thirty-one years later to meet demands of the mid and late twentieth century. By the 1950s, the motor vehicle had long since graduated from novelty to necessity.

After a distinguished career that included serving as Supreme Allied Commander in Europe during World War II, then as General of the Army and Army Chief of Staff, later as President of Columbia University, and finally as NATO Supreme Commander in Europe, five-star General Dwight Eisenhower officially retired from active military service on May 31, 1952. Four days later he announced his candidacy for the Republican Party's nomination for president. In November, he was elected and on January 20, 1953, sixty-two-year-old civilian Dwight Eisenhower began his eight-year presidency. "Ike," as he was popularly and affectionately called by Americans, had never forgotten his sixty-two-day convoy trip across America in 1919 and his conversation with Harvey Firestone. Nor could he forget the impression that the fast and efficient German autobahns had left on him during his war years in Europe. The old soldier put his administration to work on a plan.[11]

That new highway plan took time to design and by 1955, Harvey Firestone's frustration was growing. His company bought full-page ads in several newspapers under the bold headline "Let's Build Them Now" and with the warning "America's Future Progress Depends on Better and Safer Highways." The Firestone ad claimed 53 million vehicles would travel 525 billion miles in 1955 and 36,000 people would be killed. With injuries and fatal accidents increasing, "the nation," the ad warned, "is facing a serious traffic situation costing $10 billion a year." Firestone complained, "We are trying to drive 1955-model cars over 1925-model roads."[12]

What President Eisenhower proposed to Congress in 1956 was a nationwide system of interstate highways that would allow high speed travel on multi-lane, limited-access roads that would run both beside and through towns and cities.[13] The system would connect the country and eliminate the stop-and-go caused by traffic lights. Travel would be easier, faster, safer. In this era of the Cold War, Eisenhower argued that a modern highway system was needed to "meet the demands of catastrophe or defense, should an atomic war come." Years later, two catastrophes would prove the value of Ike's interstate highways. After the terrorist airplane attacks on New York City, the Pentagon and in eastern Pennsylvania on September 11, 2001, highway historian Dan McNichol recalled, "When every airplane (in the United States) was grounded, we were able to move goods and people on the interstate system and keep the economy moving."[14] Four years later, in advance of and following the deadly 2005 hurricanes Katrina and Rita, more than two million residents evacuated Gulf Coast cities on interstates leading inland.

Congress approved Eisenhower's highway plan and on June 29, 1956, the president signed a bill creating the National System of Interstate and Defense Highways. It would be paid for largely by the Federal Highway Trust Fund. Known popularly as the Federal Interstate Highway System, it would eventually include more than forty-seven thousand miles of highways that would be owned, built and operated by the states in which they are located. On all those miles of asphalt and concrete ribbon across the nation's forty-eight contiguous states, one common fixture and frustration of travel is absent: the traffic light.

By the time the interstate system was created in 1956, there were a few limited-access toll roads across the country, but they all eventually became part of the new system. By 1991, the system was officially considered complete even though some short sections and spurs were still being added in the early years of the twenty-first century. In 1993, the highway system that helped change America by attracting more travelers and truckers to the roads was officially named the Eisenhower Interstate System in memory of the president and general who had forged the idea decades before. Interestingly, the five stars on the system's highway signs commemorate Eisenhower's five star rank as General of the Army, to which he was promoted in the closing months of World War II.

Dwight Eisenhower died March 28, 1969. He is buried at his presidential library in Abilene, Kansas, the town where he grew up, one hundred forty miles west of Kansas City. His grave is only a couple of miles from Interstate 70, part of the National System of Highways about which the revered soldier had so long dreamed since his military convoy journey in 1919. That dream of a better road system for his country had brought to Americans unlimited mobility.

GSP's STRATEGIC LOCATION

The story of America's interstate highway system is important because it is one of the vital keys in the GSP airport story. Airports attract large numbers of people and huge amounts of automobile and truck traffic, so most airports are located near major highways, especially interstates. One of the first interstates to be built was I-85. Stretching 668 miles from Montgomery, Alabama, northeast to Petersburg, Virginia, I-85's location was a key to the late 1950s selection of the site for Greenville-Spartanburg Airport. Deciding on final routes for proposed interstates was not easy, especially when neighboring states could not agree on where an interstate would cross states' boundaries.

In late 1956, it became obvious that South Carolina and Georgia had different ideas about where Interstate 85 should be built. A meeting in Columbia on October 30, 1956, between representatives of the two states produced no agreement on a state-line crossing location. At a meeting in Atlanta on January 14, 1957, a route was proposed that would approximate a line from Gainesville, Georgia, to just south of Toccoa, then roughly follow Highway 123 into South Carolina and go just south of Seneca and Clemson, then on to the Greenville area. Z. W. Meeks, executive secretary of the Anderson Chamber of Commerce, was concerned about the proposed route and sent a letter to 3rd District Congressman Bryan Dorn. Noting that the South Carolina Highway Department and the Federal Bureau of Public Roads "have for years and years indicated this inter-regional highway would follow the general course of U.S. 29," Meeks told Dorn the South Carolina Highway Department wanted that route but was "encountering some political opposition in Georgia." Meeks was concerned because of what he saw would be the negative economic impact on Anderson if the new interstate highway were built fifteen or more miles to the north of the city. He urged Dorn "to do everything possible to see that the original course of this highway is not disturbed for purely political reasons."[15]

Four days after the nonproductive Atlanta meeting, the regional engineer for the Bureau of Public Roads, noting that "joint action is required, progress is at a standstill," wrote to the highway engineers of the two states. In the January 18, 1957, letter, B. P. McWhorter proposed "a complete road user benefit analysis of all reasonable and logical alternate routes." He suggested a working committee with engineers from the two states and the Bureau of Public Roads. The committee would also work with each state on estimating costs. "Let's find a solution," wrote McWhorter, "that will stand up under the closest scrutiny and most penetrating questioning of all who are interested and affected."[16]

It wasn't until 1959, with prompting from Congressman Dorn, 4th District representative Robert Ashmore and other members of the South Carolina congressional delegation, that the issue between Georgia and South Carolina was resolved. Only then was the exact route for Interstate 85 between Atlanta and Greenville established, bringing it south so that it crossed the state line near Fair Play, skirted the northern edge of the city of Anderson and continued northeast passing nearby Greenville, Spartanburg and Gaffney on its way to Charlotte and beyond. By the spring of 1959, rights of way had been purchased, grading for the interstate was underway and several interchange bridges were being built.[17] I-85 across Upstate South Carolina would be completed in time for GSP's opening in 1962.[18]

The South Carolina Upstate's other major highway, Interstate 26, was completed in the 1960s connecting the international port of Charleston with the booming business climate of the Upstate. The value of Interstates 26 and 85 cannot be overstated. They connect GSP and the Upstate with the rest of the nation and allow rapid shipment of cargo west via 85 South, which connects with I-20 and I-75 in Atlanta, and via 85 North, which connects with I-77 in Charlotte and I-95 in southeast Virginia. I-26 originates in Charleston and connects a short distance north with I-95 and then with both I-77 and I-20 in Columbia, then with I-85 in Spartanburg, with I-40 in Asheville, North Carolina, and with I-81 in southwestern Virginia. Using those connecting highways, travelers and trucking companies can quickly and easily reach a large percentage of the nation's residential and business population within two days.

CHAPTER 12

Moving Cargo

Business and pleasure travelers know GSP and its airlines as *people* movers. Industry knows GSP and its carriers as *cargo* movers and the airport moves plenty of cargo. The reason is that from its earliest planning days, the Greenville-Spartanburg Airport Commission intended the airport to be a cargo hub. By the decade of the 1990s, air cargo "throughput"—as it is called in airport talk—was experiencing double-digit growth at GSP, almost fifty-four million pounds in 1996.

GSP's fifty-year master plan, prepared by Bechtel Infrastructure in 2003, predicted that by 2053, GSP may handle more than half a million tons annually.[1] The prediction was based partly on GSP's strategic location (see Chapter 11) and on its impressive cargo facilities. Two large cargo buildings, a customs port, large cargo aprons and staging areas, an 11,001-foot runway and enough property to accommodate growth are advantages that the airport offers. Air cargo carriers UPS, FedEx and DHL provide regular cargo flights to and from the airport.

FedEx explored the possibility of a major facility at GSP, but ultimately decided to build its mid-Atlantic hub at Greensboro, North Carolina. However, in August 2001, FedEx opened a 3K facility at GSP, large enough to handle three thousand packages an hour. It occupies a 120,000-square-foot facility leased from the airport. With a 325,000-square-foot apron and a 126,000-square-foot adjacent paved staging area, the facility sits near the end of the 11,001-foot runway and alongside four-lane Highway 101. Just two miles from Interstate 85, it serves a

35,000-square-mile area of the western Carolinas. Two flights arrive each weekday morning between 5:45 and 6:15. It takes a team of fourteen workers about twenty minutes to unload 40,000 to 60,000 pounds of packages from each of the Boeing 727-200s. That cargo is sorted and transferred to large trucks that drive it to local terminals in Greenville, Spartanburg, Anderson and in Asheville, North Carolina. Trucks leave those terminals early each weekday evening and from 7:00 to 11:00 at GSP the sorting and loading process has the two planes loaded and ready for takeoff between 10:45 and 11:15 p.m., flying the local cargo to the main FedEx hubs in Memphis and Indianapolis. Meantime, large trucks drive second-day freight deliveries to hubs in Memphis, Indianapolis, Atlanta and Charlotte. On average in early 2007, FedEx handled approximately 200,000 pounds of inbound and 225,000 pounds of outbound cargo daily at GSP.[2] Facilities manager Jonn Harris said that by 2007, more than eighty were employed at the company's facility.

As preparations were being made in 1993 for construction of BMW's huge automobile manufacturing plant, United Parcel Service (UPS) contacted officials of GSP. The company was looking for a location to build a multi-state hub and wanted to consider several airports, including Greenville-Spartanburg. It would provide several hundred jobs and a facility that would handle dozens of incoming and outgoing flights each day. The timing of such a request could not have been worse. UPS had two needs that GSP would have difficulty accommodating. The shipper wanted to proceed expeditiously and it needed a facility that would have a runway available all the time. GSP had only one runway in 1993, as it still does in 2007. The property on which to build a second runway was available but GSP officials thought finding money to build it would be virtually impossible. The airport had just applied for more than $40 million in federal and state funding to strengthen and lengthen the existing runway to accommodate the perceived needs of BMW. It would be difficult to make another multi-million request now or in the near future. There also would be inevitable associated costs that the airport would have to shoulder. The airport's commissioners were unwilling to commit to those expenses at that time or to apply for more federal funding that would run into the tens of millions of dollars.[3] The commissioners passed on the opportunity and UPS ultimately established its facility at the Columbia Metropolitan Airport, a hundred miles to the south.

The loss of the UPS hub to Columbia created dissatisfaction among some local leaders. Donaldson Center would have liked an opportunity to bid for the hub. Its leaders had hoped that acquiring such a facility would help them gain more federal aid to improve the center's air facilities. Donaldson's executive director, Phil Southerland, told *The Greenville News* in October 1994, "If GSP sits out there and takes the ones it wants and refuses the others, nobody will come to Donaldson."[4] Greenville County councilman Richard Ashmore called for more communication and coordination among the airports. "Those involved in development need to decide how we're going to use these assets to best promote development so we are not competing against each other," Ashmore told reporters.[5]

In July 1999, UPS opened a small cargo operation at GSP. Planes arrive each weekday morning between six and seven from Philadelphia and Charlotte with cargo from throughout the Northeast, from Columbia with Southeast cargo and from Louisville with cargo from the rest of the country and throughout the world. It is sorted and soon on its way to UPS terminals throughout the South Carolina Upstate and western North Carolina. The operation comes alive again in early evening when those familiar brown trucks, eighteen-wheelers and smaller ones, begin arriving with thousands of packages and, sometimes, larger freight. One large B-757 can accommodate most nights' cargo. It leaves GSP no later than 11:20 p.m. for the fifty-seven minute flight to Louisville where it is placed on flights bound for destinations worldwide. Air operations supervisor Randy Johnson says about forty are employed at the GSP operation.[6]

UPS observed its one hundredth anniversary in 2007. It began as

American Messenger Service in August 1907 providing parcel delivery for retailers. By the 1930s it was delivering some packages by air.[7]

DHL is a global cargo carrier that serves GSP with one round-trip DC-8 flight weekdays. It arrives from the company's national hub in Ohio each morning about 6:30 and leaves at 10:00 p.m. DHL's conspicuous gold and red trucks serve thirty-six hundred customers throughout the South Carolina Upstate and north to Asheville and Franklin, North Carolina, delivering and picking up an average of eleven thousand shipments each weekday.[8]

DHL began in 1969 when three young San Francisco men—Adrian Dalsey, Larry Hillblom and Robert Lynn—activated a unique idea. They began shuttling bills of lading between San Francisco and Hawaii. They would carry the shipping documents on commercial flights and then begin customs clearance of the ship's cargo to reduce in-harbor waiting time when the ship arrived. Their international express service grew rapidly and within two years they expanded into the Far East and the Pacific Rim, eventually worldwide. It was ten years before they added package delivery to their document delivery service. In 2003, DHL bought Airborne Express and became the third largest express provider in the United States.[9]

General Electric built its huge gas turbine manufacturing facility on Greenville's east side near Interstate 85 in 1968. Since then, most of those turbines have been delivered by truck and train to ports in Charleston and Newport News, Virginia, and then shipped to locations across the world. Occasionally, because of changes in power plant construction schedules or changes in equipment needs, a power provider requires a large gas turbine component quickly.[10] Usually that is the rotor portion of the turbine that can weigh well over two hundred thousand pounds. If the shipment is needed quickly, it has to go by air. There aren't many cargo aircraft in the world that can handle a shipment that heavy and bulky. The Antonov 124 can.

Several times each year since 2002, General Electric has reserved the Antonov 124 for a shipment out of Greenville-Spartanburg Airport. The Russian crew usually flies the huge, four-engine heavy transport into GSP a day early. This crew, specialists in handling unique, oversized and heavy-weight cargo, can load the huge shipment in about four hours. The entire process is arranged and coordinated at the company's Greenville plant by Bobby Brown, the company's transportation specialist.

When the huge aircraft lands, it parks at a large shipping apron near the end of the 11,001-foot runway. One spring day in 2007, the Antonov 124 arrived at GSP from South America with nineteen crew members to pick up a gas turbine rotor assembly. The crew members, as usual, stayed at the nearby Marriott Hotel and visited nearby stores to shop. The next morning, while the six pilots rested and relaxed, the mechanics on the crew, who double as the loading team, raised the nose portion of the huge plane and assembled a long ramp from the front of the plane's cargo hold. Then two 130-ton cranes were positioned on either side of the ramp. Meanwhile, a nineteen-axle, fifty-tire truck was slowly being escorted the nine miles north on I-85 from the GE plant to GSP where it pulled up to the Antonov's ramp.

Workmen connected the shipment to the two cranes' rigging mechanisms. The cranes slowly hoisted the steel crate containing the rotor off the flatbed as the truck pulled out of the way. Then the two cranes carefully maneuvered the expensive cargo on a ninety degree turn to line it up with the aircraft's ramp. "It looks like the ballet of the behemoths," GE licensing manager Mary Rankin commented as she watched the delicate movements of the huge cranes with their 218,000-pound load. Moments later it had been lowered onto the ramp and was slowly being winched into the airplane and secured. About 8:30 that evening, the Antonov 124, gross weight of 782,000 pounds—plane, cargo and fuel—lifted off GSP's 11,001-foot runway. Its destination was China.

There are only twenty-three Antonov 124 aircraft in the world. Volga Dneper, a Russian cargo airline, owns seventeen of them. The airline's load analyst, Todd Cox, explained that sending this GE shipment the usual way—by truck or train to an East Coast port and then by ship—would take about fifty days. The flight to China from Greenville-Spartanburg could have the shipment to China in just sixty-five hours with four refueling stops en route.

GE's Bobby Brown, the man in charge of arranging the transportation details, is pleased that the Greenville-Spartanburg Airport is close to the GE plant. "A thirty-minute truck run up the interstate, easy access to the airport, ample parking and loading area," says Brown. "It would be tough to find anything more convenient."

CHAPTER 13

The Economic Engine

Since its opening in 1962, the Greenville-Spartanburg Airport has been a major contributor to the economy of South Carolina's Upstate, helping to attract both domestic and foreign firms. Hoechst came in 1966, General Electric in 1968, Michelin in the mid-1970s, Adidas in the 1980s. Dozens of others, big and small, from across the United States and Canada and from several countries throughout Europe and Asia have built plants. Some, like Michelin, established their North American headquarters here. As Converse College archivist Jeffrey Willis observes, "GSP made possible the diversification of industry in the Upstate."

The Michelin move was an historic occasion for economic development in the Upstate. Here was one of the world's best known and most successful business firms deciding that its needs and plans fit with the people and potential of this region. Michelin built several facilities; its North American headquarters is just two miles from the Greenville-Spartanburg Airport. That proximity has been a good fit. "When Michelin arrived in the Upstate in the mid-1970s, the company needed a mobility partner to supply aviation services," says Michelin North America's chairman and president Jim Micali. "GSP Airport has played—and continues to play—a key role in Michelin's success in North America, providing a convenient, efficient and friendly gateway to our global business needs." Michelin has aviation offices and aircraft at, and its planes are serviced by, GSP's fixed-base operator Stevens Aviation.

Almost forty years after moving to the South Carolina Upstate,

General Electric continues to expand its presence in Greenville. In addition to its large gas turbine manufacturing business, it has moved the engineering headquarters for its GE Energy Division to Greenville.

The Greenville-Spartanburg International Airport's designation as an inland port of entry and the easy access to interstates 85 and 26 were keys to attracting Adidas, the world's largest maker of athletic footwear and apparel, to Spartanburg County. The German firm opened a half-million square foot distribution center in 1988 and in the spring of 2007 was considering the possibility of establishing another distribution complex in western Spartanburg County not far from GSP. South Carolina Commerce Department secretary Joe Taylor called the presence of Adidas "another example of marquis companies, world-class companies, that have international reputations choosing South Carolina and the Upstate for distribution."[1]

Two decades after Michelin arrived, BMW opened its North American plant four miles north on Interstate 85 on the other side of GSP and intensified the national and international media spotlight on the Upstate. "South Carolina hills are alive with European commerce" blared the headline in the *Washington Post* on December 26, 1992, as construction on the BMW plant began. Writer William Booth noted the 185 foreign firms that had moved into the Greenville-Spartanburg-Anderson corridor and the area's claim of having the highest per capita foreign investment in the nation. The story quoted Clemson University economist Bruce Yandle describing the Upstate as an example of an area that had retooled itself by luring overseas investment while improving infrastructure and worker training. The article recognized Dick Tukey's "relentless pursuit" of European investment in the 1960s and 1970s, calling the Spartanburg Chamber of Commerce head, "a one-man Welcome Wagon for the European community." While the article took its swipes at some aspects of the Upstate's life and culture, it also quoted former Greenville mayor Max Heller as saying "This community is wide open and I am proof of that."

Heller is an Austrian-born Jew who escaped the Nazis and moved to Greenville in 1938, learned English, became a successful business owner and was later elected mayor. Governor Dick Riley in the 1980s appointed Heller as chairman of the South Carolina State Development Board. In that position, Heller became a popular ambassador and effective industry recruiter for South Carolina, especially in his native Europe. He was also a believer in the Greenville-Spartanburg Airport's contribution to the growing economy of South Carolina's Upstate. "We used it much to our advantage when we met with industry leaders," Heller remembered years later. "We talk about the quality of our area and its people. The airport was a good example of quality-plus. GSP moved us forward in our economic development. BMW's decision to come here and locate next to the airport is a good example."[2]

In May of 2007, BMW announced that annual production at the company's plant next door to GSP would soon increase to more than two hundred thousand vehicles, including the BMW X3 to be launched in 2008. By the spring of 2007, employment at the plant already stood at 4,500.

The Impact

While GSP enhances the economic development of the area by the services it provides and the business it helps to attract, it is a business in itself. The airport, including its on-site businesses, provides more than five hundred jobs and it purchases a significant amount of its supplies, services and equipment from the area.

The airport is a political subdivision of the state. Members of the Airport Commission that was created by the state legislature in 1959 to oversee airport operations receive no remuneration. The airport pays no property taxes. Neither does it require any property tax. The only property tax it has received paid off general obligation bonds that were issued to build the airport in the early 1960s. Since the day the airport opened in October 1962, it has been self-sustaining. Revenue for its operations is generated from operating fees paid by scheduled passenger and cargo airlines, as well as from parking fees, leasing fees for rental car and limousine operations, food and retail concessions, and from its fixed-base operator leasing fees and other miscellaneous income. Funding to meet FAA requirements and to help pay for capital improvements comes from the airport's share of the Aviation Trust Fund. That fund is supported by the federal tax on airline tickets, fuel and other aviation-related items.

Almost every viable commercial airport has a positive economic impact on the area it services. Airports need a method of calculating and reporting that impact in clear, definite terms. The FAA has developed such a method, which has been evolving since the 1980s and is now recognized as the standard for conducting economic impact studies of America's airports. It uses an *impact* approach that measures the importance of the airport as an industry. It looks at the airport's employment, the earnings it generates and the locally-produced goods and services it uses, all expressed in jobs and dollars. The study surveys three kinds of impacts. Direct impacts are local expenditures incurred by the airport and by firms at or near the airport such as airlines, fixed-base operators, flight schools, the control tower, as well as manufacturing and service firms that provide aviation-related products and services. The survey includes those entities' direct payroll, capital and operating expenses. The study also looks at indirect impacts, the expenditures of airport users. That category includes money that commercial and general aviation passengers and crews spend in the region, and spending by business firms dependent on the aviation industry, including travel agencies. The other important category included in the study is the multiplier impact. It traces money as it flows through the regional economy, passing from one source to another over and over. The longer money stays in the region, the more the region's economy benefits, the higher the multiplier. For example, an airport or airline employee uses her salary to buy groceries, gas, clothes and other items to pay for rent and utilities, to make a car payment, to eat out, to donate to charity. All of those receiving that money from the airport or airline employee are using that money to pay their employees, their utilities, their other personal bills. The money has multiplied. If GSP and the business firms that operate at or near GSP—airlines, shipping companies, rental car operators, other concessionaires, Stevens Aviation, taxis, limousines, and others—account for several thousand people who live in the area, or who visit here regularly, the multiplier effect is significant in helping to determine GSP's economic impact on the region.

In 2005, the Airport Commission retained the nationally-known planning firm of Wilbur Smith Associates to conduct an economic impact study on GSP. The firm surveyed GSP, aviation-related firms at and nearby GSP, and more than thirteen hundred arriving and departing passengers of whom 69 percent were residents of the area and 31 percent were visitors. The passenger survey results, together with the surveys of the thirty-two area business firms and government agencies, were extrapolated to reflect a full year's estimated economic impact.

The direct economic impact totaled almost $72.8 million. Indirect impacts totaled more than $150 million. That included the spending impact of almost 1.5 million passengers arriving at or departing from the airport during 2005 and money spent by those who stayed in the area, bought tickets here, rented cars or used travel agencies and other services. The multiplier impact was $186.4 million.

The Wilbur Smith study estimated that GSP in 2002 had a total annual aviation-related impact of $410 million in economic activity; $150 million of that were the earnings paid to 5,911 workers.[3] It was an encouraging report considering the decline in commercial passengers and general aviation operations during 2002 in the wake of the September 2001 terrorist attacks. The GSP Airport Commission periodically funds such economic impact studies.

Another aspect of GSP's economic impact on the region is more difficult, perhaps impossible, to measure accurately. How many business firms move to—or expand in—the Upstate at least in part because of the airport's presence and the services it offers? One prime example is BMW. As noted in Chapter 10, BMW's top leaders preferred being next to, or even on, airport property. South Carolina in 1992 was competing with Omaha, Nebraska, in its attempt to lure BMW. Had GSP not existed with its facilities and services, its extra space to build a longer runway and available land next to the airport, BMW may not have chosen the Upstate. Considering the size to which the BMW plant has grown, the number of jobs it has created and the significant number of suppliers it has attracted to the area this region would not be as economically vibrant as it has become if BMW had located elsewhere.

There is another economic impact that marquee firms like BMW and General Electric, Michelin and Adidas have on this area. Its measurement may be more elusive, but it is an economic impact nonetheless. That is the business name recognition, the statement about quality, economic vibrancy and pro-business attitude that such entities give to the region by being here and investing so heavily and permanently in the life of the South Carolina Upstate.

It is an image not lost on many business leaders who visit here to observe, explore and consider the Upstate. It is an economic impact appreciated by anyone who promotes this region and understands the necessity of vigorous and wise business development. As CEO of the Spartanburg County Economic Development Corporation, Carter Smith is constantly looking for business firms that will consider locating in the area. He says GSP plays "a significant role" in his efforts. Smith says the airport's size and its location along the I-85 business corridor, and not far from Spartanburg, make it easy for busy clients to get in and out of the area quickly and efficiently. "The growth of nonstop destinations has also been fairly significant," Smith observes. In August of 2007, airlines serving GSP had nonstop flights to airports serving sixteen major cities where connections can be made to business centers worldwide. Smith also believes the airport and its cargo facilities help to give this area "tremendous potential" as a major cargo distribution center.[4]

Airport Commission vice chair Minor Shaw believes it is "more important than ever before" to position GSP as an economic engine for the Upstate. "We live and work in a global economy," says Shaw. "Many people can live anywhere in the world they wish. They just need to have ready access to the world." For transportation, Shaw says GSP provides that ready access by connecting people and companies with reasonably easy and quick access to almost anywhere for personal or business reasons. She notes the growth of the Upstate real estate market and the number of upscale communities built in recent years.[5] Developments like those along the lakes in Oconee and Pickens counties, like Carolina Country Club in Spartanburg, and like the Cliffs Communities in Greenville and other counties attract people who move here, sometimes bringing their companies, many times to enjoy an early and long retirement. Many are attracted by the beauty of the mountains and lakes, the probability of year-round outdoor activities, including the lure of golf. It helps that a world-renowned golfer like Gary Player would become an investor and enthusiastic promoter of one of the new Cliffs Communities in northern Greenville County and that one of the retired masters of the game, Jack Nicklaus, has designed courses in at least two other Cliffs Communities. Most of those new, upscale communities are less than an hour from commercial and private flights available at Greenville-Spartanburg Airport. For people with their own airplane transportation, some of those new communities are only a short distance from GSP or a smaller airport in Pickens or Anderson, downtown Greenville or downtown Spartanburg. With their ability to help people stay easily and quickly connected with the world by air, GSP and local airports in the years ahead will make the South Carolina Upstate an even more attractive place for those "who could live anywhere" to consider.

Chris Stone heads Greenville's Convention and Visitors Bureau. Conventions are a growing segment of the area's economy. "In order to attract conventions," Stone says, "you need good transportation infrastructure and the airport is an important part of that." Stone says conventions will not select a community unless they know they will have easy and convenient access in and out of it.[6] With two major interstate highways, a regional airport served by several major airlines and a general aviation operator and local airports for private and corporate fliers, the Upstate does offer easy and convenient access.

The Upstate Alliance, the economic development group that markets all ten Upstate counties, had its "best year yet in generating leads and prospects," *Greenville News* business editor Woody White reported on

March 28, 2007. President Hal Johnson told the Alliance's annual meeting that thirty-three prospect visits had been generated through the group's "global marketing initiatives" in 2006 and that it was working on 347 leads and prospects, a 14 percent increase over 2005.[7]

GSP became eligible for designation as an international airport in the early 1970s after it gained its customs port, agricultural inspection station and immigration office. Since the airport did not receive any regularly scheduled international flights, it did not promote its international designation until 1995 when BMW was building its plant next to the airport and was planning to have frequent international cargo flights. In the years since, BMW's plans changed and the company only infrequently flies heavy equipment through GSP. However, occasional international flights use the airport. At least, say officials, the airport can handle international passenger service—scheduled or charter—and they believe international cargo shipments will eventually increase as well.

Telling the story: marketing GSP

In its first thirty-five years of existence, GSP had little reason to spend money on marketing. Sure, the airport had competition. It did lose some passenger traffic to the larger hub airports on either side of it, Atlanta one hundred sixty miles to the west and Charlotte seventy miles to the east. However, what the airline industry calls "passenger leakage" was due primarily to fares and connections and there weren't many ways to market around that. So the goal was to keep the GSP name in the public's mind. That was accomplished by traditional public relations tactics like generating media stories and features, making speeches, and participating in community organizations and efforts. GSP officials always worked hard to expand name awareness, to build public and political appreciation for the airport and its services, and to maintain good relations with airlines and other on-site business interests.

In GSP's early years, those duties fell to the airport commissioners and executive director. As the airport grew, the part-time position of public relations director was created. Its first occupant was Jack Norris, a former longtime local newspaper reporter who served for several years until his death in 1992. His successor was Chris Reddick, who had been at GSP for several years as Delta Airline's station manager, the man responsible for directing Delta's operations at the airport. Shortly after Reddick retired from Delta, he returned to GSP to take the part-time public relations job, which he held until retiring for good in 1999.

When Rosylin Weston came to the public relations director's position in October of that year, the job was made full-time. Growing competition and complexity were presenting challenges that required sophisticated marketing to complement the traditional, and still needed, public relations efforts. GSP still was not big or busy enough to compete with the variety of flights, and sometimes the lower fares, that its neighboring airports in Charlotte and Atlanta could offer. But it could provide the South Carolina Upstate one important value: convenience. Weston and her colleagues decided to make convenience GSP's main selling point.

As early as 1979, executive director Dick Graham had used highway billboards to advertise the airport. It was in the months following deregulation when the airport was looking for more airlines and more passengers. Graham bought several billboard locations along I-85 in Greenville and Spartanburg counties with the catchy theme *We Have Connections in High Places.* In 2003, during another period of intense competition, the airport launched another major billboard campaign with the theme *Think GSP First.* It was aimed at business and tourist travelers who looked at cheaper fares and more nonstop flights offered from Charlotte and Atlanta. The campaign reminded area travelers that there were advantages other than fares to consider in choosing an airport from which to fly. Especially aimed at business travelers, GSP's message was that the relatively quick and easy drive to GSP was less stressful and saved time in comparison to the time required to drive, park and wait at the bigger hub airports. GSP's first billboard—placed along busy Interstate 85 on either side of the airport—showed a harried driver and carried the provocative message *If you'd flown into GSP airport, you'd be home by now.* To impress drivers headed home from Atlanta, the billboard facing the northbound lane showed a well-worn club bag and an Atlanta luggage tag. The board just north of the airport facing the southbound lane showed a "CLT" luggage tag. Response was positive enough that the billboard campaign evolved into wider advertising efforts.

"We don't have a huge marketing budget," Weston explained, "but we are strategic in our marketing efforts." Enough minds were changed and enough attitudes adjusted to minimize the loss of passengers. Nevertheless, during periods when GSP has no low-cost carrier to influence rates, some rate-driven passengers will embark elsewhere, no matter the extra drive time. To many business travelers to whom time is money, the matter of convenience and ease of travel keeps them using GSP. Jerry Howard, president of the Greenville Area Development Corporation, thinks convenience is perhaps GSP's greatest asset and one of its most powerful and legitimate claims. His organization's job is to recruit business firms to the area.

Ben Haskew would agree with Howard's assessment of GSP's value to the area. Haskew has had a unique vantage point from which to view GSP's influence. He was for several years president of the Spartanburg Chamber of Commerce before moving away and then returning to the Upstate as president of the Greater Greenville Chamber of Commerce. "GSP," says Haskew, "has been a centerpoint for development, an economic development asset and tool for the entire region." In fact, Haskew notes, "the airport has been the venue for many presentations to business prospects looking at the area." He agrees that convenience is one of the airport's major assets.

Rosylin Weston says GSP's convenience can be measured in several ways. Compared to larger airport terminals, she says GSP's walking distances are relatively short from parking to ticketing, from ticketing areas to gates, from gates to baggage claim to rental car areas. Once planes leave the gates, she says, they are usually in the air quickly, barring occasional weather problems or last-minute "holds" imposed by hub airports.

Over the years since its introduction in 2003, the *Think GSP First* campaign has been broadened. Ads have been carried, among other places, in the *Greenville, Spartanburg* and *Anderson Journals*, on the Clemson Football Radio Network, and in Convention and Visitor's Bureau publications. The Greenville Chamber of Commerce carries GSP ads online.

Online promotion has been a successful effort for the airport since it introduced its website in April of 2002. Its value was nominal for the first three years; however, its rebirth in early 2005 kick-started the effort. The website has not fallen below twenty-seven thousand hits in any month since March of 2005. By early 2007, monthly hits were averaging above forty-five thousand. Rosylin Weston knows why. "The reason is its breadth of information and services. Our website users like being able to make reservations easily and quickly. We utilize the same database as Orbitz and Priceline," she explained. "Our users can also book hotels and cars." The website's *Flight View* feature has also proved popular. It allows users to track flights and to check on current weather and forecasts. Best of all, as Weston sees it, the website is a vital way of maintaining GSP's visibility in a world that increasingly relies on electronic communications.

The website, gspairport.com, is all part of promoting—and proving—GSP's convenience. Weston says it is convenience that extends to providing customer service agents who help people into the terminal at peak travel times, that provides free carts in front of the terminal and in parking lots, that makes available wheelchairs and bilingual services. While Weston and the airport's other officials promote GSP's convenience of location, access and services, they are most proud of its convenience in flight schedules. Even though GSP is a regional airport, it offers nonstop flights to sixteen cities, many of which contain the nation's main hub airports for direct connections to dozens of major cities throughout the world. In 2007, the airlines serving GSP offered nonstop flights to New York (La Guardia), Newark, Washington, D.C. (Reagan and Dulles), Chicago, Dallas-Ft. Worth, Detroit, Memphis, Orlando, Cincinnati, Philadelphia, Tampa, Las Vegas, Cleveland and Houston, as well as to the nearby hubs of Atlanta and Charlotte.[8]

GSP is heavily dependent on business travelers. In 2006, they represented 55 percent of the airport's traffic. "Cost is relative to value," Weston claims. "Time is money to the business traveler." GSP, she says, can save people time and stress whether they are traveling for business or fun.

From 1953 to 1963, Donaldson Air Force Base near Greenville was the home of the USAF 63rd Troop Carrier Wing, whose huge C-124 Globemasters took personnel and equipment to research facilities in Antarctica and to the Cold War-era Distance Early Warning (DEW) radar line in the Arctic. COURTESY OF RON COPSEY.

This plaque was embedded in the runway just before the project to extend the runway to 11,001 feet ended in the spring of 1999. PHOTOGRAPH BY GREG MOSS.

Airport Executive Director A.R. (Dick) Graham and Alex Crouch, president of Piedmont Engineering Services, look at a horseshoe that was found on the airport property and placed in the original runway. Before the runway was resurfaced and lengthened in 1999 the horseshoe was removed and replaced in the runway. COURTESY GSP ARCHIVES.

Airmail at Greenville Municipal Airport, 1930. COURTESY OF THE GREENVILLE COUNTY (SC) HISTORICAL SOCIETY.

A.R. (Dick) Graham retired in 1989 after twenty-three years as GSP executive director.

J. Garrett Jackson became GSP's executive director in October 1989 after serving three years as deputy director.

CHAPTER 14

Passing Through GSP

Personalities

In the years since it opened in 1962, many of the world's celebrities have passed through the Greenville-Spartanburg Airport. Some have even stopped a while to make a speech or hold a news conference, for a campaign stop or a media interview, for a short visit with local friends or a quick look at the Milliken garden. One couple even stopped for a wedding.

Executive director Dick Graham had the privilege of getting two sports legends together for a picture when he learned that Glenn Cunningham and John Wooden would arrive at GSP on different flights at the same time. Cunningham was America's greatest distance runner of the 1930s. He set a world-record mile of four minutes, 6.7 seconds in 1934, and he won a silver medal in the 1,500-meter run at the Berlin Olympics in 1936. His success as a runner was remarkable since he had been badly burned in a fire at his school when he was eight. Doctors recommended amputating his legs but his mother refused. The doctors said he might never walk normally again. John Wooden was an All-American player at UCLA and coached the school's basketball team for twenty-seven seasons. He led the Bruins to 665 wins, four perfect seasons and ten national championships.

One of America's most famous crooners of the mid-1900s was Perry Como. He and his wife often passed through GSP on their way to visit friends in nearby Saluda, North Carolina. Como and Robert Pace, longtime owner of M. A. Pace General Store on Main Street, became good friends. "When Perry Como first showed up in Saluda, jaws dropped,"

Pace remembers.[1] In the "great old days" of radio and the exciting new days of television, Perry Como was a household name, as well known as Bing Crosby. He eventually bought a house in Saluda and in the early 1980s built a second one there. For years he and his wife, Roselle, were often seen at GSP. Octavia Williams met them several times. She was GSP's longtime information director, the person who staffed the information booth in the center of the terminal. One day when Como stopped by the booth, Mrs. Williams asked if he would be good enough to talk to her sister in Atlanta. When her sister answered the phone, she was shocked to be greeted by none other than Perry Como. Another time, a World War II veteran who was passing through the airport and heard Mrs. Williams' voice on the pager, walked up and told her she sounded like Tokyo Rose.[2] In her almost thirty years at GSP, until her retirement in January of 1992, Octavia Williams met or saw many famous personalities. She even remembers Ronald Reagan visiting back in the days when he was a spokesman for General Electric, long before he entered presidential politics.

The list of famous people who have passed through GSP since its 1962 opening goes on and on: Bill Cosby, James Earl Jones, Richard Pryor, Beverly Sills, Billy Graham, Bob Hope, pianist Liberace, baseball ambassador Tommy LaSorda, dancer Gene Kelly, Eva Gabor, Dolly Parton, Olivia de Havilland, Dick Clark and many of the great performers who have starred at the Peace Center or other university and community venues throughout the Upstate, even Maria von Trapp of *Sound of Music* fame and dozens of other entertainers, writers, politicians, and notables. Of course, one of Hollywood's longest-married couples, Paul Newman and Joanne Woodward, have been through the airport many times. Ms. Woodward lived in Greenville in some of her teenage years and attended Greenville High School. One still-famous TV celebrity made the mistake of visiting GSP on a Sunday. Bar closed, no drinks, Regis Philbin wasn't happy. Airport staffers were able to find something to quench his thirst.

Famous people are more frequent now than they were in the early days of GSP. So their passing through may not attract as much attention. In fact, as more entertainers come to the area to perform or famous golfers come to play in charity tournaments, many of them arrive in private aircraft and never walk the halls of GSP's terminal.

Paul Fesperman and Gayle Kurtz wanted all their families and friends at their wedding. Problem...their families were all over: Florida, Wisconsin, Arizona, and South Carolina. They decided to take their wedding—or weddings—to them. So on Saturday, September 28, 1985, Paul and Gayle were married three times. They started with a 9:00 a.m. ceremony conducted by Paul's dad, a Lutheran minister at Newberry College. Other Fesperman family members came from Florida. The first wedding was held on the patio of the garden between the runway and GSP's terminal. That was convenient because it was just a short walk to the Delta jet for a flight to Atlanta and on to Minneapolis for wedding number two for Gayle's parents and Wisconsin friends to witness. Finally, a nonstop flight to Phoenix and wedding number three at the home of Gayle's sister, followed by an Arizona honeymoon. The Fespermans live not far from GSP.

Presidents and Air Force One

United States presidents always attract attention and their visits require plenty of airport preparation. Unlike visits during the early days, intense security now surrounds presidents at GSP. Air Force One parks at a remote site away from the terminal where public contact is minimal and carefully arranged. Presidents no longer "work the line," shake hands with admirers and hold babies for camera bugs. Now, when Air Force One is scheduled into GSP, airport officials and police work with area police, sheriff deputies and other local, state and federal officials, coordinating security with Secret Service and White House advance personnel. There is no longer a possibility that excited followers can break through police lines as they did when Republican presidential nominee Barry Goldwater came to GSP in 1964. Security personnel are everywhere, visibility is limited, contact, except for a select and carefully screened few, is nonexistent. Nevertheless, with South Carolina's rising importance in national politics, presidents and would-be presidents still pass through GSP as they have for years.

Richard Nixon and his wife, Pat, stopped in October of 1968 amidst his election campaign. The crowd was kept to five hundred at the airport but thousands greeted the president in downtown Greenville where he was welcomed by his state campaign manager, General Mark Clark. Clark was one of the powerful army generals of World War II and years later served as president of The Citadel in Charleston.

Our only nonelected president—Gerald Ford—visited on October 19, 1974, on his way to a "salute to the president" rally at Greenville Memorial Auditorium. He had moved into the White House just two months before, following the resignation of President Nixon. Future governor Jim Edwards, Secretary of Commerce Fred Dent from Spartanburg, and a young, promising Republican, future governor Carroll Campbell, were all there along with Senator Strom Thurmond, who introduced the president. Another Spartanburg County native, retired General William Westmoreland, also spoke that day.

Firemen are famous for keeping their fire trucks clean and shiny. On the morning of Tuesday, September 16, 1980, the firemen at Spartanburg's central station were busy washing, but not a fire truck. It was the presidential limousine. A U.S. Air Force cargo plane had delivered the president's sleek black Cadillac to GSP Monday night. Secret Service agents drove it to the central fire station where it was guarded overnight and washed the next morning. A short time later, the sparkling limousine was back at GSP to pick up President Jimmy Carter and deliver him to several campaign stops. Ronald Reagan came more than once for campaign visits and as president. George Bush Sr., Bill Clinton and George W. Bush also flew into GSP on Air Force One.

From Local Boy to Presidential Pilot
The Story of Gary Nelson

"We have probably one of the best airports in the world. Greenville-Spartanburg has good facilities, is well-maintained and attractive. As a pilot, I like it because it's safe and has a long runway. GSP is a good representation of the people of this area."

Gary Nelson has plenty of experience to judge airports, GSP in particular. Since 1995, he has flown in and out of GSP on his way to and from Louisville and his international cargo carrying missions for UPS. Before that, he spent twenty-one years in the U.S. Air Force, the last five of those years flying Air Force One and taking the president of the United States on more than two hundred fifty trips. He flew the backup Air Force One on another two hundred fifty presidential trips. During his air force and UPS careers, Nelson has landed at hundreds of airports throughout the world.

Gary Nelson's interest in aviation began when he was about ten. A brief ride out of Greenville's downtown airport in a twin-engine Piper Comanche was all it took. Soon after his education in Greenville public schools—Overbrook-Eastover, Greenville Junior High and Greenville High—he joined the ROTC while studying administrative management at Clemson University. After Clemson, he entered the air force and earned his wings. After six years of flying C-130s on special missions, he was transferred in 1980 to Germany and piloted a DC-9 "flying hospital" transporting sick and injured military personnel, spouses and premature babies from bases throughout Europe, Asia and Africa to military hospitals in Germany.

In 1983 Nelson was assigned to the 89th Military Airlift Wing at Andrews Air Force Base outside Washington, D.C. For the next six years he flew American officials and visiting dignitaries across America and the world. Nelson wanted, someday, to be one of the president's pilots. You could not interview or lobby for the job. The leader of the elite group was officially "the president's pilot." When he flew a mission with the president, he was always in the cockpit's left seat. He was the captain. However, all four of the pilots certified to fly the president had to have captain's rating. Nelson knew if he were ever to make it into the small elite group of presidential pilots he would just have to wait and hope. Meantime he was paying his dues. He flew many types of planes. He had even earned his master's degree in aeronautical sciences at Embry-Riddle Aeronautical University in Florida; but Nelson wanted the opportunity to fly Air Force One.

"I want you to do me a favor," Colonel Bob Ruddick told the thirty-seven-year-old pilot. It was the fall of 1988. The official president's pilot explained the favor he needed. "I want you to go to school and get qualified for the new Boeing 747." Gary Nelson knew exactly what that meant. He was being chosen to be one of the pilots who would fly the president. Presidents from JFK to Ronald Reagan had used a Boeing 707. Recognizing that the president now needed a bigger, faster, more technologically-advanced plane, President Reagan had ordered Boeing to design and build a new Air Force One, a B-747. Colonel Ruddick needed Nelson to spend two months at Boeing's plant in Edmunds, Washington. He would watch the last of the plane's construction, study all of its systems and be one of the first to test fly it. Eventually he would train the other pilots on the new plane.

Having answered Col. Ruddick's request to do him a favor, Nelson was ecstatic. He went home and broke the news to his wife. Katrina Blair Nelson is the granddaughter of former Greenville mayor Jess Helms.

After his two months at Boeing, Nelson spent several months in Wichita, Kansas, watching every detail of the new Air Force One's interior upfitting. Meantime he was occasionally flying the new president, George Herbert Walker Bush, in one of the small Gulfstream jets that are used for short trips to smaller airports that cannot accommodate the large presidential jet. Nelson's dream of flying the president on the new Air Force One Boeing 747 was realized on September 7, 1990, when he took President Bush to Helsinki for a summit with Soviet President Mikhail Gorbachev. They returned to Andrews Air Force Base two days later. The last flight he captained was September 4, 1994, when he flew President Clinton to New Orleans to address the Southern Baptist Convention.

"It was a tremendous responsibility," Nelson recognized. "There's no room for error when you are flying anyone, particularly the president of the United States." Years after his last presidential flight, Nelson still is excited when he sees the huge Boeing 747, with its brilliant blue and white color, the American flag on its side and the words "United States of America" emblazoned on both sides. "Air Force One is a symbol of America's power and prestige and the office of the president," says Nelson. "I am grateful and proud that I had the opportunity to fly the president. I miss it and I think I always will," Nelson reflects. By the end of 1994, it was time to hand over the responsibility, Nelson says, "and come back home to Greenville."[3]

CHAPTER 15

Completing Forty-Five Years: 2000–2007

The day the skies emptied: 9-11-01 and the good story of Gander and Lewisporte

August 22, 2001—Tri-County Technical Education College President Don Garrison and his wife, Carol, leave GSP bound for a Norwegian vacation.
September 8, 2001—Interim Healthcare owner Ray Schroeder flies out of GSP with his family to attend a business meeting in Halifax, Nova Scotia.
September 9, 2001—US Airways pilot Mike Martin drives from his Greenville area home to GSP and catches a flight to Philadelphia. His crew flies an Airbus the next day to London. He does it almost every week. A routine flight for Martin. A routine out-of-country business trip for Schroeder. A routine overseas journey for the Garrisons. Their trips this time will be anything but routine and their return to GSP will be much later than expected.
September 11, 2001—7:58 A.M. United Air Lines Flight 175 departs Boston for Los Angeles, fifty-six passengers, two pilots, seven flight attendants on board the Boeing 767.
7:59 A.M. American Airlines Flight 11 departs Boston for Los Angeles, eighty-one passengers, two pilots, nine flight attendants on board the Boeing 767.
8:01 A.M. United Air Lines Flight 93 departs Newark, thirty-eight passengers, two pilots, five flight attendants on board the Boeing 757.
8:10 A.M. American Airlines Flight 77 departs Dulles, fifty-eight passengers, two pilots, four flight attendants on board the Boeing 757.

The picturesque entry drive looks particularly beautiful this clear, late summer morning as Gary Jackson drives into the airport he has managed for almost twelve years. It's shortly after 8:30 on Tuesday, September 11, 2001. The terminal at Greenville-Spartanburg is busy with hundreds of people boarding flights to Atlanta, Charlotte, Cincinnati and other cities. A few hundred feet away, in the Airport Commission offices near the control tower, Jackson sits down at his desk. A short time later the phone rings, a call from his fire department. An airplane has just struck the north tower of the World Trade Center in New York. Jackson notices the time. It's just before 9:00.[1] Moments later, another call. Another plane has struck the south tower of the Trade Center. They were big planes, passenger jets. Both towers are burning. All New York area airports are closing.

9:45 A.M.—The FAA grounds all domestic flights and orders flights coming to the United States to divert. Gary Jackson's job, like that of every other commercial airport manager in the country, is about to change. From now on, it will be much more difficult. Airport life—for *everyone*—will be different.

The curtains of the crew rest seat part suddenly. A colleague tells the chief flight attendant to go to the cockpit immediately. The captain shares the printed message just received. "All airways over the continental United States are closed. Land ASAP at the nearest airport. Advise your destination." Atlanta-bound Delta 15 is more than five hours out of Frankfurt, already over the western North Atlantic. The captain's request to turn right and head for Gander is approved immediately. Delta 15 will soon be in Newfoundland.[2]

In the eastern Canadian port city of Halifax, Ray Schroeder's meeting is interrupted by a rapid knock on the door. Schroeder's wife has been watching television in the hotel room and has come with a terrible message.

"Our country has been attacked," she tells the group. "Two planes have struck the World Trade Center and both towers are burning." Moments later Schroeder's meeting breaks up. It doesn't resume.[3]

At Greenville-Spartanburg, Gary Jackson and his staff are busy. Chief Tommy Watson has called all of his airport police to duty. Passengers waiting for canceled flights are leaving for homes or hotels. The airport is on alert to accept diversions. All vehicles are being moved from near the terminal. Within two hours, Watson and his officers have shut down the airport.

On Philadelphia-bound US Airways 99 Mike Martin and his two flight deck crew mates receive a printout from US Airways' Pittsburgh operations center: "All U.S. air space has been shut down. Need to divert to Gander or return to Gatwick. Please advise." Now, almost to the midpoint of the North Atlantic, most of the passengers are resting, unaware they are returning to London…or why.[4]

GSP's terminal is growing eerily quiet. So are American skies. For the first time in our nation's aviation history, all civil aviation aircraft are being grounded. Except for military pilots who are patrolling the skies for enemies, protecting our country, America's skies are rapidly growing empty, silent. Most Americans are watching television, at home, in offices, in store showrooms, anywhere. Every television has the same shocking pictures: New York City; now the Pentagon, where American Flight 77 crashed at 9:45. And there is one plane still unaccounted for. Some Americans are watching television far from home.

Having just returned from an enjoyable cruise along the west coast of Norway, Don and Carol Garrison begin their last afternoon in Oslo with a walk. It is a walk cut short. They pass a group of people standing on the sidewalk watching television in a store window. That's when the Garrisons first hear the story. That's when they begin to feel very far from home. They return to their hotel room and for the next four hours sit on the bed, staring at the TV, like everyone else wanting not to believe what they are seeing and hearing. The fourth plane that had been missing has crashed in a Pennsylvania farm field. The Garrisons had already packed most of their luggage but they realize they will not be leaving Norway tomorrow.[5]

~

As Mike Martin's US Airways flight heads back to London, Delta 15 approaches Gander, its passengers still unaware of exactly what is happening. Soon they will know the real story, some of it. As their plane touches down the passengers see more than twenty other big jets already parked at Gander. They know something is terribly wrong. As soon as he can, Captain Michael Sweeney shares what few grim details he already knows. His calm demeanor keeps everyone else calm. In the hours that follow, he updates his passengers with information he has received from monitoring the BBC. It is 11:00 a.m. Eastern time, *12:30 p.m.* Gander time. It will be a long time before the passengers of Delta 15 leave their plane.

~

"Things will never be the same again," manager Gary Jackson is telling reporters at GSP. "This has been too big a strike against our way of life." Jackson warns there will probably be many changes depending on what measures the FAA determines are needed to prevent anything like this from happening again." He has no way of knowing just how many changes there would be.

~

It is 6:00 p.m. in London as US Airways 99 finally lands at Gatwick. On the long taxi to the gate, the passengers are given what few details the crew has. The passengers are in London instead of Philadelphia. At least they are safe. They can leave their plane.

In Gander, the crew and their 218 passengers aboard Delta 15 are safe too, but still on their plane. They come from several countries: Germany, Switzerland, India. There is a large group from Ukraine. Gander airport is jammed with jets from many airlines. They are being inspected one at a time. DL 15 is number fourteen in the U.S. category. Its passengers and crew will deplane at 11:00 *tomorrow* morning.

Five hundred miles west of Gander, dozens of flights have diverted to Halifax as they have to other major Canadian airports. His meeting suddenly disbanded, Ray Schroeder and his family have nowhere to go. Halifax airport is closed. All flights are canceled indefinitely. Rental cars for crossing into the United States are unavailable. Halifax is to be the Schroeder family's home for the next four days.

At Greenville-Spartanburg Airport, not only are the aprons in front of the terminal quiet, so are the aprons in front of the cargo buildings. The cargo carriers are having to move all of their packages and heavy freight by truck. Just like passenger planes, all the cargo aircraft have been grounded as well, except for one. On orders from the federal government, a UPS jet carrying needed equipment and supplies from the West Coast to the East Coast is on a long and lonely flight through America's empty skies.[6]

Wednesday, September 12, the day that Tri-County TEC's president and his wife were to fly home. Instead, Don and Carol Garrison take another walk in downtown Oslo, amazed at the kindness and sympathies extended by Norwegians. With American air space closed indefinitely, the Garrisons' Norwegian vacation is being extended several more days.

Normally, GSP would have been busy on this Wednesday morning, but Operations Supervisor Fred Bright finds it strangely quiet as he walks through the deserted terminal. Only GSP employees—security personnel, firemen, others—are here. There were some visitors last evening. Family members and employees from nearby restaurants had brought meals for the employees who were guarding the empty airport.

At 10:30 Wednesday morning at Gander, thousands of "visitors" are adjusting to the odd time. Newfoundland is in a special time zone, an hour and a half ahead of Eastern time. The crew and passengers who have been sitting on Delta 15 for twenty-four hours are told to prepare for deplaning. The crew is taken to one section for immigration and customs and then driven in vans to a small hotel in Gander. The passengers are processed and driven twenty-five miles to the town of Lewisporte. In both communities, the people from DL 15 are about to experience the unique and generous hospitality of Newfoundlanders. Mayor Bill Hooper had received the call for help at 4:00 p.m. Tuesday. Within an hour, he had assembled leaders from the community and they began planning for their visitors.

Newfoundland is a mountainous island in the Atlantic, discovered in 1497 by explorer John Cabot who called it "New Found Isle." About the size of two South Carolinas, along with mainland Labrador it is the easternmost of Canada's ten provinces, known officially since 2001 as the province of Newfoundland and Labrador. Its major industries are energy, fisheries, mining, forestry and tourism. The economy can be challenging, the weather difficult, but the indomitable spirit and generosity of its people are legendary, especially in times of crisis.

Most who landed in Newfoundland on 9-11—like many Americans—had likely never heard of Gander. None will ever forget it. Yet anyone who has flown the North Atlantic route has been on a plane under the watchful eye of air traffic controllers at Gander, Newfoundland. In the days of propeller-driven aircraft, a flight from London or other European cities to any of the airports in eastern Canada or the northeastern United States required a refueling stop at Gander. The airport was originally built as a military base, shared by Canada, the U.S. and Great Britain. When it opened in 1938, Gander was the largest airport in the world. With long, thick runways it could accommodate the world's heaviest planes. American planes bound to and from World War II stopped in Gander for refueling. The town of Gander was developed *after* Gander airport was built. Some of its streets are named for famous aviators like Charles Lindbergh, Admiral Richard Byrd, and American Chuck Yeager, the first pilot to break the sound barrier.[7]

Since Gander is both a military and civilian airport, it has often been a safe haven for military, commercial or private planes that have encountered difficulty on the North Atlantic route. It was also the site of the worst air disaster in Canadian history. On December 12, 1985, a charter transport crashed just after takeoff from Gander killing all 248 members of the U.S. Army's 101st Airborne Division who were on board. It was also near Gander that famed Canadian medical scientist Dr. Frederick Banting was killed when the military airplane in which he was flying crashed after takeoff in February of 1941. Banting was the co-discoverer of insulin. He was just forty-nine.[8]

The thirty-eight jets that landed at Gander on September 11, 2001, carried 6600 passengers and crew. The town of Gander has only ten thousand residents, but they and their neighbors in nearby towns cared for everyone.[9] The visitors could not believe it!

It is early afternoon when the buses carrying 773 passengers from DL 15, DL 129, and a plane each from Continental and American begin arriving in Lewisporte—population four thousand! The passengers have nothing; their luggage is still on their planes. No matter. The people of Lewisporte have all the passengers will need. Every large public place in town—the high school, Kiwanis and Kinsmen clubs and two church halls—is prepared. Food, beverages, cots, mats, sleeping bags, blankets, pillows, linens, toiletries, everything is ready. All of it provided by families, organizations, stores. Families are kept together. Women who wish are taken to a women-only facility. Elderly passengers have no choice. They are kept in private homes. A young pregnant passenger is placed in a private home across from a twenty-four-hour urgent care facility. Nurses and DSS workers stay with the passengers. Everyone can make a phone call or send an e-mail once a day. Passengers are offered "excursions" to shop, see the countryside, take a boat ride. (Lewisporte sits on the Atlantic coast.) They are given tokens to the laundromat. They are taken to eat in restaurants and invited into homes for meals. Residents of Lewisporte and surrounding towns have rolled out the red carpet, just like Gander, Appleton, and other nearby towns. Airplane crews are kept at hotels in Gander so they can be quickly available if needed at the airport.

On Thursday, September 13, airports across America begin coming to life again. At 12:34 p.m. ET, the FAA says flights may resume. Word spreads. Passengers begin arriving. At GSP, as at all other American airports, life is suddenly different. Cars are searched before reaching terminals, no curbside luggage check-in, passengers only to the gate areas, knives and other items no longer allowed. Passengers soon discover they must arrive early, at least two hours before flight time the FAA says. Security personnel are everywhere. There are new and tighter procedures. Processing passengers requires much more time than ever before. At GSP, it is 4:39 p.m. before the first flight departs. Gary Jackson was right: *things will never be the same again.*

It is Friday, September 14. By noon, Mike Martin's US Airways flight will be leaving Gatwick after three days of waiting. Flights have been rearranged, though, and this time Martin's plane is flying to Pittsburgh instead of Philadelphia. It will be one of the first flights returning to the United States since Tuesday's attacks. Despite natural feelings of anxiety, the flight is uneventful. The landing in Pittsburgh is greeted with applause from relieved passengers grateful to be safely back in the United States.

Later that day Mike Martin catches a flight home to Greenville. He has the feeling shared by many whose lives have been disrupted and changed this week. "It's great to be home again," he thinks as his plane taxis toward the terminal. As Martin drives out of GSP toward his Greenville area home, Ray Schroeder is still in Halifax where he has finally managed to rent a van. Tomorrow he and his family will head for the border, cross over into Maine and begin their four-day drive back to Greenville.

Friday morning is a happy time for the crew and passengers of DL 15. The *plane people*—as the Newfoundlanders called their visitors from all the jets that had landed at Gander—are boarding their plane for the flight to Atlanta. The passengers are telling their stories about the people of Lewisporte—their hospitality, kindness, generosity, sharing. They tell the crew about the facilities, the excursions, the shopping trips, the home-cooked meals.[10] They discuss how Mayor Hooper had arranged for everyone to have the opportunity to make calls and send e-mails back home. As the trip to Atlanta begins, two of the passengers, Shirley Brooks-Jones, a retired employee of Ohio State University and Dr. Robert Ferguson, a physician from Winston-Salem, North Carolina, begin talking about establishing a scholarship fund to help Lewisporte Collegiate students wanting to continue their education beyond high school. After some discussion and with the help of several other passengers, they quickly design and distribute pledge cards and Shirley Brooks-Jones from Columbus, Ohio, receives permission from Captain

Sweeney to read a statement to the passengers that Dr. Ferguson had written. It explains a scholarship fund will be established and asks passengers to make pledges as a way of thanking their Lewisporte hosts. By the time the initial descent into Atlanta begins, the passengers and crew of DL 15 have pledged almost fifteen thousand dollars, that would be worth twenty thousand dollars in Canadian funds. The campaign didn't end there. Delta added a generous corporate gift and Shirley Brooks-Jones began making speeches and collecting donations all around Columbus. Having fallen in love with the people of Lewisporte, she returns every year for September 11 and for the June high school graduation. In 2006, the faculty and students made her the school's first honorary alumna. In its first six years, the fund, administered by the Columbus (Ohio) Community Foundation, had provided sixty-nine scholarships. By the spring of 2007, there was almost seventy thousand dollars in the fund.[11] "It means a lot to our students," says assistant principal Rex Clements.[12]

Lewisporte received help in others ways too. Mayor Hooper says a Rockefeller Foundation official who was aboard one of the flights made arrangements for a seventy-five thousand dollar donation to the middle school for computers, and he says a Delta official aboard Flight DL 129 made arrangements for provision of a community room at the Calypso Centre, a facility for handicapped people.[13] Meanwhile, Shirley Brooks-Jones has bought a life insurance policy. The beneficiary: the collegiate scholarship fund. She intends for it to grow and help students there for a long time because the people of Lewisporte are special. Bill Hooper, the town's mayor since 1995, tries to explain. "We live in a small town where most everyone knows each other. That's the way we help each other. So when someone in need comes along, we help them too." On September 12, 13 and 14, 2001, 773 from many countries needed help. So the people of Lewisporte and neighboring towns did what they always do. Just as the residents of Gander and other Newfoundland towns did.

In Oslo, Don and Carol Garrison are still impressed with the continuing kindness and caring of the Norwegian people. Around the King's Palace and in front of the American Embassy in Oslo they have watched — Americans and Norwegians — leaving flowers, writing messages, saying prayers, some crying, many fighting back tears.

Now it is early Tuesday morning, September 18. The Garrisons are boarding a Lufthansa flight, finally leaving Oslo. When they land in Frankfurt, they are checked three times before reaching their Delta flight. The pilot's words are comforting and welcome. "Ladies and gentlemen, everything has been checked. We'll get you home to America safely." Moments later, Don and Carol Garrison are on their way to Cincinnati and then the short hop to Greenville-Spartanburg. "GSP. This is home," Garrison says to his wife as their plane lands. They love the sense of security, the feeling of being safe again.

~

Ray and Charyl Schroeder and their family are nearing the end of their emotional journey. Flags everywhere. *We love America* signs unfurled on overpasses. Bumper stickers extolling the strength of America. They pass New York City and see the smoke rising from Ground Zero. They are saddened by the destruction at the Pentagon. As they drive south toward their Spartanburg County home, the feeling, the whole traveling family agrees, is surreal. They feel the comfort of being in their own country, but a country that is at war, not as safe and impenetrable as it had once been.

~

Indeed, airports were reminders that America was in a new war. Sheriff's deputies and area police had been helping at GSP. On September 26, just two weeks after the terrorist attacks and on order of President Bush, the states' governors ordered the National Guard mobilized to help protect the nation's airports. Governor Jim Hodges deployed guard members to all six of South Carolina's commercial airports. They arrived at GSP on

October 3, their main job to search the 2,500 to 3,000 vehicles entering the airport each day. At a security post erected on the entry road between the front lawn and a parking garage, guardsmen inspected back seats, trunks, tool boxes—any place where forbidden items could be hidden, or placed by mistake. The National Guard was on the job for weeks. Meanwhile, GSP was increasing its own security. There were sixteen security posts throughout the airport instead of just three before 9-11. Gary Jackson said GSP was adding twenty-three security employees.

While security officers were being added, GSP's police chief Tommy Watson and officer Jackie Mathis were called north to help counsel New York City officers who had lost so many of their colleagues. Forty-five policemen, 343 firemen and thirty-seven officers of the Ports Authority of New York and New Jersey died in the September 11 attacks. Watson and Mathis had received crisis counseling training from the National Organization for Victim Assistance. They were needed in New York City. Less than two weeks after the attacks, they spent a four-day weekend there. Two of those days they counseled officers right at Ground Zero.[14]

In the weeks and months following 9-11, while costs were increasing, passenger traffic was decreasing. All of GSP's airlines had reduced flights. Midway Airlines had ceased operations in the market. By the end of September, the airport's daily seat capacity had dropped by a thousand, from 5,300 to 4,300.

In the months ahead, airports would change even more as they tried to find room for large, new baggage checking machines and more space to check passengers. They would need space to accommodate dozens, in some airports hundreds, of new employees. All the changes were costly. Many of the mandated ones would eventually be covered by federal funds. Others would be paid for by the airports. Just the additional security people that Gary Jackson had said he needed at GSP would cost an initial one hundred thousand dollars. Passenger revenues had declined but cargo was back to normal and strong. Airport Commission Chairman Roger Milliken assured the public that GSP was still "in a very strong position" financially.

One fact was clear: life at America's airports would never be the same, or as easy, again; but everyone was working hard to keep the nation's aviation system safe. Airports *were* changing. The need for tighter security and greater protection prompted most of those changes.

Transportation Security Administration

Just two months after 9-11, Congress passed the Air Transportation Security Act on November 19, 2001. It created a new agency, the Transportation Security Administration, within the new Department of Homeland Security. Hiring began in early 2002. By December of that year, 55,000 Transportation Security Officers (TSOs) had been hired and trained. Dressed in dark blue and white uniforms they "federalized"—as the department called it—the nation's 469 commercial airports, screening all passengers and inspecting all baggage.

By late 2002, GSP had as many as 128 TSOs. By the spring of 2007, the number of full-time and part-time agents, all employees of the federal government, had been reduced slightly. By then, procedures had been streamlined and the majority of fliers were grateful for, cooperative with and resigned to the realization that the security measures were permanent. "Passengers have a responsibility to assist with the security process," Mike Tarman tells organizations which he frequently addresses. Tarman is the Federal Security Director, the man who hires, trains and supervises the TSOs at GSP. "The speed with which we can process through x-ray," says Tarman, "depends on the cooperation of passengers." Almost six years past 9-11, Tarman observed in April of 2007 that many passengers still do not know—or forget—the rules. Sometimes those rules change.

After the London transit scare in late 2006, for example, most liquids were banned. Security lines grew long again at GSP and most airports while fliers grew accustomed to the new restrictions.

With new government rules always come new passenger reasons—or excuses—for carrying illegal substances through screening. When a university student had his bottled water taken away at GSP, he complained, "I didn't know water was a liquid." Another student's backpack contained a hairless rat. Tarman said his officers made other arrangements so the student didn't lose his pet. Another of Tarman's agents at the airport had a surprise. In a passenger's bag, the agent found three frozen squirrels. They passed inspection. Dead squirrels pose no harm. Tarman is still amazed at the number of pistols, knives and lighters his officers confiscate. The most common excuse: "I forgot I had it." "Thirty to forty containers of liquid are confiscated at each checkpoint on each shift," Tarman explained. That, observed Tarman, speaks to the need for more passenger responsibility. He says 90 percent of passengers are informed, cooperative and polite. "Another five percent are, as well," says Tarman "but they think we are wasting time. It's the other five percent that cause TSOs the most problems." The safety director says his officers have been cussed at, pushed, kicked and verbally threatened. He says almost two-thirds of the airport's passengers are business travelers. "They fly frequently, know the rules and have the process down pat," says Tarman. "It's the occasional and leisure traveler who has more difficulty keeping up with the rules and requirements."[15]

A retired, career military policeman, Mike Tarman was one of the first federal safety directors hired in 2002. While still living in Arizona, he and his wife studied possible airport locations, visited the Upstate, applied for the job and arrived at GSP on July 26, 2002. "We have no regrets about coming here," says Tarman. "This is a great airport. In fact, we plan to retire in this area." Not bad for a couple who had already bought a retirement home in Arizona before they found an unexpected opportunity and a new area they could call home in the South Carolina Upstate.

More than an airport

"Consider the Upstate without GSP. It would be incredibly different." On this morning of October 30, 2006, the mayor of Spartanburg is reflecting on the regional airport and its influence on the area.

"GSP is not just an airport," says William Barnet III. "It is a beautiful space, strong on aesthetics and functionality. It is a melding of buildings and landscaping, a most attractive place, beautifully conceived." The mayor's appreciation for GSP goes far beyond beauty. This urbane, international businessman says the airport is at the core of the region's success in attracting business, especially investment from overseas. "Who we are today," Barnet claims, "is in large measure impacted by the influence of so many foreign firms. It has been healthy for Spartanburg and has sustained our economy."

Mayor Barnet's appreciation for the positive impact of business development in his city, particularly that from overseas, is driven by his own experience. His father first ventured south and opened a plant in nearby Tryon, North Carolina. Then Barnet moved from Albany, New York, in 1976 to establish the company's international headquarters. He sold the fourth-generation firm to a group of associates in 2001 before becoming mayor. During his thirty-one years in Spartanburg, Barnet has been a supporter of recruiting overseas firms. In his view, that vision to attract international business has made Spartanburg a better city. "It is tough," says the mayor, "to picture BMW in a lesser community." And BMW, he believes, makes the area even better. "We have a sense of pride that they selected this area and that they run such a professional company. That reflects well on all of us. It lifts us all up."

That pride, says the mayor, has helped him and Spartanburg's leadership to "refocus on the resources and potential of our city's central business district." He points to the number of Fortune 500 companies in the city, the private capital raised for the Chapman Cultural Center, the number of people moving back to downtown, and the "huge international flavor" of his city. "Firms from more than thirty countries have plants in and around Spartanburg," the mayor says proudly. He knows one of the reasons why. He had been out at GSP one day and saw a 747 land on that 11,001-foot runway. "And I thought," said Barnet, "GSP is an enduring gift that Roger Milliken, Charlie Daniel and other leaders who had the vision made possible. It's a source of great pride. And," says the mayor, "I love going to GSP and welcoming guests. The airport makes a statement about the pride of our people and our focus on quality."[16]

Milliken field, 10-15-04

More than two hundred invited guests were gathered in Windows restaurant. On October 15, 1962, Airport Commission chairman Roger Milliken had addressed GSP's opening day crowd. Now, forty-two years later, Milliken was still chairman and he would have another opportunity to speak. On this evening, October 15, 2004, several people wanted to talk to and about *him*. Everyone was there to recognize Roger Milliken for his long years of service to the airport. Indeed, by the fall of 2004, it had been forty-seven years since Charlie Daniel, Walter Brown and Alester Furman Jr. had met with Milliken and asked him to lead the effort to establish a regional airport. Then at the first meeting of the newly appointed Airport Commission, in 1959, he was elected chairman.

The printed program for the evening included the text of a concurrent resolution that both houses of the South Carolina General Assembly had adopted on June 2, 2004. It honored Milliken "for his contributions to the Greenville-Spartanburg International Airport" and requested that the Airport Commission name its airfield "Roger Milliken Field." Executive Director Gary Jackson introduced a video that had been produced for the occasion. It showed highlights in the development of GSP and featured comments from Jackson, retired executive director Dick Graham and others. Commissioner Valerie Miller, state Senator Verne Smith of Greer, and Representative David Wilkins of Greenville, speaker of the South

Carolina House, paid tribute to the chairman and shared their thoughts and memories about Milliken's leadership of and commitment to the airport.

The program also included a resolution adopted by the Airport Commission on June 15. Vice chair Minor Shaw announced the naming of the airfield in Milliken's honor and unveiled a statue, conceived by Wallace Storey, approved by the commission and sculpted by Dennis Smith, the same Utah craftsman who had sculpted the figures in the airport's garden. Called *Boy Aviator*, it depicts a young boy, with goggles propped on his head, holding an old two-engine biplane at his side in his left hand and raising high above his head in his right hand a modern, swept-wing, two-engine jet; the boy is looking up at the jet. The face of the boy is a likeness of Roger Milliken in his youth. Except during the Christmas season when the poinsettia tree sits in the terminal's atrium fountain area, the statue stands on a pedestal in the middle of the atrium's lighted pool surrounded by eight jets of water. A plaque says the statue commemorates Milliken's "vision of a modern and greater airport for the Upstate of South Carolina."

Roger Milliken was moved by the tribute. As he typically does when he is recognized for his work on behalf of the airport, he gave credit to his friend and cofounder Charlie Daniel and to the team of visionaries and leaders who made the airport possible and have operated it for more than four decades.

In the years since the statue's placement amidst the atrium's pool, it has attracted the attention of fliers and visitors. It is not unusual to see a child staring at the little statue, perhaps developing a fantasy for airplanes and a desire for the excitement of flight. (See the story of sculptors Dennis Smith and Jim Dolan in Chapter 7.)

New entrance, new roads

As automobile traffic in and out of GSP grew and truck traffic increased around the next-door BMW plant, already busy I-85 between Highways

14 and 101 grew even busier and more dangerous. The Airport Commission wanted Exit 57 off I-85 more streamlined to provide easier and safer access to the airport. The commission also had long-range plans to widen its entrance road to four lanes. Chairman Roger Milliken had had discussions with State Department of Transportation director Elizabeth Mabry about the possibility of improving the Exit 57 interchange. However, no funding was available at the time. Meanwhile, the State Department of Commerce had been working with BMW on plans for developing a new interchange at Brockman-McClimon Road, about halfway between Highways 14 and 101 and not far from the airport entrance. The state legislature had already allocated funding for that interchange.

DOT's Mabry and Federal Highways administrator Bob Lee discussed the possibility of combining the projects. They believed BMW and the airport could benefit by working on a project that would improve safety and ultimately save both entities time, trouble and perhaps money. Mabry reopened discussions with Roger Milliken and the Airport Commission. The commission agreed to make available two million dollars worth of land, three million dollars of its FAA entitlement funds and provide help with landscaping. As a result of the Airport Commission's offer of assistance on the airport's interchange, highway officials determined that the Brockman-McClimon Road interchange and the airport's interchange could be built at the same time.[17]

While that construction was in progress along I-85 in front of the airport, Exit 57 would have to be closed and traffic would be rerouted into GSP off Highway 14 just north of the interstate. That prompted another idea. The Airport Commission moved up its long-range plans and decided to widen the airport entrance road while it was going to be closed for about a year during the interchange improvements project. It was an efficient and cost-saving decision.

In less than a year, McMillan-Carter, Inc. had completed the four-laning of the entrance road, Aviation Drive, from I-85 to the airport terminal.

Bad weather had lengthened the project by a few weeks but the drive and Exit 57—complete with new landscaping—were ready in time for the scheduled ceremonies on Thursday, December 15, 2005. The weather was cold and damp; the area had been hit overnight by an ice storm. Throughout the dedication program—which began at 9:59 a.m.—state, local and airport officials along with their invited guests could hear the snapping and falling of ice-laden limbs and trees.

Weeks before, deputy director Larry Holcombe had told reporters that landscapers had saved more trees than had originally been thought possible. He promised the widened entrance road had been "fashioned after the Blue Ridge Parkway" with plenty of lush landscaping and trees along the half-mile entrance. Jim Triplett of United Contractors added to the beauty of the entrance road by his $100,000 donation toward uplighting of the trees along Aviation Drive. The highlight of the drive into the airport is the last gentle curve of the road when the waterfall comes into view, set against the background of the tall fountain, the spacious lawn and the flags in front of the terminal.

Elizabeth Mabry remembers that the GSP December ceremony was on "the coldest day of the year." By contrast, she recalls that six months later the opening of the Brockman-McClimon interchange a mile north "was on the hottest day of the summer." The new interchange takes pressure off the heavily-used Highway 101 interchange two miles north on I-85 and serves as a second option for trucks going to BMW. The project had also included four-laning Brockman-McClimon Road from I-85 to Highway 101.

The entire $45 million project had made I-85 safer on the busy four miles between Highways 14 and 101 past the airport. Mabry called it a "perfect example of partners working together" to overcome a problem and meet a need. GSP Chairman Roger Milliken echoed that appraisal, expressing gratitude to Elizabeth Mabry, Bob Lee and the other officials, engineers and contractors who had designed and implemented a solution to an important safety and convenience need.

The low cost airline search

The last years of the twentieth century and the first of the twenty-first century saw an increasing number of regional and national "no frills" low cost airlines, among them Southwest, America West, Air Tran, Jet Blue, Independence Air. Even they, however, were not immune from the weight of high costs for fuel and labor contracts and the rigors of competition. Independence Air was an example.

Serving several cities primarily up and down the Eastern part of the country, Independence Air in 2004 entered the GSP market. With its low rates, aggressive marketing and efficient operation, its eight regional jet flights a day had a dramatically positive effect on GSP's business. Many who flew other airlines were attracted to GSP by more competitive rates, which all airlines serving GSP had started offering. Those good times didn't last long. As the local business weekly *GSA Business* observed, "It was fun while it lasted." On January 8, 2006, Independence Air's last flight took off from GSP, bound for Tampa, and another low cost airline slid into bankruptcy.

"If all our markets had been as good as GSP," said an Independence Air official, "we would still be flying." Once again, GSP officials were looking, with the help of area business leaders, for a successful low-fare airline. They liked Jet Blue and Southwest.

Ten months after Independence Air left GSP in January of 2006, another newer and smaller airline began limited service. Allegiant Air offered a few flights a week to Orlando and Tampa. Response to the low rate flights was strong enough that by early 2007, Allegiant was considering additional service. However, without a high volume, low cost airline, GSP was once again going through a cycle of losing some passengers to the big airports on either side of it, Atlanta and Charlotte.

Frank Newton has been a consultant to airports across the nation for many years. He has advised both Greenville-Spartanburg and Charlotte. Newton believes smaller, medium-market airports like GSP offer great advantages. "As major airports become more of a mass transit experience," says Newton, "airports like Greenville-Spartanburg become more attractive to many people." He says as the travel experience erodes at busy, crowded airports, many smaller regional airports will reap the benefits. "GSP," says Newton, "is a very user-friendly airport. It is uncrowded, pleasant, convenient, comfortable and it has good amenities." He believes those are advantages for which more travelers will be looking. Newton also believes that GSP's growth will be steady but gradual. "The airport will grow," he predicts, "as the population and the economy of the area grow."[18] According to the U.S. Census Bureau the metropolitan population of Greenville alone grew 7.5 percent between April of 2000 and July of 2006 to 601,986.

Another startup in the low cost airline market launched service in May 2007. From its base in Columbus, Ohio, Skybus was planning initial nonstop service to Oakland; Burbank; Bellingham, Washington; Portsmouth, New Hampshire; Greensboro; Ft. Lauderdale and Kansas City. It had major capital support from investor groups and hometown companies like Nationwide Insurance and promised unbundled services in return for nonrefundable low fares. There would be separate charges for everything from checked baggage and pillows to food and drinks. The airline's Airbus A319 jets might even serve as flying billboards. CEO David Diffenderfer told *USA Today*, Skybus would likely expand to other markets.[19]

2007: FORTY-FIFTH YEAR

By the early months of GSP's forty-fifth year, the world was facing international tensions just as it had a century before. The United States once again was at war, in Iraq and against international terrorism. April 6, 2007, was the ninetieth anniversary of America's entry into World War I. Of the 4,734,991 Americans who had served in that war, there were only *three* survivors, ages 106, 107 and 108.[20] The United States and the world, however, were still living in the long beam cast by one of the Great War's legacies. Aviation had helped to make the world smaller and transform its economy. On March 16, 2007, aviation again made history. The most passengers ever to ride in an airplane—550—traveled that day from Frankfurt, Germany, to John F. Kennedy Airport in New York on the European-made Airbus A380, the first complete double-decker jet.

Growth at Stevens Aviation

Perhaps the most significant business development at GSP in the early months of 2007 was the January opening of Stevens Aviation's new Turboprop Center in its newly refurbished, football-field-size hangar at the airport. It is the same hangar that was built for the airport's opening in October of 1962. Now its thirty thousand square feet is equipped to park and service more than a dozen planes. Its upper floor accommodates dozens of employee work spaces.

Stevens Aviation in 2006 signed a new ten-year lease at GSP. It continues the company's role as GSP's fixed-base operator, concentrating on fuel, catering and minor repair services for tenant firms and visiting aircraft as well as providing air charter services. Stevens also provides FBO services at airports in Nashville, Dayton and Denver. Company headquarters and jet maintenance, military work, paint operations and refurbishing services remain at nearby Donaldson Center.

In addition to the FBO line services, the new lease consolidates the company's Turboprop Division at GSP. A significant portion of the nation's King Air equipment and other types of general aviation aircraft will receive heavy maintenance, repair, hot engine and avionics services at GSP. Vice President of Operations Larry Baker says the six-month, two million dollar hangar renovation and the experienced staff "makes Stevens Aviation the premier turboprop service department in the country." Baker has been with Stevens only thirteen years. "But I can tell you," he says, "pilots know that having the Stevens name in your log book carries weight with OEMs (Original Equipment Manufacturers). Stevens has a great reputation." Baker said by May of 2007, just four months after consolidating its operation at GSP, the Turboprop Division was regaining former customers and attracting new ones. "We are confident of our future."[21] Stevens already employed almost six hundred companywide. (More on the early days of Stevens at GSP in Chapter 3.)

CHAPTER 16

Looking Ahead: The Fifty-Year Plan

Master planning is critical to airports. They are large, complex facilities that demand substantial amounts of land, intensive infrastructure support and a wide variety of land-side and air-side services. Airports also require many levels of local and federal approval, user concurrence and satisfaction, and local political and community support. So master planning requires adequate time, broad input and attention to details.

For busy, growing airports, master planning never stops. GSP officials are constantly implementing recommendations of past master plans while looking ahead to meet future growth requirements. The LPA Group, aviation consultants with offices in Columbia, South Carolina, and several cities nationwide, in 1991 looked at GSP's short- and long-term needs. Among its recommendations were lengthening the runway to eleven thousand feet and adding five gates to the concourse building. Those recommendations were implemented by the mid and late 1990s.

Airport Commission Chairman Roger Milliken also wanted a comprehensive long-range plan extending fifty years. He asked a longtime friend, Riley Bechtel, for a favor. California-based Bechtel Corporation would normally not provide consulting services for an airport of GSP's size. Bechtel is one of the world's largest engineering and construction firms with decades of experience designing and building some of the largest airports in the world. Airports like Dallas-Ft. Worth, Dulles,

San Francisco—and many large international airports overseas—are Bechtel clients.

Bechtel Corporation's first study, completed in March of 1996, looked at second runway land acquisition needs, and use of land already owned. A year later, the firm completed an update of the LPA Group's 1991 master plan. It revised growth strategies needed for the airfield, terminal, cargo, ground access and parking to improve operations and service. It also recommended more land acquisition for additional buffers from noise and for future improvements of access points.

Then in 2001, the September 11 terrorist attacks on United States planes and buildings changed aviation. Travel declined. Several major airlines faced financial calamity and new low-cost carriers entered the market. Costly new government security procedures were imposed. New electronic ticketing technologies were launched. All of these changes drastically affected airport facilities and operations. Space had to be found for increased passenger and baggage processing and equipment. Ticketing areas had to accommodate new electronic kiosks. Many airports, including GSP, had to scramble to find new airlines to provide service that had been curtailed—or removed—by the large legacy airlines. If ever careful master planning had been needed, it was after 9-11. Since most of the changes in airport and airline life would be permanent, long-term—as well as short- and mid-term—planning was necessary.

Following the events of 2001, the Airport Commission retained Bechtel Corporation's Infrastructure Division to update the 1997 master plan to meet the evolving needs of GSP and its service to the South Carolina Upstate. Consultant Omran Assa and his team studied the seven main systems of GSP's operations: airfield, passenger use and facilities, general aviation facilities and services at the airport, cargo facilities and services, and all of the airport's support facilities and services. Conducted with input from airport staff and statistics, the detailed twelve-chapter master plan update was completed in December of 2003 and presented to the Airport Commission. It offered a preferred configuration for each system with analysis to support its recommendations. The plan's development concept presented the ultimate configuration for the airport: how GSP would look and operate through 2053.

In 2003, when the master plan was completed, GSP had seventeen nonstop direct flights to and from seventeen cities. It was an airport primarily for domestic flights but able to accommodate unscheduled international flights. The plan said the airport's long-term vision must be to fill four critical roles: first, as a gateway to the United States marketplace and the rest of the world, and as a cargo distribution center that serves as an important tool in supporting existing businesses and attracting new ones. The plan also said that GSP's long-term vision must be to remain a regional economic engine with modern facilities and frequent flight schedules that would promote the growth of trade, enhance the competition of local business, and attract new manufacturing, distribution, services and technology, which would ultimately stimulate additional investment, trade and job growth. Finally, the plan urged that the long-term vision of the airport should be to present GSP as a showcase of South Carolina's success, a "front door" for air passengers visiting the Upstate. Short-term goals, the plan suggested, should include networking the passenger terminal for intelligent systems, enhancing terminal concessions, increasing the capacity for parking and studying the need for more land acquisition. Several of those and other short-term goals were acted upon within the first three years after the plan's adoption. New concession facilities and free wireless internet access were provided in the concourses; further security measures were implemented; and, in cooperation with the State Department of Transportation, improvements were made on I-85 at the South Carolina Highway 14 and Brockman-McClimon Road interchanges. In addition, the airport continued to acquire additional small tracts of adjacent land.

Annual passenger traffic at GSP had reached 1.6 million in 2000 but had dropped to 1.4 million in 2002 in the aftermath of the September 2001 terrorist attacks and the resulting economic slowdown. In July 2002, passenger traffic reached an average of 4,200 passengers a day. The fifty-year plan published in 2003 projected GSP's annual passenger growth rate at 5.3 percent between 2004 and 2023 and at 3.8 percent from 2024 to 2053. It estimated the airport's annual traffic volume could reach 3.3 million by 2010. Cargo traffic in 2002 reached almost 22,000 tons and the plan estimated that growth over the next fifty years should continue at its historical rate of 5.1 percent. At that rate, GSP would be handling 79,000 tons of cargo by 2023.

The study for the fifty-year master plan also conducted a runway demand/capacity analysis to project when GSP will need a second runway. The Federal Aviation Administration generally requires that an existing runway reach 60 percent of its capacity before an airport can apply for federal funding for a second runway. Capacity is based on projected peak-hour fleet mix (passengers, cargo, general aviation), distribution of arrivals and departures, and visual flight rule (VFR) and instrument flight rule (IFR) conditions. Bechtel's 2003 analysis indicated that GSP's existing 11,001-foot runway could reach that 60 percent capacity level between 2010 and 2015, if growth levels projected in 2003 held steady. As of 2006, growth levels were on track. Once that 60 percent threshold is reached, the length of time from applying for funding to having a second runway completed could be several years. The airport already has land for the second runway, which would be positioned between I-85 and the terminal, and between the main entrance road and Highway 101. It will be 8,200 feet long with a required 4,300-foot parallel separation from the existing runway. Construction of the second runway could be prompted either by the existing runway's capacity constraints or by the Airport Commission's decision to provide carriers (passenger and/or cargo) with the added flexibility of simultaneous takeoffs and landings.

The Airport Commission plans to retain the single-story design of the 90,000-square-foot terminal where airline ticket counters, baggage claim and rental car counters are located. In 2007, the adjoining 150,000-square-foot, two-level concourse complex had eleven operational gates with loading bridges. The south end of the concourse had two additional gates not yet in service.

Bechtel's 2003 plan projected that if GSP maintains the 5.3 percent annual passenger traffic growth averaged since 1965, the airport by 2023 will be serving more than five million passengers.[1] If the airport maintains a long-term growth rate of 3.8 percent during the next thirty years, by 2053 it could be serving 16.4 million passengers.[2] To accommodate that many, the terminal would have to be enlarged by sixty thousand feet, more than two-thirds its current size, and the concourse would have to expand almost five-fold with gates on both sides. The current linear configuration is considered user-friendly because it keeps walking distance relatively short. Since GSP is mostly an origin to destination airports, the crucial distances to consider are those between loading curbs outside the terminal and the concourse gates. Where walking distances from curb to gates exceed one thousand feet in future expansions, moving walkways will be installed. If and when GSP has as many as sixteen million passengers a year, there could be as many as sixty gates. There would also be up to four bridges connecting the concourses with the terminal.

The fifty-year plan also recommends that additional retail and food and beverage space be added on the airport's air side, in the concourse areas where passengers go after clearing security. Following that recommendation, in 2006 a small concession and small gift shop were added in each of the north and south concourses next to the escalator and near the departure lounges. As the airport grows, new food and retail areas will be located in the space between the concourses and in the lengthened concourses themselves.

GSP's cargo business grows every year. The fifty-year plan projects that the airport will become a major cargo distribution center in the years ahead. That will be good for airport business and for the drawing power a larger cargo-processing airport will have to attract more business and industry to the Upstate. GSP has ample room for additional cargo buildings, larger aprons for parking planes and more space for non-apron cargo staging areas. Most long-range cargo expansion will be to the north side of the airport property. When the second runway is built, a new apron will be provided adjacent and parallel to it. That will provide contiguous parking to the main cargo processing area and direct access to taxiways with moderate taxiing distances.

By 2053, it is projected that GSP could experience almost fifty thousand general aviation and military operations a year.[2] If so, that could require sixty covered parking positions in 258,000 square feet of hangars, fifty thousand more than in 2003, and many more tie-down and staging positions along with much larger aprons. Most of that expansion will be to the east of the current general aviation area with hangars next to each other parallel to the runways. There would also be room for a second fixed-base operator terminal.

All of these additional services and facilities will require large airport support operations. To minimize required new investment, new facilities will be located and grouped as efficiently as possible. More planes, flights, buildings, passengers and cargo will require larger facilities for airport fire and rescue, maintenance and repair, utilities, custodial, warehousing, staging and parking services. For example, consider catering. Long-range forecasts project that 50 percent of GSP's flights will be regional, 40 percent mid-range and 10 percent long-range domestic and international.

The idea of investing in a fifty-year plan for an airport may seem extravagant and unnecessary to some. However, careful long-term planning usually prevents problems and saves money. Roger Milliken promised the state legislators in 1958 and dedication day crowds in 1962 that the airport would serve the area's needs "for many years to come." That is why planning in 1958 and 1960 and 1989 was able to meet the needs of 2007. It is the reason that the fifty-year master plan study of 2003 will be the basis for planning to meet Upstate South Carolina's regional airport needs in the years through 2053.

Afterword

As the charts in the Appendix show, there have been gains in both passenger numbers and cargo tonnage during most of GSP's forty-five years of operation. That steady growth testifies to the vision of the airport's proponents and the wisdom of the legislators who supported its creation. The airport's leaders also want GSP to make a statement and leave an impression of quality, beauty, regional cooperation and vision. They believe that GSP's ability to help ignite those kinds of impressions will ultimately produce as much benefit for the region as will the number of passengers served or the amount of cargo handled. They believe people will tell others about, want to transact business in, and perhaps move a business—or themselves—to a region like this that is visionary, productive and welcoming.

Jim Anthony appreciates GSP's value to the Upstate. "It offers easy access for many of our clients who want and need to travel," he says. As founder and CEO of The Cliffs Communities, Anthony and his staff talk with wealthy people, many of whom could live anywhere they wish. "For people with whom we talk who are considering a purchase in this area," Anthony says, "the airport is one of the top five factors."

Whether welcoming newcomers or saying good-bye to travelers, Greenville-Spartanburg International Airport looks forward to being their gateway to the world.

GSP Milestones

1950s/1960s

11-11-58 Plan for regional airport unveiled in meeting with Greenville and Spartanburg county legislators

11-25-58 Greenville and Spartanburg legislative delegations approve the airport plan

3-25-59 South Carolina General Assembly approves legislation creating the Greenville-Spartanburg Airport Commission

3-27-59 Governor Ernest F. Hollings signs legislation creating the Greenville-Spartanburg Airport Commission

4-06-59 Governor Hollings appoints the first airport commissioners

1-18-61 First federal funds for airport announced

7-7-61 Groundbreaking for new regional airport

10-15-62 First airline flights in and out of airport

11-4-62 Dedication of the airport

9-13-64 Cofounder Charlie Daniel dies at sixty-eight

9-17-64 GOP presidential candidate Barry Goldwater speaks at campaign rally

4-25-65 The first jets begin service

1-23-67 Executive Director Andy Andrews dies

5-1-67 A.R. "Dick" Graham starts as executive director

1968 First departure lounge constructed for Eastern Airlines

1970s

7-3-70 Senator Thurmond dedicates customs port; fountain dedicated in memory of Charlie Daniel

4-71 Air cargo building opens

10-15-72 Tenth anniversary

1973/4	Rental car service center constructed, allowing quicker turnaround for rental cars and increasing number of cars available to the public
1975	South concourse extended for additional passenger lounge
7-3 to 7-6-77	Runway repaved and strengthened over July 4 weekend using almost 48,000 tons of asphalt
10-78	President Carter signs airline deregulation bill
7-25-79	Airport commissioner and Spartanburg chamber executive vice president Dick Tukey dies of cancer at sixty-one

1980s

1980	Air freight building expanded to 40,000 square feet and cargo road added
8-3-81	Nation's air traffic controllers strike; Reagan issues ultimatum and eventually fires most of them
10-15-82	Twentieth anniversary
12-31-82	Delta flies Boeing's new B-757 jet on its first commercial flight from Atlanta to GSP with sixty-five passengers. (GSP was selected for the inaugural revenue-producing flight because it would be used as a backup airport when the B-757 had to be diverted from Atlanta due to bad weather.)
1983	Stevens Aviation ramp for general aviation expanded and additional parking space provided for general aviation aircraft; south concourse extended and three gate positions added
1984	New parking lot added bringing total spaces to 1,500
4-85	Delta and American begin service to GSP
8-2-86	Small hijacked commuter plane lands at GSP
1988	1,600-car parking garage added bringing total spaces to 3,000
9-28-89	$40 million terminal expansion opens and longtime executive director Dick Graham retires
10-2-89	J. Garrett Jackson assumes executive director's position

1990s

1-91	Eastern Airlines ceases operations
6-23-92	BMW announces it will build its North American plant adjacent to GSP
10-15-92	Thirtieth anniversary
2-94	Work on extending runway begins
5-95	New regional weather station building opens at GSP
6-95	South Carolina General Assembly enacts zoning legislation to protect airport's environs
1-96	New Airport Environs Planning Commission adopts airport zoning ordinance
5-99	Runway extension to 11,001 feet completed
10-11-99	Historical marker given by GSP and BMW, erected at BMW's Flatwood Fields Athletic Complex; dedicated to the Flatwood community, on which GSP and BMW were built

2000–2007

9-11-01	All civilian aircraft in the United States grounded for more than two days following terrorist strikes on the country
9-13-01	GSP reopens
2-02	gspairport.com website goes online
10-15-02	Fortieth anniversary
10-15-04	Roger Milliken Field dedicated and *Boy Aviator* statue unveiled in honor of airport's cofounder and chairman
1-8-06	Low cost Independence Air goes out of business
3-07	Airport Commission promotes Larry Holcombe from deputy director to airport manager; Gary Jackson remains executive director
10-15-07	GSP's forty-fifth anniversary

Appendix

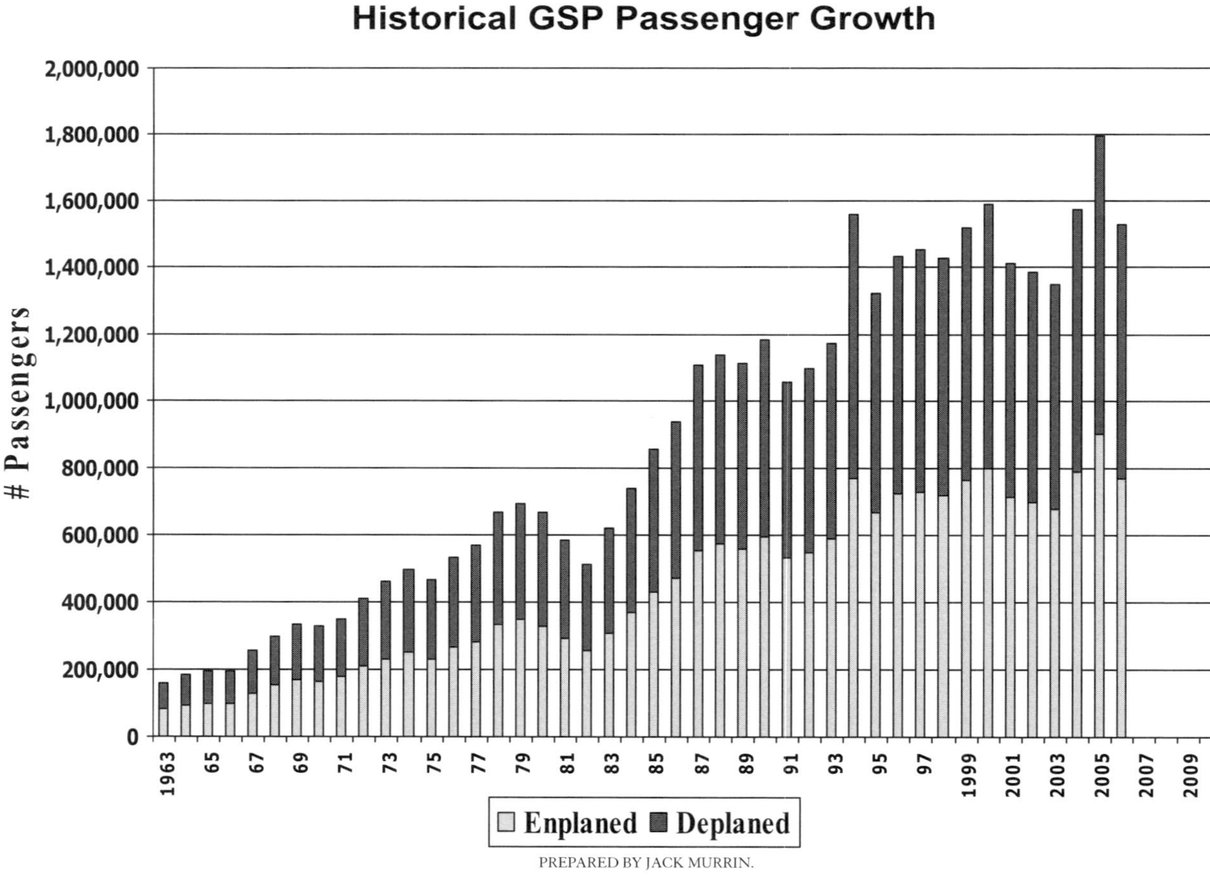
Historical GSP Passenger Growth
Passengers
2,000,000
1,800,000
1,600,000
1,400,000
1,200,000
1,000,000
800,000
600,000
400,000
200,000
0
1963
65
67
69
71
73
75
77
79
81
83
85
87
89
91
93
95
97
1999
2001
2003
2005
2007
2009
Enplaned
Deplaned
PREPARED BY JACK MURRIN.

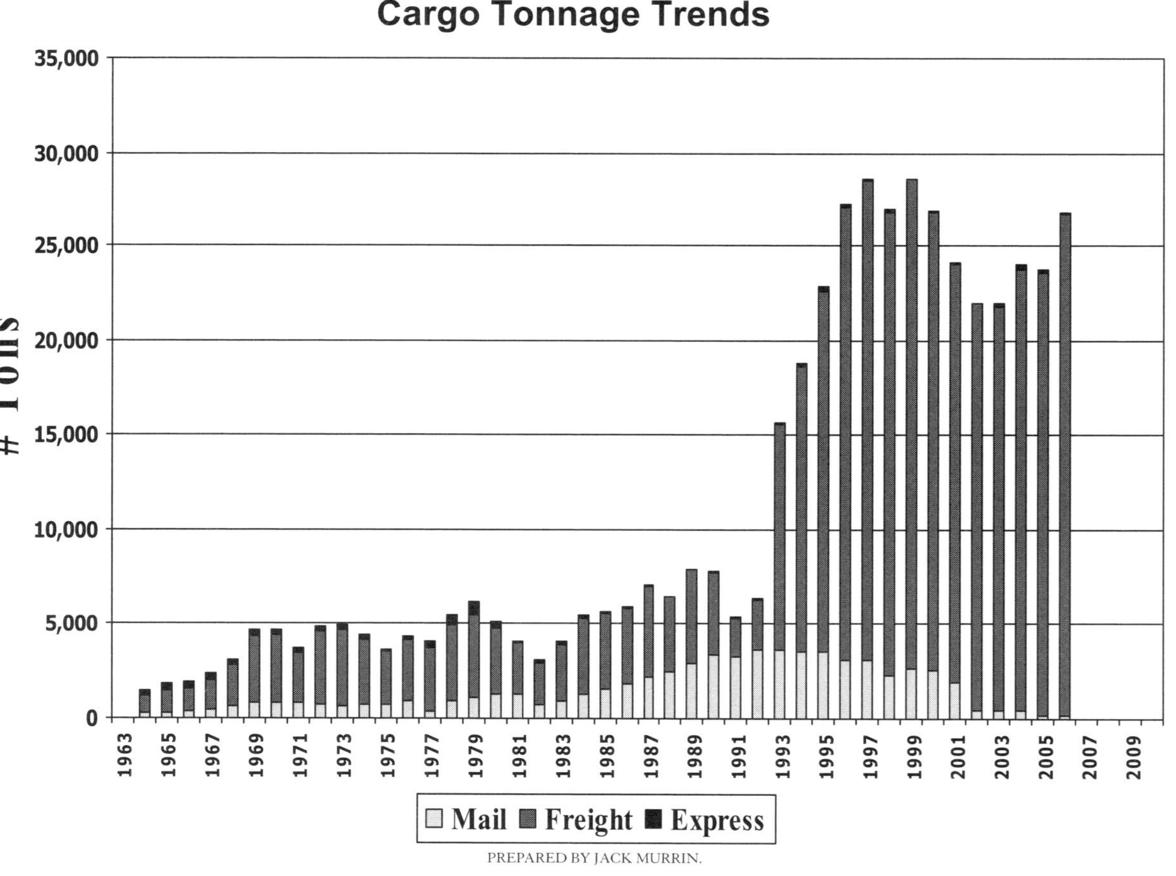
Cargo Tonnage Trends
Tons
35,000
30,000
25,000
20,000
15,000
10,000
5,000
0
1963
1965
1967
1969
1971
1973
1975
1977
1979
1981
1983
1985
1987
1989
1991
1993
1995
1997
1999
2001
2003
2005
2007
2009
Mail
Freight
Express
PREPARED BY JACK MURRIN.

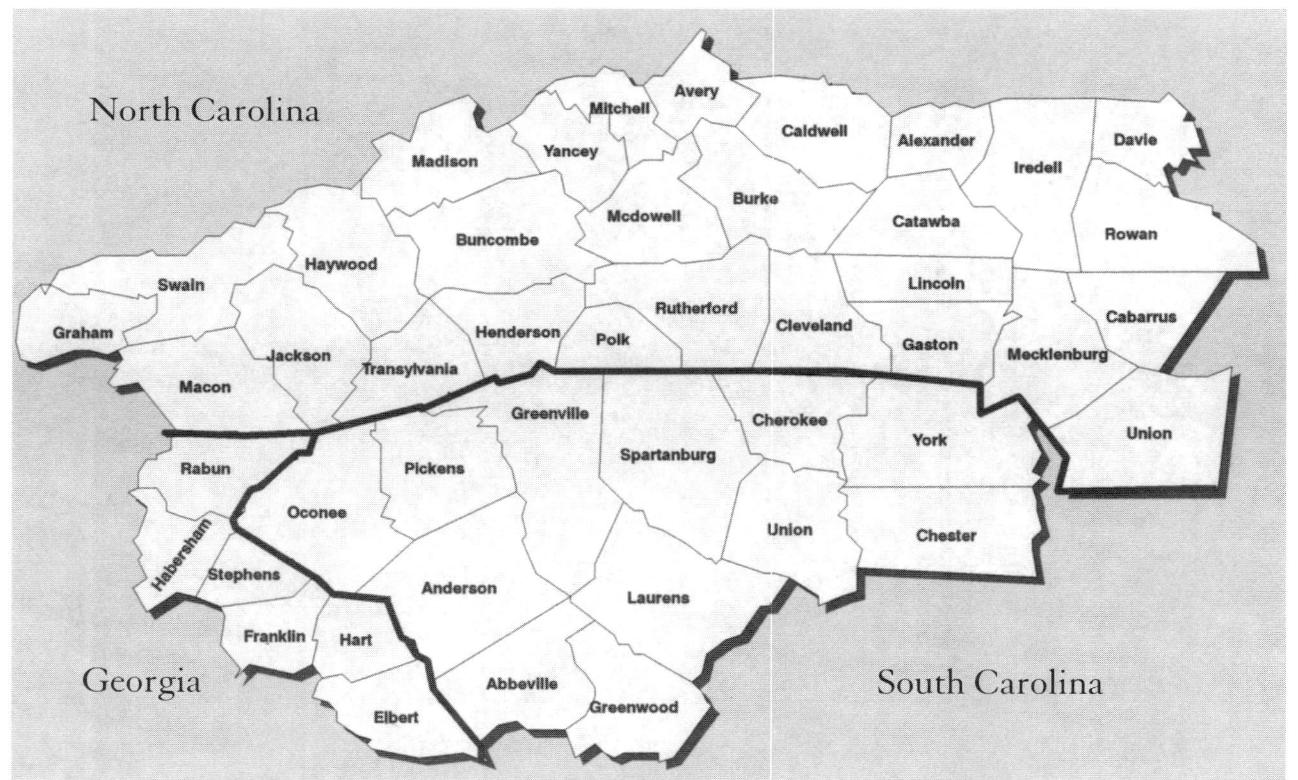

WEATHER MAP *The National Weather Service's Forecasting Office (WFO) located at Greenville-Spartanburg Airport serves forty-six counties: twenty-eight in North Carolina, twelve in South Carolina and six in Georgia.* COURTESY WEATHER FORECASTING OFFICE AT GSP.

GREENVILLE-SPARTANBURG AIRPORT COMMISSION

Six-year renewable terms; three nominated by the Spartanburg County legislative delegation, three by the Greenville County legislative delegation; appointed by the governor of South Carolina. Members serve without remuneration.

Members serving in 2007

Roger Milliken, chair	Spartanburg County	1959–
Minor Shaw, vice chair	Greenville County	1994–
Leland Burch	Greenville County	1985–
Valerie Miller	Greenville County	1998–
Henry Ramella	Spartanburg County	1981–
Wallace Storey	Spartanburg County	1989–

Alphabetical listing of former commissioners

William T. Adams	Greenville County	1959–1981
Hugh L. Aiken	Greenville County	1959–1977
Ed A. Burch	Greenville County	1978–1985
Robert E. Coleman	Greenville County	1990–1997
Wiley M. Crittenden Jr.	Greenville County	1981–1985
George Dean Johnson Jr.	Spartanburg County	1980–1989
Jean M. Little	Spartanburg County	1969–1981
Allen M. Lowdermilk	Greenville County	1965–1993
L. A. Odom	Spartanburg County	1959–1977
John Ratterree	Greenville County	1959–1969
Thomas H. Suitt	Greenville County	1985–1990
James O. Thomason	Spartanburg County	1963–1969
Richard E. Tukey	Spartanburg County	1974–1979
S. J. Workman	Spartanburg County	1959–1963

GOVERNORS OF SOUTH CAROLINA

Members of the Greenville-Spartanburg Airport Commission are nominated by their county legislative delegations (Spartanburg and Greenville) for appointment by the governor. Governors of South Carolina who have served since the Airport Commission was created by state law in March of 1959 are:

1959–1963	Ernest F. Hollings
1963–1965	Donald Russell
1965–1971	Robert McNair
1971–1975	John West
1975–1979	James Edwards
1979–1987	Richard Riley
1987–1995	Carroll Campbell
1995–1999	David Beasley
1999–2003	Jim Hodges
2003–present	Mark Sanford

AIRPORT ENVIRONS PLANNING COMMISSION

Nine members serve renewable two-year terms with two appointees from both Greenville and Spartanburg counties, two from the city of Greer, one from the town of Duncan and two appointed by the Greenville-Spartanburg Airport Commission.

Members serving in 2007:
Gary Lee and Carter Smith—Spartanburg County
Brad Medcalf and Van Swofford—Greenville County
Chris Aiken and Steven Siler—Greer
Jacqueline Moore—Duncan
Les McCraw and Wallace Storey—appointed by the Greenville-Spartanburg Airport Commission

Former members:

From Spartanburg County: Danny Allen and Robert Hitt

From Greenville County: Bob Leach, Wade Cleveland, Eddie Harbin, Dick Reid

From Greer: E. M. Compton, John Hannah, John McManus, Jack Titano

From GSP Airport Commission: Robert Coleman

From Duncan: Jacqueline Moore has served since creation of the commission in 1995.

Note: Until representation on the commission was reduced from eleven to nine in 1996, David Moore represented Mauldin and Carter Smith represented Lyman.

Notes

For additional information on the sources cited in the notes, please consult the Bibliography.

CHAPTER I ※ BEFORE THE AIRPORT

1 Hendrix, *Flatwood Memories*, 40–43
2 Meacham, *Franklin & Winston*, 6
3 *World Book Encyclopedia*, Vol. 21, 377
4 Smith, Odegard, Shea, *Airport Planning & Management*, 1
5 Author interview with Bill Rafferty; *USA Today*, 10-2-06, 9B
6 Ibid.
7 1920–1935 History, Aviation Resource Center, www.geocities.com/capecanaveral/4294/history/1920_1935.html#airlinegrowth
8 *The Greenville (SC) Municipal Airport Story*, George D. Barr, typewritten at Cedar Mountain, NC, July 10, 1971, (Greenville Downtown Airport and GSP archives). Note: The exact amount of land purchased is uncertain. Barr wrote: "A big piece of farmland about 200 acres, more or less." In *The Greenville News* "City People," 6-28-06, historian Judith Bainbridge said the land was "a 100-acre level field near Wood's fishing pond (Wood's Lake Road) off Laurens Road."
9 Author interview with Jeffrey Willis
10 Formal minutes of the 2-21-1928 meeting of Greenville City Council
11 *Lindbergh: U.S. Airmail Service Pioneer*, http://www.charleslindbergh.com/airmail
12 *Lindbergh Flies the Atlantic, 1927, Eyewitness to History*, www.eyewitnesstohistory.com (1999)
13 Wakefield, Betsy, ed., *Textile Town, Spartanburg County, South Carolina*, 116
14 Brewster, Jennings, *The Century*, 136
15 Author interview with Bruce Littlejohn
16 Author interview with Tom Hartness
17 http://enwikipedia.org/wiki/Eddie_Rickenbacker
18 Ibid. and author interviews with Frederick B. Dent and Joe F. Jordan
19 *Spartanburg Herald*, 4-16-45, 1 and *The Greenville News*: 4-6-45, 1
20 *Spartanburg Herald*, 4-6-45, 1
21 *The Greenville News*, 4-13-45, 1
22 Minutes of Abner Creek Baptist Church "Board Conference," 2-18-45
23 Author interview with Dr. Doyle Boggs
24 Wakefield, Betsy, ed., *Textile Town, Spartanburg County, South Carolina*, 228

CHAPTER 2 ❖ FROM DREAM TO DESIGN

1 Author interview with Frederick B. Dent
2 Canup and Workman Jr., *Charles E. Daniel*, 56
3 Ibid., 4
4 Ibid., 30, 36, 59, 62
5 Ibid., 30
6 Huff, A. V., *Greenville: The History of the City and County in the South Carolina Piedmont*, 398, 334
7 Author interview with Tad Brown, grandson of Walter Brown
8 Author interview with Roger Milliken
9 Canup and Workman Jr., *Charles E. Daniel*, 27, and author interview with Roger Milliken
10 Muson, *Remembering Mr. Kingsley*, 65
11 Author interview with Roger Milliken
12 Canup and Workman Jr., *Charles E. Daniel*, 26
13 Author interview with Robert Yeargin
14 Author interview with Dr. Robert C. Edwards
15 "Malcolm Baldrige National Quality Award 1989 Winner," http://www.quality.nist.gov/milliken_89.htm
16 Canup and Workman Jr., *Charles E. Daniel*, 101, 102
17 Ibid., 171, and author interview with Roger Milliken
18 Author interview with Roger Milliken
19 Ibid.
20 Hilderbrand, ed., *Making a Landscape of Continuity*, 74
21 Ibid., 13
22 Ibid., 14
23 Ibid.
24 Author interview with Roger Milliken
25 Ibid.
26 Canup and Workman Jr., *Charles E. Daniel*, 172
27 Author interview with Roger Milliken
28 Author interview with Mike Keselica
29 Author interview with Richard C. Webel
30 Author interview with Roger Milliken
31 Ibid.
32 Ibid.
33 Author interview with Mike Keselica

CHAPTER 3 ❖ BUILDING THE AIRPORT

1 *Spartanburg Herald*, 11-12-58, 5
2 Author interview with Rex Carter
3 *Spartanburg Herald*, 11-12-58, 1
4 *The Greenville News*, 11-24-58

5 Author interview with Larry Holcombe
6 "Jet Airport Committee," *The Greenville News*, 11-21-58
7 Author interview with Rex Carter
8 Ibid.
9 Legislative Act 99 of 1959, Code of Laws of SC 1976: 55-11-110
10 Bainbridge, Judith, "Donaldson Center," SC Room, Greenville County Public Library
11 Biography in Donaldson Center and GSP archives and on a plaque outside the Donaldson Center headquarters building
12 Copsey, Ron, *The 63rd Troop Carrier Wing & Donaldson's Golden Decade of Global Airlift*, 2 (GSP Archives)
13 Ibid., 3–8
14 Walker, Ruth, *The Greenville News*, 4-15-61
15 Author interview with Roger Milliken
16 Only a limited amount of military housing was available on the base. Many houses had been built and subdivisions established on the south side of Greenville within three or four miles of the base. As a result, word of the potential closing of the base resulted in hundreds of houses coming on the market within a short period of time, causing concern in the local real estate market.
17 Author interview with Roger Milliken
18 Author interview with Milton F. Smith
19 Workman Jr., W. D., *The Greenville News*, 4-21-61, 1
20 *The Greenville News*, 4-23-61, 1
21 Smeltzer, Robert, *Greenville Piedmont*, 7-25-61, 1
22 Ibid.
23 Author interview with Howard Suitt
24 Author interview with Herb Howell
25 *The Greenville News*, 6-17-62
26 Author interview with Gaynelle Cuthbertson
27 "Engineer Lauds Speedy Finish," *Spartanburg Herald-Journal*, 11-4-62
28 *The Greenville News*, 10-14-62, 1

CHAPTER 4 ❖ THE EARLY YEARS: 1962–1969

1 http://en.wikipedia.org/wiki/Najeeb_Halaby
2 *The Greenville News*, 10-16-62
3 "An Overview of the Crisis," http://library.thinkquest.org/11046/days/index.html
4 Author interview with William D. Workman III
5 Author interview with Cary Fondren
6 "Cold War: Cuban Missile Crisis," http://www.loc.gov/exhibits/archives/colc.html
7 From information at the Anderson Memorial in Greenville's Cleveland Park
8 Author interview with Cooper White Jr.
9 Author interview with Dan Foster
10 *Spartanburg Herald*, 11-5-62
11 Ibid.

12 Author interview with Betty Thompson
13 "History Made," *Spartanburg Herald*, 12-14-62
14 Author interview with Bill Orders
15 "Jetport Considers Appeal," *Greenville Piedmont*, 3-16-69
16 "Service Curtailed," *The Greenville News*, 4-3-64
17 *Greenville Piedmont*, 9-17-64; *The Greenville News*, 9-18-64
18 Author interview with Bruce Littlejohn
19 Author interview with Knox White
20 Lucille Green, *The Greenville News*, 7-11-64
21 Edgar, Walter, ed., *The South Carolina Encyclopedia*, 982
22 Author interview with Paul Foerster
23 Author interview with Ernest F. Hollings
24 Edgar, Walter, ed., *The South Carolina Encyclopedia*, 982
25 "Spartanburg: Portraits of the Good Life & Profiles in Excellence"
26 Author interview with Governor Robert McNair
27 Author interview with Pinckney Spencer
28 Edgar, Walter, ed., *The South Carolina Encyclopedia*, 982
29 Author interview with Pat Tukey
30 Author interview with Henry Ramella
31 Author interview with Rex Carter
32 McConnell III, F. C., "Watch That Criticism of Our Airport," *Greenville Piedmont*, 9-20-66
33 Author interview with A. R. (Dick) Graham
34 Author interview with Skip Shelton
35 Ibid.
36 "Good Afternoon, This is Gil Rowland," column, *Greenville Piedmont*, 5-28-69
37 Workman III, W.D., "Report Forecasts Air Traffic Needs," *The Greenville News*, 8-28-69
38 The airport's fiscal year begins July 1 and ends June 30.
39 Sargent, Alice, "Local Jetport Up," *Greenville Piedmont*, 7-11-69
40 Workman III, W.D., "Report Forecasts Air Traffic Needs," *The Greenville News*, 8-28-69

CHAPTER 5 ✻ THE 1970S

1 "Aviation Security," www.centennialofflight.gov/essay/Government_Role/security/POL18.htm
2 Bearak, Barry, "Hijackers—They're Still Flying High," *The Los Angeles Times*, 8-4-83, www.latinamericanstudies.org/hijackers/flying-high.htm
3 *The Greenville News*, 12-4-71, 11
4 Author interview with Dick Graham
5 Ibid.

6 The average retail price of gasoline in the United States in 1978 was sixty-five cents a gallon according to apachecorp.com.
7 "20th Anniversary of Deregulation: Cause for Celebration," 1998, www.heritage.org/research/regulation/B&G1173.cfm
8 Author interview with Dick Graham
9 www.aa.com
10 *The Wall Street Journal*, 10-5-04, 15A
11 www.aviationexplorer.com/eastern_airlines.htm
12 University of Miami Libraries, Special Collections Division, http://scholar.library.miami.edu/panam/history.html

CHAPTER 6 ❧ THE 1980S

1 Author interview with Dick Graham
2 Pels, Rebecca, "The Pressures of PATCO," *Essays in History*, vol. 37, 1995, University of Virginia Department of History, etext.virginia.edu/journals/EH/EH37/Pels.html
3 Author interview with Dick Graham
4 Author interview with Wallace Storey
5 Author interview with Roger Milliken
6 Author interview with Mike Keselica
7 "The Snow of '88," insert, *The Greenville News*, 1-19-88
8 Author interview with Wallace Storey
9 Author interview with Louise Nelson
10 *The Greenville News*, Airport section, 9-24-89, 2, 3
11 Author interview with Dick Graham

CHAPTER 7 ❧ THE ART AND BEAUTY OF GSP

1 Author interview with Larry Baker
2 Author interview with Dick Graham
3 Author interview with Gary Jackson
4 Author interview with Dean Knox
5 Author interview with Dennis Smith
6 Ibid.
7 Cornelison, Jimmy, *Greenville Piedmont*
8 Author interview with Gary Jackson
9 Cornelison, Jimmy, *Greenville Piedmont*
10 Author interview with Richard C. Webel
11 Author interview with Jim Dolan
12 *Landscape of Continuity*, 149
13 Author interview with Richard C. Webel

CHAPTER 8 ※ THE AIRLINES

1 http://www.aviationexplorer.com/eastern_airlines.htm
2 http://www.historycentral.com/aviation/airlines/delta.html
3 http://www.usairways.com
4 http://www.aa.com
5 http://www.united.com
6 http://www.continental.com
7 http://www.nwa.com

CHAPTER 9 ※ THE AVIATION CLUSTER

1 Author interview with Michael O'Donnell
2 *The Economic Impact of Spartanburg Downtown Memorial Airport*, brochure prepared by Wilbur Smith Associates for the South Carolina Department of Commerce, Division of Aeronautics, 2006
3 *The Economic Impact of Greenville Downtown Airport*, brochure prepared by Wilbur Smith Associates for the South Carolina Department of Commerce, Division of Aeronautics, 2006
4 *Donaldson Center Industrial Air Park*, brochure prepared by Donaldson Center Industrial Air Park, 2006
5 *The Economic Impact of Greenville-Spartanburg International Airport*, brochure prepared by Wilbur Smith Associates for the South Carolina Department of Commerce, Division of Aeronautics, 2006
6 *Donaldson Center Industrial Air Park*, brochure prepared by Donaldson Center, 2006
7 Author interview with Michael O'Donnell

CHAPTER 10 ※ THE 1990S

1 Author interview with Paul Foerster
2 *Spartanburg Herald-Journal*, 9-24-89
3 Author interview with Paul Foerster
4 Ibid.
5 *Spartanburg Herald-Journal*, "BMW Special Report," 6-24-92, 11
6 Author interview with Foster Chapman
7 "BMW Story," *The Greenville News*, 6-24-92, 8A, 10A
8 Author interview with Roger Milliken
9 Ibid.
10 Author interview with Wallace Storey
11 Ibid.
12 Author interview with Jack Murrin
13 Author interview with Gary Jackson
14 *Spartanburg Herald-Journal*, 3-31-92, 9A

15 *The Greenville News*, 4-2-92, 5A
16 Author interview with Wallace Storey
17 "Nebraska Officials Visit Germany," *The Greenville News*, 5-15-92
18 "Measuring the Cost," *The Greenville News*, 5-3-92, 1A
19 Author interview with Foster Chapman
20 *The Greenville News,* 4-8-92, 1
21 Author interview with Phil Davis
22 McAllister, Bob, "Other Views" Column, *The Greenville News*, 3-13-06, 7A
23 *Spartanburg Herald-Journal*, 5-21-92, 1A
24 *The Greenville News*, 5-23-92, 1A, 11A
25 *The Greenville News*, 5-30-92, 1A
26 Ibid.
27 Ibid.
28 Associated Press report in *Charlotte Observer*, 4-2-92 and *The Greenville News*, 5-13-92, 5A
29 *Spartanburg Herald-Journal*, 6-4-92, 1
30 *Spartanburg Herald-Journal*, "BMW Special Report," 6-24-92, 13
31 Ibid.
32 Author interview with Paul Foerster
33 *Spartanburg Herald-Journal*, 6-20-92, 1
34 *Spartanburg Herald-Journal*, 6-23-92, 7A
35 *Greer Citizen*, 6-24-92, 1
36 *Spartanburg Herald-Journal*, "Special Report," 6-24-92, 1
37 *Greer Citizen*, 6-24-92, 1, 3
38 *The Greenville News*, 7-1-92, 9A
39 Wood, Mark, "Greer Residents Happy The Wait Is Over," *Spartanburg Herald-Journal*, BMW 3, 6-24-92
40 "Campbell BMW chief sign declaration," *The Greenville News*, 7-7-92, 1
41 Ibid.
42 "BMW History," *Greer Citizen*, 7-1-92, 23
43 Ibid., 20
44 *Greer: From Cotton Town to Industrial Center*, 25–27
45 Author interview with Don Wall
46 Ibid.
47 Ibid.
48 *Greer Citizen*, 12-7-94, 1
49 "Airport Commission to Fight Annexation," *The Greenville News*, 1-24-95
50 *Spartanburg Herald-Journal*, 1-29-95, 1A
51 "Annexation Suits," *The Greenville News*, 3-5-95, 1B
52 Author interview with Lewis Vaughn
53 Author interview with Wallace Storey
54 Author interview with Frank Newton
55 The Environs legislation became final with Senate passage on June 1, 1995.

56 The Environs Planning Commission was created by S.C. Code of Laws (1995) 55-11-230. The Zoning Ordinance was actually adopted on 3-24-66 and amended on 3-31-97 and 4-22-99.
57 Author interview with Wallace Storey
58 "Airport Zoning Board Approved," *The Greenville News*, 6-2-95, 1D, 2D
59 Author interview with Lewis Vaughn
60 Author interview with David Wilkins
61 Author interview with Larry Holcombe
62 Author interview with Gary Jackson
63 Author interview with Larry Estridge
64 Author interview with Les McCraw
65 Author interview with Rick Danner
66 According to the FAA, the ten busiest commercial airports in the U.S. in 2006 were: Atlanta, Chicago O'Hare, Dallas-Ft. Worth, Los Angeles, Las Vegas, Denver, Houston Intercontinental, Phoenix, Philadelphia, Charlotte. GSP in August 2007 offered nonstop service to seven of those airports: Atlanta, O'Hare, DFW, Las Vegas, Houston Intercontinental, Philadelphia and Charlotte. The world's ten busiest airports in 2005 were Atlanta, O'Hare, Heathrow, Haneda (Tokyo), Los Angeles, DFW, Charles de Gaulle, Frankfurt-main, Schiphol (Amsterdam) and Las Vegas.
67 Author interview with Elizabeth Patterson
68 "Weather station's hours may be cut," *Spartanburg Herald-Journal*, 1991 (in GSP's scrapbook 5.88–9.91, 43)
69 "Hollings Makes Bid to Keep Weather Station Open," *The Greenville News*, 7-10-91
70 Ibid.
71 Author interview with Larry Gabric
72 Author interview with Wallace Storey
73 Ibid.
74 Airport Commission minutes, 7-23-92
75 "Aviation," *The Greenville News*, 10-23-94, 14A
76 Copy of a letter to Roger Milliken given to the author by the writer F. E. Hendrix
77 Francis Earle Hendrix videotape of dedication ceremonies

CHAPTER 11 ※ THE TRANSPORTATION NETWORK

1 Lief, *Harvey Firestone, Free Man of Enterprise*, 190
2 Ibid., 171
3 Ibid.
4 Ibid., 188, 190
5 Ibid., 190
6 Giffels, David, "Rubber Meets the Road," Akron, OH, *Beacon Journal*, 6-27-06
7 Ibid., 190, 191
8 Lief, *Harvey Firestone, Free Man of Enterprise*, 191

9 "History of the U.S. Highway System," http://www.gbcnet.com/ushighways/history.html
10 Ibid.
11 http://www.enwikipedia.org/wiki/interstate_highway
12 Firestone Company newspaper ad, 1955
13 Reid, T. R., "The Super Highway to Everywhere," *Washington Post*, 6-28-06, 1A
14 Ibid.
15 January 18, 1957 letter from Z. W. Meeks to Rep. Bryan Dorn, Dorn papers, SC Political Collection, University of South Carolina Libraries
16 January 18, 1957 letter from B. P. McWhorter to S. N. Pearman and M. L. Shadburn, Dorn papers, SC Political Collection, University of South Carolina Libraries
17 *The Greenville News*, 3-29-59, 1D
18 "Vandiver," *The Greenville News*, 8-21-59, 1-2

CHAPTER 12 ※ MOVING CARGO

1 "2003 Master Plan Study," Bechtel Infrastructure
2 Author interview with Jonn Harris
3 "Airport Commission," *The Greenville News*, 9-11-94, 3-4A
4 "Airport Coordination," *The Greenville News*, 10-23-94, 1A, 14A
5 Ibid.
6 Author interview with Randy Johnson
7 www.ups.com/history
8 Author interview with Marty Griffin
9 DHL-USA.com
10 Personal correspondence to author from Mark Reilly, spokesman for GE gas turbine plant, Greenville, SC

CHAPTER 13 ※ ECONOMIC ENGINE

1 "Adidas," *The Greenville News*, 9-7-07
2 Author interview with Max Heller
3 "The Economic Impact of Greenville-Spartanburg International Airport," (2005), Wilbur Smith Associates Study for the South Carolina Department of Commerce, Division of Aeronautics
4 Author interview with Carter Smith
5 Author interview with Minor Shaw
6 Author interview with Chris Stone
7 *The Greenville News,* 3-28-07
8 As of August 2007. The number of cities to which GSP has nonstop service fluctuates slightly depending on airlines serving GSP and their schedules at any given time. The number has held between fourteen and seventeen cities for several years: GSP records.

CHAPTER 14 ✻ PASSING THROUGH GSP

1 Rogers, Freeman, "When Perry Como Serenaded Saluda," *Bold Life*, November 2005
2 Author interview with Octavia Williams, 3-10-06; "World War II, Psychological Warfare," *World Book Encyclopedia*, vol. 21, 1976, 408. Iva d'Aquino was an American propagandist broadcaster for Japan during World War II. Dubbed "Tokyo Rose" by military personnel, she was convicted of treason following the war and sentenced to prison.
3 Author interview with Gary Nelson

CHAPTER 15 ✻ COMPLETING FORTY-FIVE YEARS: 2000–2007

1 This account and other mentions of Gary Jackson in this chapter are from author interviews with him.
2 This and most other references in this chapter to Delta Flight 15 on 9-11-01 from Frankfurt to Atlanta, with the diversion to Gander, were taken from the fax of a flight attendant on board which was provided to the author and from an author interview with Shirley Brooks-Jones.
3 This account and all other mentions of the Schroeder family in this chapter come from an author interview with Ray Schroeder and from a written account of the family's experience given to the author.
4 This account and all other mentions of US Airways Flight 99 from London and back on 9-11-01 come from author interview with Mike Martin.
5 This account and all other mentions of the Garrisons in this chapter come from author interview with Don and Carol Garrison.
6 Author interview with Randy Johnson
7 *Gander's Historic Street Names: A Biographical Guide to Pioneers of Aviation*
8 *Crossroads of the World: Recollections from an Airport Town*, 22–25
9 Defede, Jim, *The Day the World Came to Town*, 7
On page 6, Defede notes that more than 250 aircraft were diverted to fifteen Canadian airports including Vancouver and Calgary in the west, to Ottawa, Montreal, Halifax, Gander and St. John's in the east. Defede says they carried 43,895 passengers and crew members. Most of the large jets stayed in those airports between two and four days.
10 Details from DL 15 flight attendant's fax
11 Author interview with Shirley Brooks-Jones, DL 15 passenger
12 Author interview with Rex Clements, Lewisporte Collegiate assistant principal
13 Author interview with Bill Hooper, Lewisporte mayor
14 Author interview with Tommy Watson
15 All quotes in this section from author interview with Mike Tarman
16 Author interview with William Barnet III
17 Author interview with Elizabeth Mabry
18 Author interview with Frank Newton

19 *USA Today*, 4-25-07, 5B
20 "Last Known WWI Navy Vet Dies," Associated Press, *The Greenville News*, 4-2-07
21 Author interview with Larry Baker

CHAPTER 16 ※ LOOKING AHEAD: THE FIFTY-YEAR PLAN

1 Bechtel Infrastructure's Master Plan Update, December 2003, 4-1
2 Ibid.

Bibliography

BOOKS AND ARTICLES

Bainbridge, Judith T. *Greenville's Heritage*. Greenville, SC: J & B Publications, 2006.

Belcher, Ray; Hiatt, Joada. *Greer: From Cotton Town to Industrial Center*. Charleston, SC: Arcadia Publishing, an imprint of Tempus Publishing, Inc., 2003.

Canup, C. R. (Red); Workman, W. D. Jr. *Charles E. Daniel: His Philosophy and Legacy*. Columbia, SC: The R.L. Bryan Company, 1981.

Defede, Jim. *The Day the World Came to Town: 9/11 in Gander, Newfoundland*. New York, NY: HarperCollins Publishers, 2002.

Edgar, Walter B. *South Carolina: A History*. Columbia, SC: University of South Carolina Press, 1998.

Edgar, Walter B., ed. *The South Carolina Encyclopedia*. Columbia, SC: University of South Carolina Press, 2006.

Goff, Roderick B. *Crossroads of the World: Recollections from an Airport Town*. St. John's, NL: Flanker Press, Ltd., 2005.

Gordon, Debra. *The Kindest of Strangers*. Page 60, *Family Circle Magazine*, March 12, 2002.

Hendrix, Francis Earle. *Flatwood Memories*. Duncan, SC, 1998.

Hendrix, Francis Earle. *Abner Creek Baptist Church: An Historical Account*. Spartanburg, SC: The Reprint Company, 2007.

Hilderbrand, Gary R., ed. *Making a Landscape of Continuity: The Practice of Innocenti & Webel*. Cambridge, MA: Harvard University Graduate School of Design, 1997.

Huff, Archie Vernon. *Greenville: The History of the City and County in the South Carolina Piedmont*. Columbia, SC: University of South Carolina Press, 1995.

Jennings, Peter; Brewster, Todd. *The Century*. New York, NY: Doubleday, 1998.

Lief, Alfred. *Harvey Firestone: Free Man of Enterprise*. New York, NY: McGraw-Hill Book Company, Inc., 1951.

Littlejohn, Bruce. *Political Memoirs*. Spartanburg, SC: Bruce Littlejohn, 1989.

Meacham, Jon. *Franklin and Winston: An Intimate Portrait of an Epic Friendship*. New York: Random House, 2003.

Muson, Howard. *Remembering Mr. Kingsley*. Lansberg, Gersick & Associates.

O'Neal, Peggy; Gould, Scott. *Spartanburg: Portrait of the Good Life and Profiles in Excellence*. Spartanburg, SC: Towery Publishing, Inc., 1993.

Racine, Philip N. *Seeing Spartanburg: A History in Images*. Spartanburg, SC: Hub City Writers Project, 1999.

Ropp, Theodore. *World War II: The Secret War*, Volume 21, Page 408, *The World Book Encyclopedia*. Chicago, IL: Field Enterprises Educational Corporation, 1976.

Searles, Robert A. *NBAA's Tribute to Business Aviation*. Washington, DC: National Business Aviation Association, 1997.

Seaward, Greg; Dyke, Rhonda, eds. *Gander's Historic Street Names: A Biographical Guide to Pioneers of Aviation*. Gander, NL: Printmaster Limited, 1991.

Smith, Donald I., et al. *Airport Planning and Management*. Belmont, CA: Wadsworth Publishing Company, 1984.

Teter, Betsy Wakefield, ed. *Textile Town: Spartanburg County, South Carolina*. Hub City Writers Project, Spartanburg, SC, 2002.

Willis, Jeffrey R., Greenville County Historical Society. *Remembering Greenville: Photographs from the Coxe Collection*. Charleston, SC: Arcadia Publishing, 2003.

Young, Peter. *World War I*, Volume 21, Page 377, *The World Book Encyclopedia*. Chicago, IL: Field Enterprises Educational Corporation, 1976.

PUBLIC AND PRIVATE DOCUMENTS

Public papers of William Jennings Bryan Dorn
University of South Carolina, Columbia, SC
South Carolina Political Collections, Columbia, SC
Kate Moore, Processing Archivist
Moorekv@gwm.sc.edu

Files of the South Carolina Department of Aeronautics (1940s)
South Carolina Department of Archives and History, Columbia, SC
Elaine Rohr, Reference Room Librarian
www.state.sc.us/scdah

Formal minutes of the Greenville City Council, 1926–1928
Cheryle Ratliff, City Clerk
ratlifc@greatergreenville.com

Minutes of the Greenville-Spartanburg Airport Commission's meetings: 1959–2007
Jack Murrin, Chief Information Officer, Greenville-Spartanburg Airport Commission
www.gspairport.com

Greenville-Spartanburg Airport Environs Zoning Ordinance, 3-29-96
Adopted by the Airport Environs Planning Commission
Amended 3-31-97 and 4-22-99

Discussion of future growth potential and land considerations, Greenville-Spartanburg Airport, 1-23-95
Newton & Associates, Inc., the LPA Group Inc.

Legislative Act 99 of 1959
Code of Laws of South Carolina 1976: Title 55, Chapter 11, Section 110
Approved 3-25-59

Legislative Act 100 of 1995
Code of Laws of South Carolina 1976: Title 55, Chapter 11, Section 230
Approved 6-12-95

Fifty-Year Study Plan for Greenville-Spartanburg Airport
Bechtel Infrastructure, 2003
Copsey, Ron. *The 63rd Troop Carrier Wing and Donaldson's Golden Decade of Global Airlift, 1953–1963*. Greenville, SC: Speech Manuscript.

ELECTRONIC SOURCES

"Lindbergh Flies the Atlantic, 1927." www.eyewitnesstohistory.com (1999).
"Lindbergh: U.S. Airmail Service Pioneer." http://www.charleslindbergh.com/airmail.
Dwight David Eisenhower biography. http://www.ibiblio.org/lia/president/EisenhowerLibrary/_General_Materials/DDE_Bibliography.html
History of the U.S. Highway System. http://www.gbcnet.com/ushighways/history.html
Malcolm Baldrige, National Quality Award, 1989 winner: Milliken & Company. http://www.quality.nist.gov/Milliken_89.htm
"Deregulation and Its Consequences." http://www.centennialofflight.gov/essay/Commercial_Aviation/Dereg-Tran8.htm

OTHER SOURCES

Records of the Spartanburg County Public Libraries
Debra Hutchins, Local History Librarian
http://www.infodepot.org
Records of the Spartanburg County Historical Association
Nannie Jefferies, Museum Administrator
www.spartanarts.org/history
Records of the Greenville County Historical Society
Sidney Thompson, Executive Director
www.greenvillehistory.org
Scrapbook and photo album archives of the Greenville-Spartanburg Airport Commission (1957–2007)
Rosylin Weston, Director of Public Relations, Greenville-Spartanburg Airport
www.gspairport.com
Archives of the Greenville Downtown Airport
Joe Frasher, Airport Director
www.greenvilledowntownairport.com
Archives of Donaldson Center Industrial Air Park
www.donaldsoncenter.com
Bainbridge, Judith, "Donaldson Center," South Carolina Room, Greenville County (SC) Public Library
Barr, George D. *The Greenville (SC) Municipal Airport Story,* July 10, 1971
Hendrix, F.E., videotape, October 1999 historical marker dedication

INTERVIEWS

The date and location indicate author's initial conversation with each source. Many of them answered additional questions in follow-up interviews.

Warren Abernathy, 9-16-06, Spartanburg, SC
Former aide, Senator Strom Thurmond
Jim Anthony, 5-26-07, Greenville, SC
Founder & CEO, The Cliffs Communities
Larry Baker, 5-9-07, GSP
Executive Vice President, Stevens Aviation
William Barnet III, 10-30-06, Spartanburg, SC
Mayor of Spartanburg, SC, 2000—
Dr. Doyle Boggs, 11-14-06, Spartanburg, SC
Executive Director of Communications, Wofford College, Spartanburg, SC
Fred Bright, 3-19-07, GSP
Operations Supervisor, GSP
Shirley Brooks-Jones, 5-12-07, Dublin, OH, by phone
Delta 15 passenger, 9-11-01
Bobby Brown, 3-19-07, Greenville, SC, by phone
Transportation Specialist, General Electric
Tad Brown, 4-10-06, Thompson, GA, by phone
Grandson, Walter Brown
Leland Burch, 10-19-06, Greer, SC
Airport Commissioner
Jack Buttram, 2-1-06, Rutherfordton, NC, by phone
Former aide to senators Barry Goldwater and Strom Thurmond
Vance Byars, 10-28-06, Raleigh, NC, by phone
Former Flatwood resident
Rex Carter, 3-30-06, Greenville, SC
Former SC State Representative and House Speaker
Peter Cevallos, 8-30-06, Greenville, SC
Manager, Donaldson Center Airport
A. Foster Chapman, 3-29-07, Spartanburg, SC
President/CEO, Johnson Development Associates, Inc.
Harry Chapman, 4-13-06, Greenville, SC, by phone
Former SC State Representative
Rex Clements, 5-9-07, by phone
Assistant Principal, Lewisporte (NL) Collegiate
Robert E. Coleman, 1-12-06, Greenville, SC
GSP Airport Commissioner
Airport Environs Planning Commissioner
Retired CEO, Riegel Textiles

Ron Copsey, 5-4-07, Greenville, SC
Former PIO, 63rd Troop Carrier Wing, DAFB
Retired executive, J. P. Stevens Company
Todd Cox, 3-30-07, GSP
Global Sales Agent/Load Analyst, Volga Dnepr Air Cargo Line
Flip Cuthbertson, 10-11-06, GSP
Sales Representative, Stevens Aviation
Gaynelle Cuthbertson, 4-27-07, Santee, SC, by phone
Widow of Ralph Cuthbertson
Rick Danner, 3-15-07, Greer, SC
Mayor of Greer, SC
Paul Davis, 2-15-06, Woodruff, SC
Former Flatwood resident
Phil Davis, 2-12-06, Duncan, SC
Former Flatwood resident
Frederick B. Dent, 4-27-07, by phone
Retired CEO, Mayfair Mills
Former U.S. Secretary of Commerce
Jim Dolan, 10-06, Belgrade, MT, by phone
Sculptor
Dr. Robert C. Edwards, 10-10-06, Clemson, SC, by phone
President, Clemson University 1959–1981
Larry Estridge, 10-18-06, Greenville, SC
Corporate Counsel, GSP Airport Commission
Womble, Carlyle, Standridge & Rice
Paul Foerster, 10-24-06, Spartanburg, SC
Former European representative,
SC State Development Board
Cary Fondren, 10-17-06, Greenville, SC
VP, National Bank of South Carolina
Dan Foster, 5-14-07, Greenville, SC, by phone
Retired sports editor, *The Greenville News*
Joe Foster, 3-30-07, GSP
Ramp supervisor, GSP
Lamar Foster, 3-07, GSP
Air Traffic Manager, FAA, GSP
Joe Frasher, 8-31-06, Greenville, SC
Executive Director, Greenville Downtown Airport
Larry Gabric, 4-10-07, GSP
Meteorologist in Charge, National Weather Service, GSP, 2005–present
Nathan Garner, 3-19-07, GSP
Operations Supervisor, GSP

Dr. Don and Carol Garrison, 9-14-06, Easley, SC
Retired President, Tri-County Technical College, Pendleton, SC
Peggy Gilliland, 10-10-06, Woodruff, SC, by phone
Daughter of S. J. Workman, original GSP commissioner
A.R. (Dick) Graham, 3-20-05, Greenville, SC
GSP Executive Director, 1967–1989
Marty Griffin, 5-7-07, Greer, SC, by phone
Area Manager, DHL, Greer, SC
Frank Halter, 10-17-06, Greenville, SC
Chairman, Coldwell Banker Caine
John Hansen, 3-30-07, GSP
FedEx, GSP
Jonn Harris, 3-19-07, GSP
Facilities Manager, FedEx, GSP
Tom Hartness, 10-24-06, Greenville, SC
Founder/Chair, Hartness International
Ben Haskew, 10-18-06, Greenville, SC
President, Greater Greenville Chamber of Commerce
Past president, Spartanburg Area Chamber of Commerce
Max Heller, 5-4-07, Greenville, SC, by phone
Mayor of Greenville, SC, 1971–1979; Chairman, SC Development Board, 1979–1984
Francis Earle (F. E.) Hendrix, 2-12-06, Duncan, SC
Flatwood Community historian
Author, *Flatwood Memories*
Neel Hipp, 8-30-06, Greenville, SC
Chairman, SC Aeronautics Commission
Dr. G. B. Hodge, 10-9-06, Spartanburg, SC, by phone
Former Chair, Spartanburg Chamber of Commerce
Larry Holcombe, 10-04-06, GSP
Manager, Greenville-Spartanburg Airport
Ernest F. Hollings, 4-13-06, Charleston, SC
Governor of South Carolina, 1959–1963
Former United States Senator
Bill Hooper, 5-17-07, Lewisporte, NL, by phone
Mayor of Lewisporte, Newfoundland
Josh Houston, 10-05-06, Spartanburg, SC
Manager, Spartanburg Downtown Memorial Airport
Gerald Howard, 12-9-06, Greenville, SC
President/CEO, Greenville Area Development Corporation
Herb Howell, GSP
Former station manager, Northwest Airlines, GSP
J. Garrett Jackson, 3-13-06, GSP
Executive Director, Greenville-Spartanburg Airport

Randy Johnson, 5-2-07, GSP
Facilities Manager, UPS
Joe Jordan, 10-10-06, Greenville, SC
Owner, Joe Jordan Photography
Mike Keselica, 1-19-06, Ft. Myers, FL
Retired architect, Skidmore, Owings & Merrill, New York, NY
Dean Knox, 4-27-07, Harbor Springs, MI, by phone
Owner, Knox Galleries; Avon and Denver, CO; Harbor Springs, MI
Barbara (Davis) Kohler, 3-29-06, Greer, SC, by phone
Former Flatwood resident
Bruce Littlejohn, 10-9-06, Spartanburg, SC
Retired Chief Justice, South Carolina Supreme Court
Glenn Lott, 4-30-07, Columbia, SC, by phone
CEO, LPA Group, Columbia, SC
Elizabeth Mabry, 4-07, Columbia, SC, by phone
Former director, SC Department of Transportation
Mike Martin, 10-6-06, Greer, SC
Captain, US Airways
Les McCraw, 5-11-07, Greenville, SC, by phone
2007 Chair, Airport Environs Planning Commission
Robert McNair, 5-1-07, Jamestown, SC, by phone
Governor of South Carolina, 1965-1971
Valerie Miller, 9-15-06, Greenville, SC
GSP Airport Commissioner
Roger Milliken, 5-21-05, Spartanburg, SC
Chairman, Greenville-Spartanburg Airport Commission
Retired CEO, Milliken & Company
Carol Mucci, 3-14-06, GSP
Air Traffic Controller
Jack Murrin, 10-3-06, GSP
Chief Financial Officer/Chief Information Officer, GSP
Gary Nelson, 8-28-06, Simpsonville, SC
Former presidential pilot
International pilot, UPS
Louise Nelson, 3-27-06, Greer, SC
Retired administrative assistant, GSP
Frank Newton, 4-07, Charlotte, NC, by phone
Consultant, Newton & Associates
Michael O'Donnell, 2-07, Columbia, SC, by phone
Executive Director, SC Aeronautics Commission
William Orders, 3-13-07, Greenville, SC, by phone
1963 president, Greater Greenville Chamber of Commerce
Elizabeth Patterson, 10-05-06, Spartanburg, SC
Former SC 4th Congressional District Representative

Dr. Joseph Pelissier, 7-05, GSP
Meteorologist in Charge, National Weather Service, GSP, 1995–2005
Bill Rafferty, 10-3-06, Atlantic City, NJ, by phone
City Engineer, Atlantic City, NJ
Hank Ramella, 11-10-06, Spartanburg, SC
Airport Commissioner
Vardry Ramseur, 8-30-06, Greenville, SC
Executive Director, Donaldson Industrial Center
Ray Schroeder, 10-30-06, Greenville, SC
President, Interim Healthcare of Greenville
Richard W. Riley, 4-30-07, Greenville, SC, by phone
Governor of South Carolina, 1979–1987
Former U.S. Secretary of Education
Minor Shaw, 5-3-07, Greenville, SC
Vice Chair, Greenville-Spartanburg Airport Commission
Skip Shelton, 4-09-07, Greenwood, SC, by phone
Retired Stevens Aviation pilot
Alan Sistare, 4-15-05, GSP
Fire Chief, GSP
Carter Smith, 4-26-07, Spartanburg, SC, by phone
CEO, Spartanburg County Economic Development Corporation
Dennis Smith, 9-22-06, Alpine, UT
Sculptor
Doug Smith, 3-08-07, Greenville, SC
Retired Manager, WYFF-TV
Milton F. Smith, 4-30-07, Spartanburg, SC
Spartanburg attorney
Pinckney Spencer, 10-10-06, Spartanburg, SC
Spartanburg businessman, son of Dick Tukey
Wallace Storey, 3-30-06, Spartanburg, SC
GSP Airport Commissioner
Airport Environs Planning Commissioner
Howard Suitt, 3-15-07, Greenville, SC, by phone
Former Greenville-Spartanburg Airport Commissioner
Michael Tarman, 3-19-07, GSP
Manager, Transportation Safety Administration, GSP
Nick Theodore, 4-11-06, Greenville, SC, by phone
Former SC State Representative and Lieutenant Governor
Pat Tukey, 11-06-06, Murrell's Inlet, SC, by phone
Development Director, Brookgreen Gardens, son of Dick Tukey
Lewis Vaughn, 5-6-07, Greer, SC, by phone
SC State Senator
Sergei Volodin, 3-30-07, GSP
Flight Manager, Volga Dnepr Air Cargo Line

Don Wall, 10-19-06, Greer, SC
Mayor, Greer, SC 1992-2000
Tommy Watson, 5-8-07, GSP
Police Chief, GSP
Richard C. Webel, 10-20-06, New York, by phone
CEO, Innocenti & Webel, Landscape Architects, Long Island, NY
Rosylin Weston, 2-21-05, GSP
Director of Public Relations, Greenville-Spartanburg Airport
Cooper White, 10-11-06, Greenville, SC
Mayor of Greenville, SC, 1969-1971
Knox White, 10-26-06, Greenville, SC
Mayor of Greenville, SC, 1995—
David Wilkins, 11-01-06, Ottawa, Ontario, Canada, by phone
U.S. Ambassador to Canada
Former Speaker, South Carolina House of Representatives
Octavia Williams, 3-15-06, Greer, SC
Former Information Director, GSP
Dr. Jeffrey Willis, 11-14-06, Spartanburg, SC
Archivist, Converse College, Spartanburg, SC
James H. Woodside, 10-17-06, Greenville, SC
President, Woodside Insurance Agency
William D. Workman III, 10-31-06, Bluffton, SC
Mayor of Greenville, SC, 1982–1995
City Manager, Bluffton, SC, 2006–
Robert Yeargin, 10-27-06, Greenville, SC
President, Yeargin Properties; former project manager, Daniel Construction

NEWSPAPERS AND MAGAZINES

Airlift Magazine
Atlanta Journal-Constitution
Bold Life
Charlotte Observer
Fortune
Greenville Journal
Greenville Piedmont
GSA Business
Middle Tyger Times
New York Times
Omaha World Herald
Spartanburg Herald
Spartanburg Herald-Journal
Spartanburg Journal
The Greenville News

The Greenville News-Piedmont
The Greer Citizen
The State
USA Today
Wall Street Journal
Washington Post

PHOTO CREDITS

Ron Copsey
Kathy Wood Edge
The Coxe Collection, Greenville County (SC) Historical Society
Greenville-Spartanburg Airport Archives
A. R. (Dick) Graham
Francis Earle Hendrix
Cindy Hosea Photography
Joe F. Jordan Photography
Photography by Cynthia Blair Miller
Greg Moss Photography
Spartanburg County Historical Association Museum
Herald-Journal Willis Collection, Spartanburg County (SC) Public Libraries

Index

Page numbers in italics refer to illustrations.